Following the Trail of Max Birnbaum

Following the Trail of Max Birnbaum from the Lesachtal in the Alps to Lake Wobegon in Minnesota

Told by
Otmar M. Drekonja

Collegeville, Minnesota

To
My wife Ingrid,
my children
Thomas, Natascha and Dimitri,
and my grandchildren
Alexander, Nikolaus, Andreas, and Stephanie

Typeset by Kathy Zdroik
Cover photo by Juergen Graefe
Cover design by Ann Blattner

The story of Max Birnbaum was made possible with the help of people to whom I am deeply grateful:

Mark and Judy Twomey for editing the text, Brooke Kreitinger and Josh Evans for working out soft-ware problems, Fritz Rudolf Fries from Berlin and Norene Hokett from Riverside, California, for adding important components to the narrative, Joe and Jill Farry for reading the proofs, the production department of the Liturgical Press for designing, typesetting, and arranging the printing of the book, and my wife Ingrid for refreshing my memory and her loving care while I was writing.

Contents

Otmar with his family in August 2005.
First row: Alexander, Otmar, Andreas and Nikolaus.
Second row: Natascha, Glenn, Stephanie, Ingrid, Dimitri, Kara and Thomas.

Otmar with his brother Gerhard, Professor for Latinamerican Studies at the University of Vienna, in 2004.

By Way of Introduction

If you are an ordinary mortal, writing memoirs may sound a bit grandiose. I am a rather ordinary guy. To sound a bit more fictitious, I call myself Max Birnbaum. That helps me to add or subtract and deal with reality in a more creative fashion. This is not going to be a string of lies, but sometimes I do not know how to connect the dots. Then I use the power of imagination and suggest how it may have been. It could be a fairly short or a fairly long narrative. It could be simplistic, e.g., just list the yearly Thanksgiving letters I sent out. Or I could put it all into a nutshell and publish my personal profile. Should I run out of energy and time for the rest, I will have said at least that much about myself, Max Birnbaum from the Lesachtal.

I ended up in Minnesota, and that is a longer story but not that unusual after all. The United States is a nation of immigrants. I am now a citizen of two worlds: Central Europe and Central Minnesota. Both are wonderful worlds, and I would not want to do without either one. Central Europe, after all, is the home of classical music.

Central Minnesota is the home of Minnesota Public Radio (MPR).

Central Europe is the living legacy of six hundred years of Habsburg splendor.

Central Minnesota is a splendid piece of unspoiled nature.

Central Europe shows the scars of human tragedy from Sarajevo to Auschwitz.

Central Minnesota is the place with endless winters, hot summers and no spring.

Central Europe is where my roots are.

Central Minnesota is where I feel at home.

I lead a happy life. I am very fortunate. I have a wonderful wife and three great children. Our youngest son Dimitri is an internist and the fastest marathon runner in Minnesota. Our beautiful daughter Natascha is a lawyer in Denver and in love with the mountains, like me. Our oldest son Thomas is a great orthopedic surgeon in Salzburg—but a fine American too!

I was pretty fortunate in a time that was tumultuous, the 20th century. I regret nothing. I am thankful for so many things, especially two fine grandsons, Alexander and Nikolaus.

I was a pretty good professor at Saint John's University. I was a "poster-boy" for excellence in teaching on their brochures. The Austrians gave me the *Das Österreichische Ehrenkreuz für Wissenschaft und Kunst Erster Klasse.* What more could a Central Minnesotan guy expect or say, "A fella could do worse?"

I will start with the 2003 letter because it marks an important event. It reminds me of my mortality, when I thought I was indestructible.

I loved the chainsaw, the pickup, hiking and biking. Now I must slow down. It is time. When your old pickup starts coughing uphill, gets a grinding noise in the transmission and has trouble starting, your heart breaks, because you love the old clunker.

For a while, one can ignore symptoms. Besides, Ingrid and I flew to Salzburg in February. Alex had an operation. Thomas opened his new clinic. We went skiing with Nikolaus; we spent days in a sumptuous spa with Ingrid's family. I visited Monika and Bernd in Bad Gastein. Walked for hours in the lovely mountains of the Hohe Tauern. . . .

But in March we turned to the pickup. It was me. We went to the Mayo Clinic and asked the wise men what it was that slows me down. The times were not good. Bush started his war in Iraq. And the verdict of the wise men of Mayo was, indeed, a cracked cylinder head! Cannot be fixed; just keep driving. Go slow and don't overdo it!

ALS they call it. At first, we were shocked. What a nice pickup I was! Then we turned sentimental and went to the opera at the Ordway with our kids. It was *La Traviata.* As the soprano wilted in the last act, we all cried. Then Ingrid took over, "Take all the medications that work! See Dr. Lu for acupuncture and green tea! Join a medical study group! And keep going!" That is what we are doing. Thomas, Natascha and Dimitri are so helpful. Ingrid is a saint. I am a hedonist enjoying every good day. Bob Spaeth, the former dean of Saint John's, knew the facts: Life is too short. No more *Traviata*!

On May 8th, my sister Erika died. She always was so brave and upbeat. And she was so eager to see her son Martin graduate from medical school in Vienna in June. He did!

It was also in June when Ingrid and I flew to Salzburg with the Zernatto papers from SJU in our luggage. (Zernatto was a wonderful poet who had the misfortune to enter politics at the wrong time at the wrong place and had to flee Austria after the Anschluss. He came to the U.S., and that's why the papers were here.) The University of Klagenfurt became the recipient of this gift. My brother Gerhard, a professor in Vienna, arranged a fine "Transfer Party." For thirty seconds I was even on Austrian TV during the ceremony. Professor Amann was happy. So was Vice Rector Martin Hitz, who knew that the papers were hidden here, and he wanted them back home.

On the Magdalensberg, among Roman ruins, we celebrated the 50th anniversary of my graduating class from teachers' training college. Sentimental reminiscences, nostalgia and curiosity. We all got old. Only the Romans up there are older, but we look better!

Then it was time to fly back to Minnesota. Life near Lake Wobegon is good. The boys would come soon! It had been that way for twelve years. A magnificent tradition! First Alexander would come, flying solo for the first time, and then Thomas and Nikolaus. We love them dearly, and they love us. Thomas started taking flying lessons. Ingrid takes care of the garden, the house and me. Our friends, Judy and Mark Twomey; John Merkle and Sarah Pruett; Susie and Mark McKeon; Eileen and Dick Haeg; Joe and Jill Farry; Thorpe and Cheryl Running; Bob Weber and the good Father John—you could not have better friends! Many former students see us and bring joy to our lives. On top of that, we have the very best neighbors. If only Bush would stop disgracing America! Regime change! The guy has been "misunderestimated"!

In November, we made our pilgrimage to Grand Cayman. Wind, sand, sun, waves, fish and most of our children made us happy. Thanks, Natascha and Glenn, Dimitri and Kara, Thomas and the two boys! We love you very much! Happy Thanksgiving!

The Story

I

Everyone who happens to live in the Avon Hills in Minnesota, not too far from Lake Wobegon, is fortunate. There are few places in America where the landscape is calmer, the neighbors friendlier, the colors in fall more vibrant, the water in the lakes clearer, the weather more intense and nature more pristine. The music of the Avon Hills is filled with singing frogs in the slough, loons on the lake, howling coyotes in the hills and the not so sonorous sounds of Canadian geese or wild turkeys. Once in a while, there is the sound of a noisy motorbike on Fruit Farm Road, the hushed sound of good runners, the remote sound of a distant jet up high or the healthy roar of an old pickup.

If it were not for the pickup, my contentment as a retired professor, a former Austrian country school teacher, a musician with modest talents and an almost-artist who does occasional watercolors would be perfect. I explained my condition as a guy with a pickup in my 2003 Thanksgiving letter, which went to my friends, telling them that I am not immortal. But so, I am age seventy, and I have had a wonderful life, which I am going to tell about in this lengthy story. I have a wonderful wife and three magnificent children, two fine dogs and a sensuous cat. I used to play the clarinet. I loved the chainsaw as a precision instrument. I am the proud owner of a John Deere Gator as well as an indestructible riding mower, which my son gave me many years ago from his first earnings. Those help me to get out into the hills. Let me also tell you that that Gator was a surprise birthday gift from my neighbors and friends. They are good to me, and I am so grateful. I am a lucky guy.

I will start with the end of my story. It is the story of a trip from a remote Austrian village in the Carnian Mountains near the Italian border. I come from Birnbaum in the Lesach Valley. As I mentioned, I sometimes go by the name of Max Birnbaum, who well remembers the wonderful years in this stunningly beautiful valley. But then there was WW II, during which time I lived in German-occupied Yugoslavia. From there, it was a difficult return to post-war Austria. I worked as a farmhand and went to school. I entered a teachers' training college in the provincial capital of Klagenfurt, which was still scarred from the bombs and the war. I attended the conservatory and blossomed as a promising musician. I worked as a country school teacher in Carinthia and Tyrol. I conducted singing ensembles, played the organ in church and played in the Radio Orchestra of the ORF (Austrian Radio). I went to the Universities of Vienna, Innsbruck and Salzburg and became a decent academician. I came to the U.S. as a Fulbright Fellow. I came to Saint John's University and the fine Bauhaus concrete structures of Marcel Breuer. And there were some more erratic moves—but here I am, after almost forty years at Saint John's! Time to sit down, lean back and start writing my story.

Where do I start? Oh, yes, with my pickup distress letter, because it marks a shift in gears. It also reminds you of what is important and what is trivial. The greatest modern German writer Thomas Bernhard said, "In the face of death, everything else is ridiculous."

In short, the story of my life is not going to be monumental. I am no Melville, Mozart or Michelangelo. I am just lucky to be ordinary. It is so much easier than being great. You disappoint fewer people when you talk about the weather and pickups. No pretense. No regrets. A fellow could have done worse. You betcha! And if you know when a pickup has a strange sound, you know there is a problem. Well, my Thanksgiving letter highlighted a problem. Until then, everything went surprisingly well, and I am grateful.

The story of my life fills the turbulent 20th century, not that I am that old. But it starts with my father, who was born in 1901, and about whom I know so little. Europe in the 20th century was truly what Mazower called the "Dark Continent": Whatever could have gone wrong did. My family was not the only one shaken to its foundation. But when we celebrated the arrival of the new millennium in Salzburg, the fireworks were no bombs, and the roofs of this most beautiful city gleamed in the spectacular illumination. I thought the 21st century must indeed be a better one than the last.

Besides, at the end of the 20th century, I retired after fifty-five years of teaching. I gave myself a new pickup. We celebrated the wedding of our daughter Natascha to Glenn in Aspen, and that of our son Dimitri to Kara at Saint John's. A year later, Thomas surprised us with a wedding announcement: He had married Astrid in Las Vegas! Dimitri graduated from the University of Minnesota Medical School. Thomas established a fine orthopedic practice in Salzburg. I started playing the clarinet again for the St. Cloud Opera Company, where Dimitri had occupied a cello chair for many years. I had time to read the *New York Times* daily at the lake by our fine chalet named "Kärnten," which Thomas had shipped from Austria. My wife Ingrid retired from the St. Cloud Hospital's psych ward. I went sailing with Ingrid's brother Alfred in Croatia. I enjoyed an extended visit to New York. I climbed wonderful peaks with Natascha in Colorado and accompanied Dimitri in the canoe in Voyageurs National Park in that magnificent corner of northeastern Minnesota. We planned trips back to Grand Cayman, but the 9/11 event made us delay those plans. In 2003 we did go back. And that was so good, because it was after our visit to Mayo, which is when my condition was diagnosed, and I was forced to slow down. Up until then, I would have said that the years in retirement were the best years of my life—and I still think so.

But I must admit that I run out of breath easily. I noticed this first while skiing in Aspen. Then I felt it while swimming in our lake, where at times, it got hard to reach the shore again. I had to rest my beloved chainsaw. One more reason to now focus on telling my story and the story of the turbulent century, which killed our fathers and uncles so early, and left our mothers despondent and our home country disgraced.

"Death is a master from Germany," Paul Celan says in his Auschwitz "Death Fugue." But I was lucky. I have a wonderful wife and the best grandchildren in Salzburg, Alexander and Nikolaus. They, too, love

Minnesota and come here every summer. They are the joy of my life. Otherwise, only a few things have given me so much pleasure during the last seventy years: the mountains in the Alps and the Rockies—from Mont Blanc to the Tetons; then, there was music: the Klagenfurt Madrigal Ensemble in the '50s, the orchestra playing so many less-than-famous venues, and the drifting into the world of the sounds of classical music, which is the gift from Central Europe to the world: Dvorak, Bruckner, Schubert, Mahler and Mozart. Not to forget the seductive sounds of George Gershwin and jazz, something that had fascinated me even long before my discovery of America. Finally, the joy of literature; I discovered that by teaching rather than by studying. "German Studies" has become my job over decades. It has brought me to Minnesota, to Saint John's, to the Avon Hills. Here I am, listening to Minnesota Public Radio—invented by Fr. Colman Barry, O.S.B., at SJU. Here, I read the *NYT* and enjoy the *Sports Illustrated* swimsuit models on my desk calendar. Here I work. Here I write. I love to be right here with Ingrid.

But before I start telling my story of Max Birnbaum, a man I know quite well, I would like to warn my readers with a touch of mischievous delight, that my narrative will not follow a line of chronology, a unity of time, place or character. Rather, it will be a collage which jumps back and forth, involving many people in and outside my family. As I said, it starts around 1900 and ends a hundred years later. It involves the story of the discovery of America, and the discovery of Central Europe, a place often referred to as "Kakania." Robert Musil, a man from Klagenfurt, the town where my wife comes from, gave it this name. It is a wonderful world between Venice and Prague, Budapest and Innsbruck, Ljubljana and Salzburg. Most importantly, it is centered around the Habsburg Vienna.

Thus, I ended up being a citizen of two worlds. Familiar with both, fully at home in neither, but happy to move from one to the other regularly. I have two passports. Two personas. Children on two continents, and friends on either side of the Atlantic. KLM/NW is the link. In eight hours I can get from Minneapolis to Amsterdam. Telephone and e-mail are additional bridges. Therefore, my story comes out of two languages.

This is the English version. Most of it is true. Some things that I did not know, I had to invent. It could have been that way, maybe. I do not know where and how my father died in 1944. I do not know what he was like. I do not know why he did not come home after WW I, after he had served as a sailor in the k.k Imperial Navy. I also do not know what I would have done in place of my father and my uncles during the Third Reich. They all faced difficult decisions. Some made a pact with Mephistopheles. Some died in a brutal fashion. All of them would have loved to be able to visit us here in Minnesota. Our grand-children certainly do.

So let me begin. I am the main character.

II

The year was 1953. I was eighteen. I had completed a five-year program at the Klagenfurt Teachers' Training College (LBA). I also took advanced courses in woodwinds and theory at the conservatory. Udo Jürgens, then Bockelman or Bohlan, was one of the vertical take-off *Wunderkinder* at the conservatory. He became a great pop star soon thereafter. He still is today. I had modest talent, but great ambition. I considered a teaching assignment at some country school as a demo-tion—should it come to that. They said there were no teaching jobs available, partly because the denazification process since 1948 had cleansed a good number of former teachers who were party members during the Third Reich, and partly because more and more POWs were coming back, the last ones in 1955 from Russia. So, many of the former teachers slid back into their positions. I got used to earning some money working at lumber yards and doing construction jobs. My music teacher got me a summer job as a private tutor twenty miles from home. I went there every week by bike and tutored four kids who were slow on the up-take.

Maybe my fame with slow-pokes spread, because in October the Education Department issued me a contract for teaching special ed. classes for mentally challenged kids in Kötschach—the same place where five years ago I had graduated from a very good *Hauptschule* (middle school) while working as a farmhand on the Lamprecht farm near the Italian border. The teachers still remembered me, but I felt shy, young and inexperienced in their midst.

In November, they sent me a new contract for a two-classroom school in the Lesach Valley, the place where I had spent my childhood years. It is a stunningly beautiful valley high in the mountains, close to the border of Italy. Kötschach is the last train stop. Then, a gravel road takes you to St. Lorenzen, fifteen miles further up. In summer, there is a bumpy bus service. I boarded that bus with two big cardboard boxes containing a good radio, my clarinet, some clothes and my first new winter coat. I also bought a pair of brand-new skis. I thought I was a lucky guy with those belongings.

I rented a room from a farmer. They wanted me to play in the local band, which I did. But they needed a trumpet rather than my clarinet, so I learned the trumpet. I had to teach grades 1–4. I enjoyed it very much, so did my kids. But I did not make enough progress; by Easter they should have been able to read and write. Instead, they were able to sing and paint. But the fourth graders took the first graders under their wings and helped them catch up. I was grateful.

I also had to teach agriculture for the vocational school twice a week to boys ages fifteen to eighteen. However, I knew little about cattle or grain, lumber or manure, so I faked it. In the spring, I taught them how to prune fruit trees. The trees did not bear any fruit for the next few years.

When winter came the road stayed closed for the next three months. At Christmas, I walked for four hours to the train stop. On the return trip, the local doctor gave me a ride in an old army 4 x 4 coming in from the west via Lienz. It was a difficult trip.

Above all, I missed the music culture of the conservatory, and I felt stuck in a world that looked beautiful but was utterly stifling. I applied for a different job. It worked, because in a place fifteen miles from Klagenfurt—doable by bike—they needed a choral conductor for the men's chorus and an organist for church on Sunday. On top of that, I was invited to become a member of a stellar ensemble, the Madrigal Choir, where we studied glorious 15th- and 16th- century music.

The place was called St. Filippen ob Reinegg. Again, it was a two-classroom school, in which I taught grades 5–8. I liked it very much and learned to be more demanding. But I wanted to move on to high school teaching, so I fulfilled the requirements in music. I also completed the requirements with honors for teaching grade school. Some thought I would become a great teacher.

Today, there is no more school there. However, *Gasthaus Kurath* is still there. I had a room there and ate in the fine restaurant. I spent weekends in the city—went to the opera, attended the rehearsals with the Madrigal Choir and played clarinet in the radio orchestra ORF.

I always had some notions of grandeur and knew I should move on to greater challenges. I became interested in a technical secondary school for gunsmiths and engravers in Ferlach. I had no qualifications for that kind of school, but I would eventually teach drawing and design, math and phys. ed. But what really fascinated me was the musical horizon of Renaissance music and American jazz. Yes, I started to flirt with America by listening to a wonderful AFN (American Forces Network) station. And I became a frequent visitor of the *Amerika Haus*, a magnificent library and place of discovery. Not only could you find Hemingway, Arthur Miller and Steinbeck, but all the *verboten* German exiles from the Third Reich: Sigmund Freud, Thomas Mann, Arthur Schnitzler, Bertolt Brecht and Heinrich Heine. I became an insatiable reader and a little snob. I wore American clothes that were handed down to impoverished kids by U.S. welfare organizations. I thought I looked like the young Frank Sinatra, and I liked that disguise.

I felt that my days as a country school teacher were numbered. With the madrigal ensemble, I traveled to Italy and England, where we won major competitions, and I fell in love with a soprano from the teachers' training college while in a state of awe and admiration for the architecture of Florence—and the female form. But I was a rather inhibited lover, and our affair never became an affair, even though we stayed in touch for years to come.

More passionate was a relationship with a young Israeli folk-singer named Sandra Gold. In 1954, the State Department sent an ensemble performing *Porgy and Bess* to Europe. I got tickets to the *Theater an der Wien*; the main opera house was still bombed out. The performance was one of the sacred moments of my musical experience; Gershwin in Vienna, along with Bruckner in Linz, and Monteverdi in Arezzo.

I spent a few days with Sandra in Vienna. She was so kind to me, sensuous and sweet. And I was happy. She visited me in Klagenfurt, and I was flying high in bliss. Sure, I never ever saw her afterwards, but she left a mark on my heart.

Of course, there was another woman who almost got me out of my pedestrian job of country school teacher. In 1953, Mr. Leopold Katt, a fine composer and director of a fine arts training center in Lungau, needed a secretary to run his workshops and keep an eye on the place. I came for an interview via the narrow-gauge railway to Mauterndorf and stayed for a week. There I met a young soprano, Gundi Gries. A heavenly voice! A lovely young woman. Later, she became a permanent member of the St. Augustine Music Ensemble in Vienna. We liked each other. However, I did not take the job. We never saw each other again until forty-five years later. I have her CD. Her voice is still as magnificent as it was then.

All those people struck my heart and told me not to return to my role as a humble country school teacher. Had I stayed in that job, it would have been very predictable, and my story would be over one page later. I would have married some nice farm girl. I would have lived in some scenic retreat. I would have been the director of the marching band and have worn yodeling outfits. I would have skied in the winter and hiked in the summer. I would have been happy and content, an ordinary guy, and kids would have greeted me with respect.

And I would have slowly but steadily killed my gypsy nature and become rooted in the soil of some Alpine valley filled with cows, sheep and summer tourists. But I was smitten by women I admired, by music I missed and by parts of the world I wanted to discover. Above all, I knew how little I knew, and I wanted to work on this deficit one way or another. I am glad I did.

Even though I missed all the women I had loved in a rather platonic fashion, I would make up for this later. I would find a wonderful wife while in Ferlach. I was the conductor of the Alpine Club's singing group, and she was part of it. Later she became a part of me, and she still is, fortunately.

My next chapter will lead into the world of greater teaching challenges and wonderful discoveries while in this old hunting weapons' factory of Ferlach, created by Empress Maria Theresa in the 18th century. On top of that, I now owned a Puch scooter and could retire my bicycle. That gave me a new horizon of motion and a toy that much impressed some of my girl friends and my climbing buddies. It was indeed the mountains and women, in that order, which I learned to respect, love and appreciate.

III

I have to explain my addiction to mountains. It is a legacy of my years in the Lesach Valley. There, everything either goes up or down. There is no flat part anywhere. The gravel road from Kötschach runs ten miles over many bridges and ravines to Birnbaum, where Max Birnbaum is from. There are two bars and restaurants, one post office, one grocery store and a few farm houses, plus one chapel. From Birnbaum, you walk up a steep narrow road to Kornat, where my brother, Gerhard Kornat is from. He writes columns under that name in the papers. There is a splendid Gothic church from the 14th century. There's also a yellow stone house, the school, and a blue stone house, the parish house. The parish house is now bulldozed. On the steep slopes there are a few more farm houses with fields that are more vertical than horizontal. Around that fine church is a cemetery with a breathtaking view looking south on the Carnian Ridge—a climber's paradise. There is a saddle near the Wolayer Lake with a crossing to Italy. There are still bunkers and fortifications from WW I on two sides. To the left is the mighty massif of the Plenge, where in February the avalanches thunder down with a horrendous roar. Further up behind Kornat are the grassy humps of the Griffitz with an abundance of berries. Behind the Griffitz is the majestic limestone formation of the Lienz Dolomites. There, you can pick Edelweiss in August.

As a boy, I was all over those mountains, sometimes with some adult, often alone. I could walk for hours and take in the ever-changing sights. In college, I joined the Alpine Club and did more advanced climbs, often as a guide but sometimes alone. While living in Ferlach in the late '50s, I became familiar with the latest in rock climbing techniques in the splendid Koschuta Range. Later, as a student in Vienna, I met an architect, Franz Lindner, with whom I did spectacular climbs in Austria, Switzerland and France. I developed a fine ice-climbing technique, and we did a number of north faces on the Wiesbachhorn, the Zebru in Italy, and in Chamonix, France. I stood on top of Mount Blanc, the Dom, the Matterhorn and the Ortler. We would stay up for weeks and find refuge either in a spartan shelter or a lavishly supplied hut. Those were wonderful years. They gave me the feeling that up is great, and thin air is addictive. That addiction, I would later take along to America. However, let me say in all honesty that this lifestyle conflicted with my amorous pursuits. Besides, you do not smell that great after three weeks at an altitude of four thousand meters.

There was a fine violinist from Dublin, a Jewish woman—not that attractive, but quite lively. She would have loved to see me continue on in music. We went to some formals together where Udo Jürgens played. She was a musical superstar and an inspirational person. But at that time, I also started seeing my future wife. It was not love at first sight, but she was astounding in many ways. She would ski and climb mountains with me. She would wait for weeks and then welcome me back down to the real world. When I would work hard at construction sites, she would send crates with fruit from Italy. I started to see her more often, but there were still the mountains. I was not yet ready for a steady relationship.

Most of all, I was a confused, unfocused and restless young guy, who arrogantly assumed he was called to greater things to come. To make it worse, some of the young women who looked at me with some sense of anticipation suggested I better get off my butt and do something serious.

Ruth Ticher, the splendid Jewish violinist from Dublin, said I had to quit doing silly things and focus on music. She was already playing the Bruch concerto on stage, while I labored through some lower level repertoire. Besides, if you want to be a musician and you have not yet made the stage at age twenty, you never will. My Gundi Gries from Mauterndorf said I should really go to Vienna. My Israeli Sandra Gold said I should go to America. And the love affair with Gerlinde, which started in Florence, suffered from the daily trivia of me being a teacher elsewhere. Besides, she would stay in this job, and I might not. The fact is, however, that much of my encouragement for doing something worthwhile came from women I admired. Being a child of that fatherless post-WW II generation, this is in itself not surprising. But it confirms the old theorem according to which behind each successful man stands a surprised woman.

The year was 1956. I was twenty-two years old and saw time as a country school teacher in St. Filippen working against me, so I sat down and wrote a terse letter of resignation to the Education Department, resigning from a tenured position as an elementary teacher. Not that I disliked the work; quite the contrary. I loved those kids, and they liked me a lot.

My mother turned pale when I told her that I had quit a secure job. And the education secretary of the State of Carinthia was miffed and implied I was crazy. Maybe I was. But I had my feelers out in that academy for gunsmiths and engravers, which also allowed me to teach drafting and design—neither of which I was really qualified for, but I was a good enough amateur artist. Not quite as good as Adolf Hitler was at my age, but I was okay. Most importantly, I had a knack for teaching, for being onstage, for putting together a production—for faking it. In short, I could be inspirational.

That was certainly a legacy of that fine teachers' training college I had attended from 1948 to 1953. During the Third Reich, it was a cadre school for future Nazis to indoctrinate innocent young kids. After the war, it became something of a "faith-based" conservative institution with heavy emphasis on patriotism, Catholicism and moralistic ethics in the service of a post-war society. The teachers were either denazified Nazis, like my good German professor Perkonig, or people who were being rewarded for having been harmed by the Nazis, like my Latin teacher and director, Seiwald. The religion professor, Meier, was a good-looking, sporty Hugh Hefner-type who loved virgins (not Mary). My math prof was better than his incompetent wife, who made math a horror trip. The art prof was a really good painter who liked my work.

The physical education professor was a universally gifted Renaissance man, who helped us with math and Latin. But he was also a drive nut when it came to sports. He was choleric and did not tolerate weakness of any kind. But he liked me, even though I was never Olympic material; my best grade was a C. He was a bit intense. He came from the Sudeten area in Bohemia and was strongly pro-German. He had volunteered for the *Waffen SS* as he felt he was an *Übermensch*. But they kicked him out because he had, fortunately, some Jewish blood. So he set his Faustian dreams into the center of his teaching. He was a first-rate biologist. Above all, he loved mountains and relaxed in the thin air. As fellow members of the Alpine Club, he and I felt very close

The best professors were those in music. We put on magnificent performances of everything in the classical repertoire, choral and orchestra, opera and Mass, folk songs and modern music. In addition, Professor Meier, a motherly woman, tried to take very good care of me. Dr. Schmidt was a brilliant conductor and music instructor. They were the ones who sent me to the conservatory and also paid for it. There, I met a Professor Harald Haselbach, who taught art appreciation. He opened my eyes to literature and the aesthetic dimension in life, for which I am eternally thankful. He also always brought a string of lovely young women who adored him, and he enjoyed those groupies very much himself. I guess he was a stylishly dressed master Casanova and humiliated us young guys for our relative incompetence in amorous and erotic matters. I had much to learn yet above and beyond Rilke, Trakl or Benn.

The best part of the college, however, was the practical portion. We practiced teaching on an ongoing basis in grades 1–4. The most inspirational master teacher was the brother of Harald, Volkmar Haselbach. The kids called him the "Great Volkmar." We felt likewise. I will never forget his advice on how to be a good teacher: You must master and love your subject, and you must love the kids and take interest in them; nothing else matters. He was right. It helped me throughout my erratic career. Later on, the Great Volkmar drank too much and became, unfortunately, an administrator in the state government. As a teacher he was brilliant.

Sure, there were others too. There was the cranky violin teacher who despaired seeing us go nowhere on that difficult instrument. At night, he played schmaltzy tunes as an entertainer for British occupation officers and felt as if he were in heaven when he improvised on themes from *Der Rosenkavalier*. There was a young music professor called Günther Mittergradnegger, who had survived the war in the Caucasus and the Eastern front. He was a brilliantly gifted musician who had founded the Madrigal Choir. But he became politically active in a way not in line with the conservative orientation of the LBA and was phased out, unfortunately. There were history profs, but we never learned about anything past 1900. No comment on the tragedies of the 20th century: 1914, 1918, 1927, 1933, 1939–1945. . . . Silence from Sarajevo to Auschwitz. Nothing about the Jews, totalitarian structures, *Untermenschen*, *Übermenschen*. Nothing. Total amnesia. As if they had not lived in that time and just awoke from a fairy-tale world of Greek antiquity or Babylonian cultures, which we did hear about. When we dared to ask, we were told we were lucky, had it good, should shut up and work hard. *Arbeit macht frei*!

Much later, I saw this icon over the entrance to Auschwitz near Krakow. Sure, we were alive and healthy, young and naïve. All we needed to know is how to become a decent country school teacher. But it also would have been nice to hear why, where and how our fathers and uncles had died and for what.

The year of graduation was 1953. There were no special festivities. Our mothers were relieved and grateful that their children would find what sounded like a secure, *ordentlicher* job. My mother certainly was glad to see me follow the footsteps of her MIA husband. My fine Professor Turnowsky, with whom I shared a love of mountains, invited me and a few others for a graduation trip, a climb up the north face of the Hochstadel in the Lienz Dolomites. It was splendid.

IV

The year was 1956. Austria became a free, neutral and unoccupied country in 1955. I had sent my resignation before taking a trip to Berlin on my scooter. Berlin was not yet divided. It was my first encounter with the GDR, which would become very important later while in the U.S. I enjoyed the discovery of Germany—also a topic about which we had learned absolutely nothing in school. Too hot, too complicated, too close, too uncertain, too painful for most teachers.

I had, in the meantime, received a nod from the academy in Ferlach, and in the fall, I drove my scooter south into this sleepy town on the Slovenian border where gunsmiths had been working since the 18th century. The students were mostly Austrians, but there were also some Germans, Russians and Italians. I was also the head resident of the dorm and had to provide recreational activities, that is mountain climbing tours in the Koschuta, swimming in the Drau River, playing soccer with the school team and playing jazz with some of the musicians. The work I had to do was to teach design and drafting for engravers, who otherwise added oak leaves to hunting guns of great delicacy.

Later on they also needed a math teacher, an area where I was especially weak. So my colleague Friedl Schmid, brother to a rather fine painter, Kurt Schmid, who later drank too much, coached me. He did a good job, and I enjoyed it. But he also served very fine cognac, and I would have been a drunk soon had I stayed there. Friedl was an engineer who built Messerschmitts in Vienna Neustadt during the war. He was a feared math prof. and a pretty good mountain climber.

Right behind the town were some of the most majestic peaks of the Karawanken, the border to Yugoslavia. With some of the students, I spent almost every weekend there. It was a wonderful life except that I was on a conditional contract, and it was painfully clear that for the kind of work I did, I was under qualified. That could only be rectified by four to six years of studies at the university.

I was in a dead-end situation professionally. On the other hand, every Thursday I was in Klagenfurt for the Radio Ensemble doing paid work as a clarinetist. Every Tuesday was rehearsal for the Madrigal Choir, and every Friday was my evening as conductor of the Alpine Club's singing group. There was, among others, a pony-tailed blond soprano: Ingrid Luger. She was a vivacious person, ready to do something at any time, like skipping school to go skiing during the week. Or go to some formal on the weekends in February. Or go to the theater or a concert. I usually took her back home to her upper-middle class family, where I was something of an intruder. One night she gave me a good-night kiss. From then on, she more so than I, was toying with the idea that we should stay together and get married. That was not so simple because she planned to go to Vienna and study medicine. I had plans, but no money. First, I would have to find a job with, hopefully, little work and enough time to pursue studies. I did not find one in Vienna, but in Krems, a magnificent medieval city in Wachau, the wine-producing region of the Danube Valley. There was an academy for building engineers and architects. I landed a job for architectural design and planned to commute to Vienna by train, about a one-hour trip. But what should I study? I had flirted with the art academy and thought about an art education. For the entrance examination one needed a dossier with one hundred works. I had completed almost a hundred while in Ferlach.

One day, I took my scooter and went to the river marshes to work on some water colors. On the bumpy way back, I must have lost the file because I arrived without it. I could not find it anywhere. That was the end of my artistic dreams. At least I did not suffer the fate of Adolf Hitler, who was rejected by the academy. God knows what would have become of me had I suffered the same fate!

There was some thought of studying woodwinds at the music academy, but I knew that I was too old and not advanced enough to become a first-rate musician. I went to Vienna anyway and met Ingrid there in the *Café Votiv*. She would not do medicine, she said. Instead, she planned to study German and English literature. Oh! Well, that would interest me also. So I enrolled at the university without any entrance examination and became a student of the philosophy faculty. Many of the classes I could not attend because of my work schedule. So Ingrid and I met regularly at the *Café Votiv*, and she filled me in on what I was supposed to know. It also became quite clear to me that she liked me and I liked her. But she was the much better student and a wonderful comrade in the new world of the Imperial City.

Without much thought or reflection, I had made a rather important decision, without which America, the marriage to Ingrid and the discovery of literature would not have happened. *The year was 1958.* I was twenty-four years old—almost a "non-traditional student" by that age, but eager to discover a world rather new to me. It was far from clear whether I would ever finish with a degree on that part-time student basis. It was painfully clear to me that I was out of the loop in so many parts of this new discipline. Nobody would have bet his money that anything would come of me anyway. The old star Professor Kranzmayr, who liked Ingrid and wanted her to do a doctorate with him, noticed that I was in tow and asked her in an honest and confidential moment, "What the hell do you want to do with this fellow anyway?" That was three years before we got married.

There is one more thing I have to dig up from the past before I make a jump ahead to the now in Minnesota. My brother Gerhard (Kornat) had just served in the Austrian Army after his *Matura* (diploma) in 1957. He was already noted as a brilliant kid with great potential. He had won a speech contest of the *Amerika Haus*, and he had graduated with distinction. But he was a rebellious and stubborn guy, who clearly suffered from the fatherless condition of our upbringing. He saw the confines of the petty-bourgeois environment from which we came, and he decided to do something drastic about it. He eloped from home and went to join the French Foreign Legion, which was at that time busy in northern Africa and Indochina. At the border, he was stopped by customs, and my mother brought him home. Distraught as she was, she asked me to take over some "fatherly" protective functions and be where he was. So it was good I was in Vienna, where he started to study history and philosophy. Not that I could do all that much. I was only five years older—and not as bright. But at least we were both in Vienna, so to speak. We would talk and see each other, and that was good for my mother. Maybe not so great for my independent, young superstar. For two years, at least, Vienna was the stable point for the two of us—and for Ingrid and me.

Had the departments of German and English not been so sterile and dull, we might have stayed there. But it became increasingly clear to me that I was running in circles rather than making progress. At some point, I started flirting with the Canadian Embassy, looking for a work permit there. Then Ingrid decided enough nonsense and stopped me.

V

The year was 1960. We left Vienna for Innsbruck. That may sound constructive, but it was not that simple. Sure, Ingrid prevented me, fortunately, from turning into a lumberjack in Canada. Certainly, the University of Innsbruck did not seem quite as stale in our discipline. On top of that, Innsbruck was a much nicer city with a splendid hinterland. And the cultural ambience of Vienna was not much of a loss because I always had such a sleep deficit from the combination of commuting, work and studies that I would fall soundly asleep in the second act of some play in the Burgtheater, for which Ingrid would have provided tickets. There was a good nightclub we would miss, Fatty George's (a great clarinetist) on the Petersplatz, where we had enjoyed performances by Luise Martini and Gerhard Bronner.

But in Innsbruck one would have mountains and could ski. However, I had to find a job. And our English needed some polishing. For this purpose, we had arranged a stay in England: Ingrid in Crew, and I in Llay, Wales, near Llangollan, where I was with the Madrigal Choir the year before and had won a big trophy. The good old Puch scooter was the vehicle—a long trip for such a fragile machine. We were near enough to see each other sometimes. For two months, we tried to become polished English speakers. We appreciated the hospitality of our friendly host families.

Late in August, we started moving south, to Brighton, where we wanted to catch a ferry to France. Our cash flow was marginal, but we were blissfully carefree, enjoying berry patches, limestone cliffs and a good ferry with cots on the way to Bretagne.

With our perfect English, we wanted to enjoy Paris and compensate for the Anglo-Saxon sobriety with a bit of Gallic spice. We found a quaint and cheap hotel on the hill of Montmartre. We were young, beautiful and innocent, until the night—where else but in Paris—when we saw that we were made for each other. We consumed the erotic chalice with French spice, and Ingrid became my wife. Never had Paris looked more romantic and wonderful. There were more overnights in France with the tender caresses enhanced by a good French meal with red wine. We stopped at the stunning church of Rochamp by

Le Corbusier—even though we had to fish the coins from the fountain for the entrance fee. Switzerland was close, however, and we met with Ingrid's friend Barbara Haselbach, a dancer, in Bern.

With little cash, we reached the border of Austria. We drove past a village called Haiming in the Ötztal and then via Innsbruck over the Brenner Pass into Italy and back into Austria near Dobbiaco. We were not yet within walking distance to home, but close. Our cash cushion had virtually reached the bottom when the scooter started acting up. We had been driving in pouring rain, especially in England, and now, the cables for the clutch and the gas were stiff and broken. The scooter did not do its thing anymore. We went to the train station with dis-arming smiles, showed the remnants of British, French and Swiss cur-rency and wondered whether this would get us on the train to Klagenfurt. They looked at us and knew that we would camp at their doorsteps if they would not agree to an act of charity. We got on the train, fell asleep and woke up rolling into the Klagenfurt station, where they unloaded our handicapped scooter, which we pushed home.

But we had to make plans for Innsbruck. We had few belongings but many ideas on how to live more nicely in the Tyrolean capital. I was offered a job as a high school teacher in Haiming, and I accepted. It was the last stop before Innsbruck for the incoming express trains from Paris. I enjoyed those train rides after work and then hopped on the C-bus, which took me to Arzl. There, Ingrid had found a charming apartment near Innsbruck, and we lived cheerfully together in happy harmony with the conviction that life together is nicer than celibacy, something we did not share with our families. From our apartment, we saw the peaks of the Serles and the Habicht.

The university was indeed more attractive. There was a stupendous Fulbright professor, Chester E. Eisinger from Purdue—a Jew and a charismatic teacher. We started reading the canon of English and American literature in the original. We invited him to our home, and he planted the idea of a Fulbright Fellowship, for which we would eventu-ally apply. In the meantime, we studied seriously, hiked the mountains in fall, skied them in winter, and I kept teaching in Haiming.

The German Department was less attractive, but we were used to those orgies of roaming through piles of secondary sources while ignoring the primary texts. It was a disgrace. The professors pretended that we had read something, and we pretended that we had. We did that for two years. We might have stayed there forever. Maybe we would have finished our studies or not. Maybe I would have stayed a high school teacher or a tour guide, ski bum or innkeeper at some mountain hut. We might have been content with less, lived a simple life and yodeled on the weekends on some mountain at sunset.

Then, something unexpected happened. We surprised our families, and in October 1961 we got married in the baroque cathedral of Klagenfurt. Ingrid was beautiful, and I was dashing. Our families were concerned because we were still students with an uncertain future. Did we have no moral seriousness? Was frivolity our middle name? Did we ever think about income, retirement funds and stability?

Ingrid applied for and got a teaching job at the elementary school at Stams, a village with a splendid Cistercian monastery. Father Hermann tried to intervene and insisted that no heretic Protestant had ever set foot in this holy place. But our connection in the government worked, and we surprised him. I took a position at the high school in the same place. We rented an apartment in an unfinished house next to the railroad tracks. At night, we would be woken up by the express trains from Paris thundering by, and the earth shook. Ingrid was a sublimely gifted grade school teacher. Her students, who smelled of manure and mold, loved her. I taught German, art and music. Everybody loved us. It looked like an arrangement that would last forever.

But then something changed our lives for good. We did not know it back then, but ultimately it did. Without that event, we never would have landed in the Avon Hills, where we are today. We did follow the advice of Professor Eisinger and applied for a Fulbright Fellowship. So did my brother Gerhard at the University of Vienna. We all had splendid credentials, but the Fulbright Commission told us that awarding three Drekonjas would sound fishy. How about sending my brother as a Fulbright Fellow to Cornell, me as a Fulbright Fellow to Kent State, and Ingrid as a T.A. to a National Defense Education Act (NDEA) German Institute at Kent State, where I would also T.A.? Now, Fulbright Fellows are supposed to study in the U.S. and must return home and tell about the glory of the U.S. It was one of the brilliant moves of

Senator Fulbright to build bridges to the rest of the world, and it worked well. By anybody's projection, we would not stay in the States, and we did not plan to do so. But here we are, listening to Minnesota Public Radio founded by Fr. Colman Barry, O.S.B., at Saint John's University, becoming part of Garrison Keillor's Lake Wobegon fairy-tale landscape with the concrete structures of Marcel Breuer's Bauhaus architecture at SJU and the coziness of our two-story brick house with the paintings of Bela Petheo and Ingrid's hospitable porch, the "Slough View Inn" as our friends call it affectionately.

VI

The year was 1962. We had submitted our applications to the Vienna Fulbright Commission. We looked glorious on paper and even better in reality. We had to go to Salzburg to an American doctor who would attest that we were without TB, STD or other contagious diseases and in good health. That Ingrid was slightly pregnant, he did not notice, but we knew and were happy. For the visit we paid a hefty fee. That was our early introduction to the U.S., which has no universal coverage healthcare system. Then we had to go to Vienna for an interview. We denied ever having been Nazis, Communists or political agents against democracy. We were also asked about the meaning of the Salzburg Festivals, and we said that they were too expensive for us to attend. They must have liked our unconventional mix of marriage, studies and fulltime work, and they clearly must have noticed our brilliant potential for the future. On top of that, we had stellar recommendations from Professor Eisinger and others. Many years later, I saw my file and was impressed as to what was written about me. We were told that we were recipients of two grants and a teaching assistantship for Kent State in Ohio. We even found the place on the map.

Our families were panicky. Can one really give birth to a baby in America? We thought one could since the population was on a growth curve. The travel arrangements were made by a Mr. Krasitzky at the American Express in Vienna. My ticket was paid for, but Ingrid had to pay her share. We got tickets for a first-class sleeper car from Vienna to Rotterdam. Never before had we indulged in such hedonistic luxury. Waking up in Rotterdam, we boarded the *Statendam* of the Holland America Line. It was a stormy crossing of the North Atlantic, and Ingrid did not enjoy the culinary delights of the ship. I did.

After seven days, we landed in Hoboken. A man from the Austrian Institute, sent by Mrs. Zernatto, was there to bring us to Manhattan. After all, the major emphasis of my project was to write a dissertation about an Austrian emigrant named Guido Zernatto. He was the Secretary General of the Unity Party "Fatherland Front," and after Schuschnigg, the second-highest ranking man in the Austrian government prior to the Anschluss. Unlike Schuschnigg, he advocated a militant response to the German takeover. It never came to be. He escaped Vienna as Hitler annexed Austria and came to New York in 1941 via Paris, Mentone and Lisbon on the SS *Excalibur*, together with Alma and Franz Werfel, the Zuckmayrs and other celebrities fleeing the Nazis. Zernatto then worked at Fordham University and wrote books, articles and manifestos. He tried to form an Austrian government in exile with Otto von Habsburg and Otto Bauer, the Social Democrat, but to no avail. He died in 1943. I wanted to find the papers and the materials he had left behind. Nobody knew anything about it in Austria.

We were received wonderfully at 11 East 52nd Street, at the Austrian Forum—now a brilliant little skyscraper by the Austrian architect Abraham. It was the beginning of a wonderful friendship with Mrs. Zernatto, a highly intelligent, irreverent Jewish woman of great wit and civility. We stayed in New York for a few days. After we were turned away from the 66th Tower restaurant, Ingrid bought a stylish New York outfit: a short black formal dress. That along with a single strand of pearls made a look worthy of New York's high society.

Before we left for Kent by train via Washington, D.C., we stayed for a week or so with a hospitable family in Westport, Connecticut, where we also met my brother Gerhard, who had arrived earlier. It was a splendid introduction to America. At the Unitarian Church, I met the great Dave Brubeck in person. We had admired him last at the Vienna Stadthalle. We also enjoyed the train rides from Westport to Manhattan, where we fell in love with that exuberant city. But the time had come for our trip to Kent. We hopped on a night train with a sleeper compartment, saw Washington at night and arrived in the morning in Kent, Ohio.

It was not a pretty town. A Professor Tapp picked us up in a rusty Ford. We lived in brand-new married student apartments. We were T.A.s at an NDEA German Institute of Kent State. Our students were middle-aged teachers, mostly married, who were hoping to be recycled as language teachers in order to catch up with those Russians after Sputnik and their scientific advantage. Bill Braxton was a retired air force officer, a very nice guy from Florida. The Raus came from New Jersey, and the Hoketts from Texas. Donald Hokett was very kind, but had no talent for language. Norene was a drama queen and very spirited. We stayed in touch for many years.

The best part was that we could study comparative literature with stellar professors. For the first time ever, we read the masterworks of the French, Russian and English novelists. We discovered Irish literature and the world of Melville. After years of drowning in secondary sources in Europe, we were able to read and discuss the original texts of the 19th century. It was wonderful. At the same time, my brother Gerhard was studying at Cornell in New York, and he discovered Latin America.

Most importantly, Ingrid was pregnant. By Christmas, it was visible. In spring, our first child, Thomas, would be born in the New World. There was also work, studies, teaching, and doing the daily chores of shopping, entertaining and coping with the drab looks of the industrial Midwest, which looked gray, rusty and cluttered, and a bit tacky. Sure, we took trips to New York, the splendid city. We visited the Simons in Westport. We drove to Chicago and Colorado with the Hoketts. But those were rather fleeting impressions.

In the meantime, America was sliding into the Cuban Missile Crisis. Our concerned parents in Austria wanted us to come back. There was the Bay of Pigs debacle, and John F. Kennedy tried to avoid a nuclear war. He succeeded. We were sure he would, and he did.

Peter, Paul and Mary came and sang on stage at Kent State. We tried to be good "cultural ambassadors" of the German-speaking world. And we discovered that we were rather successful teachers and pretty good graduate students. It was a given that we would return to Tyrol after one year as Fulbrighters. By Christmas, we got notification from the Education Administration in Innsbruck that we would be assigned to the *Hauptschule* in Ötz im Ötztal upon return. Further away from Innsbruck! Not back to Stams! Not able to finish our university degrees in Innsbruck from such a distance! NO! We asked Fulbright for another year in the States and told the office in Innsbruck that we resigned from our tenured positions! That was a rather bold move, and people back home thought we had lost all sense. Maybe we had. We had shed all vestiges of humility and acted like arrogant Americans.

Most of all, we were concerned about our baby, which was due in March. Ingrid's stepfather came to visit in order to greet the new Drekonja. He had only a few days time for it and wanted us to deliver on time—a command performance, so to speak. And it worked. Not because Ingrid was so respectful, but because her stepfather was plain lucky. Staying here for another year also meant that we had to find a job because Fulbright had already given out all awards for the coming year. First, we toyed with the idea of a summer job running a trading post in Alaska but then accepted a summer job teaching German at Rhodes College in Memphis, Tennessee. Then, a full-year contract was offered by a Benedictine university in Minnesota. We thought the three of us would make it somehow.

Now Norene Hokett will take over and tell how we were doing in Kent for the time being.

Meeting Ingrid

She stood at the door of our married student apartment. She was so tiny, so European. The wind whipped her heavy winter coat and scarf about her. She had been crying and looked like she was ready to break out in tears again any minute.

"Ve live next door," she explained in her Austrian accent. "Ve haven't met but I need to talk to someone."

"You must be Ingrid," I said, while opening the door wider and motioning for her to come in. "My husband said you are so very encouraging at the German Language Institute. He appreciates you and your husband so much."

"Thank you. He is very nice." It was plain she was not here to talk about the Institute.

The year was 1962. A number of families had come to Kent State University for a year of language studies to become more fluent German teachers. We had sold our new home, stored our furniture and moved our clothes and pots and pans all the way to Kent, Ohio. From the first day, my husband Don was lost, with a capital "L." He spoke very little German, although he had completed fifteen college units worth—just enough to be assigned to teach three German classes in a large high school in Forth Worth, Texas. He had spent his first year as a teacher attempting to keep over-active high school students in their chairs while he used generic language tapes that said truly exciting things like, "The teacher has a pen. The teacher likes his pen. The pen has no ink," etc. But German language teachers were difficult to find in Texas while Spanish teachers were a dime a dozen. German was truly a "foreign" language to rodeo riding cowpokes fresh off the range. "As long as I can dance the two-step and ride a stationary bull at Billy Bob's Steak House, who needs it? I ain't never heard nobody speak in German," his students would tease him. Don didn't think it was very funny.

"Those kids are making fun of me," he would worry, as he stayed up past midnight every night, getting ready for another hellish tomorrow.

The Fort Worth school system allowed him a year off to perfect his German, so desperate were they for teachers. We had put my drama department on hold for a year while we came up north for some much needed help. However, fearing we might not return, they insisted he take a three-month concentrated course in Bozeman, Montana, instead. After that year at Kent State, I often wondered what "concentrated" meant! The first day Don opened the language house door, it read, "*Deutsch bitte*," meaning "German, please," so there was no English spoken past that door.

"Take a year and you cannot come back," the administration finally decided. Being stubborn, Don chose the year-long institute. So my dream drama job, our new house and everything were gone. Don was over his ears in more German than he could handle. The young Austrian couple in the apartment next door had been the only really helpful faculty at the Institute. Most of the rest of the faculty spoke only German. We, "the Instituters," even went grocery shopping for many of them. Ingrid and Max had graciously helped translate Don's grocery list since these old-world professors asked for things not too familiar to English-speaking Americans, especially ones who had only been guests in their country for about nine months, while Don was in the army.

"Ingrid is very pregnant," Don would worry. "She is so little, but she is so sweet. You would really like her Norene. Why don't you get acquainted? It would give you something to do besides grading all those stacks of English papers." I had traded my high school drama job for a junior high school English job, and I was nearly as unhappy as Don had been the year before.

"But Don, I have trouble understanding her. Maybe she is just quiet and speaks low," I would argue.

"But she is so alone," he would worry, when he had time to think of something besides his studies. "I'm the poorest language student in the entire German Institute," he would complain.

"No way!" I tried to encourage. "What about ol' martini eyes?"

But, to Don, it wasn't funny. "Even swearin' drunk, he is better than me."

In an effort to tease him, I would suggest that he might drink a quart or two of vodka and see if it improved his German, but I would have overstepped my bounds and threatened his Christian morals. I had already overstepped my boundaries, so my encouraging remarks would cease for the day.

Now, Ingrid, still standing in our living room, was tearing up again. "I'm sure your husband has told you I'm pregnant. I'm so far from home, and I don't vant to have my baby here. I vant to go home."

I put my arms around her. We had more in common than she knew. I was homesick too. Texas was a long ways away, and I couldn't go home again, either.

"Oh, Ingrid, you'll have your baby over here, and that's better than having it in Austria."

She just looked at me and said, "For you, maybe. But Austria is home, and I'm so homesick."

I knew just what she meant. As we wrapped our arms around each other, I didn't realize that I was hugging someone who would become a lifelong friend. She and Max are all we really got out of that cold year at Kent Sate, but that warm friendship made all of the heartaches of that year worthwhile.

Holidaze

As Thanksgiving approached, Ingrid and Max and Don and I made plans for a trip to Lafayette, Indiana. We'd decided to go together even though we were visiting different sets of friends there.

"Ingrid, are you taking all of your big monies?" I laughed, as Ingrid stuffed the bills from the cabinet into her purse.

"Oh, yah, we might need it."

We were on the road early, had stopped and had a rather large breakfast. In reviewing the bill, Max laughed, "At this rate, we won't have enough big money to feed us all the way there and back! Ingrid is such a hungry one, lately. No doubt she is eating for herself and a very fine boy."

After paying, we were on the road again, and soon were asleep, except Don, who was driving. Later on, Ingrid awoke, "Max! Have you seen my purse?"

"Me? No. Vhy you ask?"

"Because I don't have it."

"You must have it somewhere here."

"No, I tell you, you have it, I'm sure."

"Vhy would I have it?"

"Max, look on the seat on the other side of you."

As Max searched all around the seat, Ingrid was becoming increasingly alarmed. "Oh no, Donald, my purse is missing. I don't remember having it after we left our breakfast place. How far is it back to vhere ve had breakfast?"

"Oh, fifty or sixty miles at least," Don replied. "Are you sure it isn't back there somewhere?"

"No, ve have looked. It is surely missing. Ve must go back. All of our money is in it."

Don pulled over to the side of the road, so a more thorough search could be made. After looking everywhere, no purse was to be found. The purse was really missing. We had to go back on the chance that we might find it. Don turned the car around, and we headed back toward the restaurant. None of us were hopeful that it would be there. If someone had found it, they probably wouldn't admit it. Finding a purse full of bills would be a "lucky find" for the finder, and too bad for the loser.

After arriving back at the restaurant, we all went in, and Max approached the lady behind the cash register. "Have you found a small purse? Ve sat right back there in that booth."

"Sorry, sir. We haven't found any purses. I remember you were here a couple of hours ago. Yes, you sat right back there, didn't you?"

"Yah, vell, I'll go back and look, but there is little hope, I agree."

Looking rather downcast, Max and Ingrid walked back to the booth where we had enjoyed our large breakfast. "Max! Here it is!" Ingrid exclaimed, holding up her purse. "Right vhere I left it. And yes, it still has all our big monies inside!"

Jubilant, all four of us laughed, and even cried a little at our happy find.

Then, we were on the road again to our destination. Each couple had good times and pleasant visits with friends that Thanksgiving. But the highlight of the trip was in the lost and found department, finding the lost purse with the big monies.

Not long after that Thanksgiving, Ingrid's Christmas box arrived from Austria. Waiting until Christmas to open it was not an option. It would be opened immediately, and it was. Ingrid's mother had sent lots of homemade pastries associated with Christmas and home. Her mother had also included a lovely little doll. Its face, hands and feet were made of doeskin. The detail was so fine, even his little tongue was sticking out. He was about three inches high, wore a tiny little shirt and lederhosen. Wrapped around him was a note in German. Translated, it said, "Remember when this was our bread and butter?"

Ingrid's father had died in the war, and her mother had been the only means of support. The mother had made up pairs of these little dolls and sold them all over Europe and later in the United States.

Each time I went to Ingrid's apartment, I visited with the little fellow. Later, when I opened my gift from Ingrid that Christmas, she had given me that little doll. It is a treasure that I still have and enjoy.

Another item in Ingrid's Christmas box that year was candle holders for the tree. In Austria, trees are sometimes decorated with real candles. Ingrid decorated her tree with them. Of course, the candles are only lit for a few minutes at a time, and only when someone is in the room.

I availed myself of a nice garden hose, just in case. I told Ingrid she should keep it near the tree. One of the last times she lit the candles, a branch did catch fire. She put it out with a small pail of water.

In the weeks before Christmas, Ingrid bought clay, and we made figures for the manger. There was a manger with all of the Christmas characters and animals. There were cows, donkeys and camels for the wise men; but she was so inspired, she even had elephants.

As I looked at her perfectly formed animals, it was apparent she had the ability of her mother. "Ingrid! That's not a donkey."

"Of course it's not. It is a fine elephant."

"An elephant? They don't belong down there."

"Vell, I don't know, but I think all the animals came."

I don't know why, but her elephants seemed to fit right in.

On Christmas Eve, Don and I and Max and Ingrid went sledding on a hill on the Kent State campus. Ingrid sledded along with us even though she was very pregnant. "Watch out and don't hit a tree!" I warned, but she was fearless.

"Don't worry, Norene. I know about such things. She took to her sled and maneuvered around the trees with the greatest of ease.

We had a festive celebration, making turkey with all the trimmings the next day. It was Ingrid's first Christmas away from home. I know she was missing home, but that is one Christmas holiday I always recall with fondness and will never forget.

Thomas Discovers America

"Norene! Norene! Are you home?" It was Ingrid's excited voice accompanying the knocking on my door. "Hurry, hurry, I have something to tell you," she cried.

I opened the front door and Ingrid rushed in. Her face was flushed, and she obviously had news she didn't really like.

"My stepfather is coming to America!" she stammered, not thrilled at the prospect.

"When?" I questioned.

"Today! This afternoon! Max must meet his plane in Cleveland. Oh, I tell you, vhy must he come? Vhy couldn't he send my mother? Oh no. Not him. This is important business. No, he has to take care of it himself."

"But Ingrid, the baby hasn't been born yet."

"Yah, and he is not a patient man. He will demand to see the baby now! Vell, I haven't seen the baby yet, either, but the kind of man he is, he will demand to see it first!" Ingrid was beside herself. This stepfather was a most overbearing gentleman, and she was anticipating the worst.

"Where's Max?" I questioned.

"Oh, he has gone to pick him up at the airport. Donald took him, I think."

"Oh, yes, Don did leave me a note, saying he was taking Max to Cleveland. So that is what it was for. I read the note, but I didn't really understand it. Now it makes sense."

"Yah, it is not good, I tell you," Ingrid said, sitting down while throwing her hands in the air.

Sitting down beside her, I asked, "Are they coming back here for dinner?"

"Oh, yah, of course. He is a big fellow, and he will stride in demanding dinner. He is always demanding things. That's the kind of man he is. I don't know how my mother tolerates him."

"Oh, he can't be that bad," I tried to encourage.

"Oh, yah, he is. You vill see. You vill be impressed. He does not speak English, so you vill hear him in his native tongue. And you have often said you think German is a harsh language, vell, just wait, it is worse when he speaks it!"

By now, Ingrid was in tears, so great was her frustration.

"For just once in his lifetime, vhy couldn't he be thoughtful and send my mother? I would love to see her. But no, he thinks of himself, as usual. He will make the trip and report back. It isn't even his grand-child. It is his step-grandchild. Oh, but he will make the big trip to America. He will be the important one, as always."

Ingrid was so tired from her anger and frustration, she buried her head in her hands but finally wiped away her latest tears, stood up and started toward the door.

"I must prepare dinner for him," she said, opening the door. Then she turned back toward me and with a wicked twinkle in her eye, said, "Do you have any poison I can borrow?"

"Only some black shoe polish!" I returned, giggling.

"No, Norene. I don't want to make him sick. I want to kill him!" With that she turned and slammed the door on her way out. But, on second thought, she opened it again, stuck her head in and declared, "You and Donald will come to dinner tonight, also."

"Oh, but Ingrid, you have enough on your mind without feeding us too," I argued.

"Ah, Norene, no, it is good. If you come, I vill be nicer to him. That vay I won't kill him, and I von't have to spend time in prison for mur-der!" With that, she was gone.

That night, Don and I went next door to dinner. As usual, Ingrid had prepared a lovely meal. The expression on her face spoke vol-umes, and she wasn't happy. She was right, the stepfather spoke no English. Max did the honors, "Norene, you vill meet Ingrid's stepfa-ther," he began, as this large gentleman in front of me took my ex-tended hand, smiled and made a small bow. I don't remember if he said anything or not. He seemed awfully big, and whether he was or not wasn't important. With Ingrid's description, he seemed huge, and his German was clipped, harsh and scary. I wanted to rush back to our apartment and slam the door.

Don's introduction wasn't any better. The man asked Don a question in German. Don was so intimidated he looked to Max for translation. Max quickly said something in German, explaining that Don was in the German Language Institute. Then Don tried a sentence in German. There was a long silence, finally followed by the stepfather's bellowed question, "Vot?" Don wasn't doing so well.

"Didn't you meet him this afternoon?" I asked Don.

"Well, sort of. He and Max did the talking; I drove the car. I think Max intended to get Dr. Catsfield to go, but he was busy." Don tried once more, but there was something pitiful about his efforts, and the stepfather stared in disbelief. He reminded me of a famous music conductor who has just heard a sour note. Evidently realizing that Don wouldn't understand him anyway, he turned and seated himself at the table.

The delicious meal was eaten in German. Max and the stepfather did most of the talking, with Ingrid offering a few remarks, all in German. Don may have understood some of the conversation, but I was at a total loss. A few times, the stepfather banged his fist on the table while speaking to Ingrid. She was respectful, but her answer sounded emotionally hot to me.

Later, after we had cleared the table, washed the dishes and returned home, she came to our apartment. "What was that all about," I inquired of Ingrid.

"Vell, my stepfather said I must produce this baby tonight. His plane returns to Austria Monday morning at 8:00 o'clock. I told him I cannot just produce this baby to fit his schedule. But he says that he is here, he cannot vait," whatever that means. "I told him that babies aren't born on schedules. They come when they come. He said, 'Take a laxative!' Can you believe that man?"

"Don't take a laxative. That wouldn't be good for the baby," I cautioned.

"Yah, I know, but that man claps his hands, and he vants the whole world to bow. That includes me and my baby.

By now Ingrid is almost in tears. "I must do something. I hope Max gets him to go to bed before I go back to the apartment."

"Listen, Ingrid, it's 10:00 o'clock on Saturday night. You might not have that baby until next Saturday night. Then what will he do?"

"Oh, I must have it before he leaves, I tell you. He stomps, and he shouts, and the world stops until he tells it to turn again! I vill have the baby before he leaves!" she said with a determined voice.

"How can you?"

"Because he will probably scare it out of me!" and with that she was gone.

It was well past midnight when there was a loud banging on our front window. It woke me up. "What was that?" I cried sitting straight up.

"Oh, it must be Max," exclaimed Don. "The baby must be coming."

"You don't suppose Ingrid took a laxative, do you?"

"I don't know, but from the sound of that front window, Max thinks that baby is on the way."

I jumped out of bed and started dressing while Don answered the door. I heard Don ask, "Max, what is it?"

"Yah, I think the baby is ready to come. Suddenly, he is a persistent little fellow from the pain Ingrid is in. The labor pains are close together and rather strong, she tells me. I think the baby comes soon."

"We'll be ready in a minute," Don said. We had offered to take Ingrid and Max to the hospital when the baby came because they had no car.

Within a very short time, the four of us had rushed down to the car and were on our way. Ravenna, Ohio, was the next little town over from Kent. It had a hospital; Kent did not. Don took the only highway leading to Ravenna.

"Max, vhere is the hospital," asked Ingrid.

"Vell, I'm not—I'm not really sure," replied Max.

"Max! You were supposed to go to the Ravenna hospital to make arrangements. You did that, didn't you?"

"Vell, not exactly. I kept intending to ask Donald to bring me, but, vell, we were all so busy."

"Max! You mean you never came and filled out the paperwork?"

"Oh, vell sure, but Ingrid I never managed to get over here."

"And we don't know how to get to the hospital, either!" fretted Ingrid.

"Donald, you will need to find someplace that is open so we can ask questions. I tell you, ve need directions."

"It would be good if we could find a public telephone. We could call the hospital," reasoned Don.

"Yah. It is after midnight," chimed in Max. "There von't be too many places open now, and the snow just keeps piling up."

Snow was piled high on both sides of the roadway. "If there is some place open, it will be difficult to get near," Don said, surveying the high ridges. "We don't have this much snow in Texas. Here, it just never seems to melt."

Suddenly, we spied a window with a light. "Oh, what is that?" cried Ingrid.

"Looks like an all-night Laundromat™. That won't do us any good," I informed.

"Vell, it might have a telephone, and somebody might be doing their laundry," Max said. "Maybe they vill know where the hospital is."

Don pulled toward the curb, which was still piled with snow, but before anyone could do anything, Ingrid jumped out and ran toward the Laundromat™ door. She went inside and talked to a young man doing his laundry. It was a hurried conversation, with Ingrid nodding several times. Don and Max were still trying to get their doors open but discovered they opened directly into snow banks. In the meantime, I had managed to get out, but Ingrid was already on the way back to the car. "We are in luck," she announced. "It is just a few blocks from here. Lucky for us it is a small town!"

As we continued on our way, I said, "That guy looked a bit surprised while you were talking to him."

"Yah, I guess he did too!" Max exclaimed. "Here was this lady, obviously ready to give birth, asking for directions to the hospital!"

"Yah, Max, I could be having this baby on the street corner. We must be getting to the hospital if my pains are any indication," moaned Ingrid.

"I see the hospital just ahead," Don said. "We'll be there in a minute."

"We don't have any time to lose, I tell you. Ingrid is having some hard pains here."

Don pulled into a parking place, as Max opened the door and ran to get a wheel chair. Once Ingrid was safely seated, he wheeled her into the lobby. Don and I ran along behind.

I looked over at Don. "Don, why don't you take over the wheel chair, and Max and I will get her checked in?" So Don grabbed the wheel chair as Max and I raced over to the check-in window.

"We have a lady here who is having labor pains, two minutes apart. We need to get her to the delivery room right now," I hurriedly told the lady.

"Have you filled out the preliminary paperwork?" she asked.

"Well, no, but if you'll take her on back, we'll take care of that right now."

"Not until the forms are filled out. That must be taken care of first," she informed us in a stern, curt voice.

"Lady," Max pleaded, "My vife is having a baby *now*."

"Well, we can't take her here until the paperwork is completed," she announced in an even sterner Brunhild-type voice. "She probably doesn't have any friends to lose," I surmised, standing there completely at her mercy. "And she probably really doesn't care."

She handed Max a pen and several pages of forms. He was so frustrated; he just stood and looked at them. I grabbed the pen and directed him to a nearby chair. In the meantime, Don and Ingrid were across the lobby, Ingrid in the chair, looking frantic, and Don holding her hand.

"Can you hurry up here?" Don called out. "Her pains are coming faster all the time."

"Hang on," I called back. "We have to get the forms filled out. No paperwork, no baby."

"Oh, there'll be a baby, all right," Don's voice was a few decibels higher. "It may arrive in the lobby if they don't let us in."

"Look, Max, answer these questions, and I will fill in the blanks. Where was Ingrid born?"

I was already in trouble. "Okay, okay, spell it."

The questions went fairly well until Ingrid became more and more uncomfortable and frantic. One or two cries of pain got our attention. Now Max was getting concerned and excited. At this point some of his answers were coming in German. "Keep it in English," I pleaded. Ingrid was too excited to remember anything, and so was I. We did the best we could under the circumstances, and it went pretty well except for when Max lapsed into German instead of English. I would remind him, and we would continue all over again. Finally, I handed the completed forms to Brunhild. Untouched by anything, she directed Max to take Ingrid to the delivery room. He raced across the lobby, grabbed the wheel chair and rushed toward the double doors leading back to the delivery area. Don and I stood there waving at them, as they sped out of sight.

"Call us when the baby comes," called Don. But it was doubtful either one of them heard. They were really in a hurry, and well they should have been.

We drove back to Kent at a much slower speed. We were exhausted. It was after 3:00 o'clock in the morning by the time we got home and in bed.

At 6:00 o'clock, three hours later, the phone rang, and I answered to find Max on the other end of the line. He was jubilant.

"It is a lovely boy!" he announced. "He is quite a handsome fellow. He has a lovely prominent nose. You should see him."

"What will you call him?"

"Ah! We shall name him Thomas Drekonja."

"No middle name?"

"Nah. Thomas Drekonja is all the name he needs."

"You could call him Thomas E̲. Drekonja. " E" for elephant to go with his outstanding, prominent nose!" I teased. "And how is Ingrid?"

"Oh, she is very tired. She sleeps now, and so does the baby. I vill be home in a little while if Donald can come and get me. However, I want Donald to go next door and tell the grandfather. He is liable to vake up and vonder where ve are. I am sure Donald can tell him the happy news; then ask Donald to come and get me. I think I'll enjoy a little sleep myself."

"Okay, I'll tell him Max. Don will be there in a little while."

Don went next door to inform the new grandfather that he was a grandfather. A few minutes later, Don retuned. "That was so dear, Norene. That man was so thrilled. He had me call Western Union, and he sent the cleverest telegram. It was simple and straight to the point.

"It said, 'I have seen the light of day. Signed Thomas Drekonja.'"

Don and I put our arms around each other. What an exciting, hectic, delightful and memorable two days.

Thomas Is Introduced to Touch Football

"Max! You are supposed to be watching Thomas," Ingrid reprimanded.

"Oh, I am a very versatile fella," Max assured her. "I can do both. It's called delegating responsibility." Max was displaying one of his most winning personality traits, his charm.

"Vell, you should have delegated the responsibility of playing touch football, not the care of Thomas. Vhere is Thomas?" Ingrid demanded. She was looking unhappier by the moment, and it was plain to see. However, she very rarely ever lost patience with Max.

"Yah, he's around here, somevhere."

Our entire section of married student housing was occupied by the German Language Instituters, so Thomas was relatively safe. In fact, most of the students preferred Professor Drekonja; he had such good rapport with the students, and that is why he and Ingrid were housed in student housing.

"Who did you give him to, Max?" By now Ingrid's chin was thrust forward, her hands were on her hips, and she wore a scowl on her face. Charm or no charm, Max was in trouble!

Ingrid and I had been grocery shopping. Upon our return, we had discovered several of the Institute men and Max playing touch football in front of our section of the married student apartments.

"Yah, he is around here somewhere, I tell you. He could not have gotten far, fortunately. He isn't valking yet. Oof! Not at the ripe old age of two months!"

"But someone could kidnap him," Ingrid protested. "He is a handsome little fella, you know." Her temper was rising and by this time, she didn't care who knew it.

"Ah, Ingrid, don't get so angry. Ve vill find him. I gave him to some nice lady on the bottom floor of the apartments, I'm sure."

"You mean to tell me you don't know who has him?"

"Ah, vell, it was someone on the bottom floor. He couldn't have gotten far."

Max is beginning to see the situation from Ingrid's perspective and realizes he has a problem. "Aw, ve vill find him, I'm sure of it. You start at that end of the apartments, and I'll start at this end." Max's efforts at charming his wife had ended. He was now in serious trouble, and he knew it.

"Max, you really did lose my baby. Ven vill you ever grow up?" By now, Max is frantically knocking on apartment doors. With a flushed face and her hands on her hips, Ingrid followed him from door to door. She was angrier than I had ever seen her. Fortunately, Thomas was discovered in the third apartment.

A couple came to the door with Thomas. "He's none the worse for the wear and tear," Max informed, but he was beginning to look a bit strained.

Ingrid grabbed her long lost baby, cradling him and talking to him in her own brand of baby speak. She thanked the couple for taking care of Thomas. "Yah, you did a better job of taking care of Thomas than my forgetful husband here."

Behind her, Max was carrying on his own monologue. "You see Ingrid, he is fine. I knew I had put him in safe hands. He is well-fed; he is happy. Just look at him! He is all ready for a nap." But Max was carrying on his conversation with thin air.

As we walked up the stairway to our apartments, Ingrid was talking to Thomas all the way in her own special language. Max was racing along behind, still explaining, "You see, I knew Thomas was fine. I am a responsible fella. I just have a little weakness for touch football."

But Ingrid wasn't having any. "Max! You are a fool. I vill condemn you to going to the grocery store from now and . . . ."

The rest of her remarks reverted to German and were totally lost on me. They weren't lost on Max, however. Her remarks intensified in volume and speed, and as they did, I noticed that Max was quickly changing strategies. He no longer appeared the happy-go-lucky fella with a touch football game to play. He was accepting the responsibility of the ne'er-do-well idiot, who all but put her young son up for adoption. Or worse, child endangerment, or desertion would be more like it.

"Yah! I am a fool! I am an idiot! It's true. How could I do it? I don't know."

As Ingrid continued her tongue-lashing, attacking in rapid German, Max continued to agree with her, vehemently.

By now we were inside their apartment. Hoping to be of help, I followed the warring couple into the bedroom. Ingrid had checked Thomas's diaper and discovered it was soaked. She placed Thomas on a changing pad on her bed and continued her diatribe, while removing the diaper and placing it in the diaper pail. She then opened the drawer and reached in for a replacement. However, something in the drawer claimed her attention. She pulled out a heavily soiled diaper, still dripping with more than adequate contents.

"Max! You put a dirty diaper in the drawer with the clean ones?" her loudest voice asked, as her astonished face turned red.

"Oh, yah, I am such a fool, I must have forgotten. My mind was on touch football, and the fellas were in a hurry to start . . . ."

His explanation was drowned out by Ingrid's explosive remarks, completely in German, delivered in a key, volume and speed I would not have believed possible for her.

Max was reacting now with complete chagrin. His head was down, he nodded repeatedly, "Is true, yah, is true. I tell you, it is true."

Ingrid wasn't finished. As she continued in deliberate fashion, she must have been delivering some well-placed verbal blows because Max's face was now almost as red as hers. Max continued to shake his head and mutter phrases in obvious agreement.

Both of them had forgotten I was a spectator to one of their most intense emotional battles. Just then, Max turned and saw me. His embarrassment quickly turned to humiliation.

"You do not understand?" he inquired, staring at me. But he had already figured out my answer, long before I shook my head "no."

"Hah! THIS TIME, I DO NOT TRANSLATE," he announced, sounding more like the charming rascal he is.

That phrase broke the tension, and suddenly all three of us were laughing. What a wonderful relief! "That's one time I'm glad I don't speak German," I giggled.

"Yah, ve are glad too," Ingrid laughed. "You wouldn't believe all the awful things I called Max."

"It was pretty bad, okay, BUT IT LOSES SO MUCH IN THE TRANSLATION!" he declared, triumphantly.

Once again, Max had come out on top, as usual.

Max Buys a Car

"Is Donald there?" I heard Max ask on the telephone.

"Oh, yes, of course. Shall I put him on?"

"Yah, please. Prepare for a shock."

I called Don to the phone, and as he listened, he exclaimed, "You did what?"

Don continued to listen, then said, "I hear you. I just don't believe you!" Then he hung up the receiver, turned around toward me, shaking his head, "Max just bought a car!"

"Oh, no! He said he couldn't drive."

"Yeah, and I'm to go over and drive the car home." Don shook his head in disbelief.

"Wow! This should be exciting. What kind of a car is it?"

"A VW Bug, of course," Don laughed. "He wouldn't dare buy anything else." Don got his jacket, and we made the trip to pick up the car. When we arrived, Max was still walking around, admiring his car. Ingrid was standing nearby, holding Thomas.

"Oh, yah, Donald, isn't it a beautiful car?" Max exclaimed, pointing to his VW Bug.

"Max is crazy," gestured Ingrid, nodding toward the bright blue purchase. "We have a new baby. Vhy must we have a new car all in the same year? If Max could drive, vell then, maybe, but breaking in a baby and a car all in one year is too much!"

"Ah, come, Ingrid. It is time to take our newest baby home," Max proclaimed, proudly. "No, me and my baby vill ride home with Norene. You and Donald can go home in the new buggy," said Ingrid as she walked toward me.

The days and weeks that followed were filled with excitement as Max learned to drive. The happenings usually took place on the street to and from the Institute, since that was the only time to learn, so busy was everyone with studies. All of us left the student housing about 8 o'clock in the morning—me for school, and Don, Max and Ingrid for the language house. I usually led the way, but not always. Sometimes they started first, and the carnival in front of me was well worth the wait.

As always, Max was eager and enthusiastic. Once everyone was on board the Bug, he and Don, and sometimes another student, pulled onto the well-salted streets of Kent. Salt was the way the little town kept its thoroughfares free of ice. On nights when there was measurable snowfall, the snowplows were out early. Otherwise, the streets would re-freeze into a glaze of ice. Then the street crews would spread a heavy coat of salt. Whatever the condition of the streets, Max approached his driving with fervor. The rest of us watched with enjoyment.

In the beginning, Max was well-aware of the gears. However, he appeared to be too busy driving to make use of them. When he did, he often didn't seem to know just when that time was. He would pick up speed too hurriedly, and whatever the gear, the car would begin to jump. The passengers were subjected to a series of jerks and jumps as the little Bug sought the right gear to match the road. The speed would vary widely. Approaching a hill, the gear often didn't match Max's enthusiasm. The car would give one final, mighty lurch and die.

At that point, everyone behind the VW had to stop. If I were driving behind them, I would see Max throw his hands up in the air, and Don would turn toward Max, talking a blue streak. I could just hear him yelling, "Max, get your hands back on the wheel!"

Sometimes, Max and Don would get out and try to push the car out of the way as much as the high drifts on the side would allow and let the cars behind pass on by. Then Max and Don would climb back in and start all over.

Max had a unique approach to parallel parking. One morning I topped the hill to find Don and Max outside the little VW Bug, and I stopped to ask questions. "Max, what are you doing?" I yelled from my window.

"Vhy, ve are parallel parking," he called back.

"Aren't you supposed to be doing that from inside the car?"

"Ah, no. This is parallel parking for beginners. Donald here grabs the front bumper, and I grab the back one, and ve just lift it into place."

As I sat there watching, that is just what they did!

"Such skills are one of the last skills of the beginner driver. I vill lift my car into place until I can overcome some of my other problems, like the changing of the gears! Donald says they are still doing a bit too much screaming, but I am making progress."

By the end of the spring semester, Max had earned his driver's license, after two tries.

The next year, Ingrid and Max drove all the way from Minnesota to northern Colorado in their Bug to visit us. When they drove into our driveway, Max was the experienced driver. We welcomed them to our new home, completed only weeks before. "Ingrid, hand me that baby," I directed, reaching for Thomas. By now, he was a husky little fellow, made bulkier by his snow suit. "Isn't he hot in this outfit?" I questioned, as I started removing his heavy outer covering as we made our way into the house. As I got the suit off Thomas, I discovered he had a nice red rash all over!

Ingrid gasped. "Max! Look vhat I've done to our wonderful boy. I covered him up so vell, he has heat rash! Vell, perhaps it is better than a bad cold."

That evening as we were all getting ready for bed, Max looked forward to a hot, relaxing shower after such a trip. He went into the bathroom to shower while we sat talking.

Suddenly, we heard a loud thump, a ripping and crashing sound, followed by a loud yell from Max. We immediately jumped up, and the three of us rushed to the bathroom door. "Are you okay in there?" Don yelled, fearing the worst.

Suddenly, the door opened, and Max stood there in his bathrobe, holding the shower curtain. "Yah, I made it," he laughed, holding up the shower curtain, "but I'm afraid the shower curtain did not. On the way down, I grabbed for it, and it broke my fall, but it is now only a memory!"

A visit from the couple would not have been complete without a little drama. During the following days, we went skiing. I kept Thomas at the lodge, while the others skied. Thomas showed his excitement of the view, as he stood at the window and squealed watching his parents crisscrossing each others' trails on the mountain above us.

On the way back to our house that evening, we picked up some Easter eggs in a restaurant where we had stopped to eat. As Don drove on home, Ingrid fed Thomas a couple of them, and suddenly, Thomas was wide awake.

"Max! Vhat is wrong with Thomas?" He was jumping higher and higher in her lap.

"I don't know. He certainly is excited about something," he laughed, watching Thomas almost hitting his head on the top of the car, he was jumping so high.

"He acts drunk!" Ingrid observed, bending forward to smell Thomas's breath. "Max! Those Easter eggs must have had liquor in them!" she declared. "Thomas is drunk!"

That was the ultimate drama of the visit. Drunk before he could walk!

A few days later, the VW Bug was repacked, and the little family was ready to leave. The visit had been all too short, as were all the visits through the years, including one we shared about thirty years later, the year Thomas graduated from the University of San Diego.

Max and Ingrid's family had grown and so had ours. But with each visit, we never had really left that wild and crazy year at Kent State. What an adventuresome beginning it had been to a wonderful friendship which lasted for a lifetime.

VII

Thomas was a magnificent U.S. citizen and a healthy boy. Our students were chipping in as baby-sitters and helpers, so Ingrid could continue with her work as a T.A. After all, we had to pay for the boy in cash—$375.00, hospital, doctor and all. We had even more cash left in our kitchen drawer, so we bought a fine blue VW from Bill Braxton, who also taught me how to drive. And at Easter, we drove all the way to Cornell to show my brother the baby for which he was to act as a godfather. He liked the guy, but we baptized him without Gerhard back in Kent at the Newman Center. The Raus were the stand-in godparents. So the guy had a name: "Thomas." We forgot a middle initial. It should have been "F" for Fulbright.

I bought an old bike for Ingrid, so she could breast-feed Thomas during the workday. We called it the "Dairy Express." Ingrid became a celebrity—she was breast-feeding. American women seemed to be eager to become Hugh Hefner's centerfolds in *Playboy* and thought sucking babies would harm their chests. Well, Ingrid's chest remained quite impressive in spite of it. We finished our courses. We got good grades. We taught our seminars, and we enjoyed our students, all of whom were older than we. We picked up and left Kent. Only a few years later, Kent State would be on the map because of violent anti-Vietnam War protests: the burning down of ROTC buildings and the National Guard coming in, shooting students where we had once sat under trees with the baby.

We hopped into the blue VW and drove south. For the first time, it dawned on us how big this country really was. Several days later, after making stops at the pools of Holiday Inns, we arrived in Memphis. No longer the city of the blues, no longer the city of cotton. Not yet the famed city of John Grisham's great novels. But it was already a city torn apart by the Civil Rights Movement. Fountains and park benches "for whites only," back entrances to doctors' offices "for blacks only."

Southwestern at Memphis was a lily-white college for affluent whites. A Haliburton tower graced the ivy campus and reminded everybody of republican values. We rented the apartment of a fine writer, Jack Jones, whose books we enjoyed. Overton Park, with the zoo, was nearby, and roaring lions provided voice lessons for Thomas.

I taught German summer courses. After work, we would mingle with a colleague, Jared Wenger, a Russian expert, and taste the best Irish whisky, Dumphy. We admired the glorious sunsets beyond the mighty Mississippi over the Arkansas Bridge. We ventured into the State of Mississippi and wanted to visit the Faulkner mansion. Alas, with our Ohio plates, we looked like northern activists who were unwelcome in the integration-resisting South. They looked at us and said, "House is closed," even though it was open. "Absalom, Absalom!" What a complicated part of America we discovered.

But they liked us down there and indicated that we would be welcome for a longer stay. But we had a fine contract from Saint John's in Minnesota. After so many hot muggy months in the Deep South, we were eager for the cooler North. Humidity and heat in Memphis drain all the energy out of you. After a while, you move slower. You talk slower. You think slower, and you live a slower pace of life.

In the meantime, *it was now August 1963;* my brother Gerhard announced that he would return from Honduras. He felt sick and weak. Could we meet him somewhere in New Orleans? By now, we had learned to live with American distances. We drove south following the ever more majestic Mississippi and arrived in the charming city of jazz, easy life and decadence. Yes, there was Gerhard, haggard and thin, but happy to be with us.

We explored the nightlife, but instead of good old New Orleans jazz as we had played it back in Krems, we ended up being entertained by women who had seen better days, wore fewer clothes but could rotate neon tassels with their breasts, clock- and counterclockwise. America was at the beginning of the sexual revolution started by Hefner. New Orleans was still caught in the seedy and contrived display of sex. But the food was good, the Gulf of Mexico was near and the architecture was still French.

From there, we headed west to Forth Worth, Texas, where the Hoketts from Kent had invited us. We did the Western museums with Remingtons and Russells, Bierstaedt and Audubon. We even did the amusement park Seven Flags of Texas.

August was running out, and Saint John's was waiting for us. We headed north to Chicago. There, Gerhard met one of his early mentors, the Austrian Jew, Professor Katz, an eminent Latin American scholar at the University of Chicago. Later on, Bruno Kreisky tried to lure Katz back to Austria and created the "Katz Chair," but Katz never did return. Thirty years later, Gerhard would inherit that position for himself. When the University of Vienna finally planned to give academic honors to this great man, it was Gerhard who found the money and arranged a splendid ceremony in the Vienna City Hall, where he also gave the honoring speech. That was at the end of his brilliant career in Latin American affairs. The beginning was in Cornell and Honduras. But without us, how would he have made it back to the First World after his plunge into the Third?

Soon after Chicago, it got greener, cooler and fresher. Refreshing Wisconsin was quite a relief after steaming Tennessee. Another night at a Holiday Inn, and then we crossed into Minnesota. The first glimpse of fall colors was already showing. The air was crystal clear. There were trees and lakes. Thomas breathed easier, and so did we. The heat of the summer was broken. Our VW was purring along. By midnight we arrived at the concrete structures of Marcel Breuer, the Hungarian Jew and Bauhaus architect. There was a solid place! Powerful, bold and promising to last forever.

Only half a year ago during the interview in winter, I had come back to Kent, and said I would never ever set foot on that desolate piece of permafrost. But the monks persuaded us otherwise. Dean Dunstan Tucker, O.S.B., a fine Dante scholar, and President Arno Gustin, O.S.B., greeted us late that night. They had already arranged a nice lake home for us in Avon. It came with a motorboat and fishing gear. It was wonderful.

Soon, the semester would start. I taught courses that interested me. I decided what would be read and studied. I started my long-lasting love affair with the German literary canon, none of which we had touched during our sterile studies in Vienna and Innsbruck. I opened the eyes of students to texts of great beauty and relevance: the dramas of Schiller, the first and last novel of Thomas Mann (*Buddenbrooks* and *Krull*) the splendid narratives of Stefan Zweig, Ödon von Horvath, the poems of Goethe, Rilke and Hoffmannsthal, the ballads of Brecht. On top of that, I was asked whether any Catholic writers deserved attention? Would Karl Kraus, the Jewish convert do? Or the Jewish convert Elisabeth Langässer? Or the quaint Karl Waggerl? Besides, they had to learn German, which would have been easy, had a stubborn local monk not insisted on writing his own textbook full of flaws and bugs.

Another Jewish convert, Fr. Roland Behrendt, O.S.B., a lawyer from Königsberg who had studied law in Leipzig, came to my rescue and helped me do damage control. I had to do the exercises for the language lab. Father Roland defended the integrity of the German heritage with his contagious civility. In protest against his stubborn confrere, he decided to teach French instead. Ingrid was one of the first women in a SJU course when she took French with Father Roland. He had great respect for her. At the end of the year, he dedicated his book *On the Consecration of Virgins* to her. Ingrid's presence in a class of an all-male university was the beginning of a promising co-operation with the women's College of Saint Benedict located four miles away.

Thomas grew. I worked. Ingrid took good care of all of us, including the neighbors and colleagues, among which was a crafty musician from Vienna named Gerhard Track. I played clarinet in the SJU Orchestra. We swam in the lake, skated on the lake and looked at the lake from our living room during sunset.

It was a very good year, except in November John F. Kennedy was assassinated in Dallas! Problems brewed in Cuba and in Vietnam. L.B. Johnson from Texas took over and became a magnificent President. He gave the nation MEDICARE and MEDICAID. He passed racial-integration legislation. He started the War on Poverty. He was a bold and civil man, but the Vietnam disaster would eventually make him the tragic hero he was when he decided not to run again in 1968.

Graduation in May was a festive event. Pomp and ritual! And then we did something very bold, something almost reckless. We lusted after a discovery expedition throughout the U.S., much of which we had never seen. So we gave our fifteen-month-old Thomas to Mel and Bob Brix and went on a three-week "99 days for $99" trip on Greyhound. First, we had to go down to Memphis, where I would teach for the summer again, and drop our belongings there, then hop on a Greyhound bus and cross the Arkansas Bridge towards Kansas, Oklahoma, Texas and Arizona on the legendary Highway 66. We stayed with host families in Flagstaff. We stood in awe at the rim of the Grand Canyon. We crossed the desolate Mohave Dessert. We came to Los Angeles and inhaled the Pacific at Portuguese Bend. We came to San Francisco with the Golden Gate. It was cold there, even in summer.

We had hardly any luggage. So, Ingrid bought a wonderful pink coat. She looked magnificent. Then on to Salt Lake City. There, our patience ran out. Mormons are something else anyway! We cancelled our stay there, and Ingrid made it back to Avon, Minnesota, as fast as possible to retrieve our "lost son." He turned away from her and turned to Melvina, his "real" mom. That almost broke Ingrid's heart.

I had, in the meantime, left for Memphis alone to start summer school. Brave Ingrid then took Thomas and came via Chicago to St.

Louis, where I picked them up with our blue VW. She had stayed overnight at the Y in Chicago and came "home" happy and tired after such an ordeal. She is an awesome woman and a wonderful mother. A brave partner and a loving wife!

Memphis had us again. Another summer term in the muggy heat of the old cotton city. At the end of that summer, we had to make plans for the return to Austria. We had to sell the VW. With the proceeds, we bought, sight unseen, an apartment in the Olympic Village of Innsbruck. We flew to New York. We stayed a few more days with the Raus in Hoboken.

At the end of August, we boarded the SS *Constitution* and left for Genoa with stops in Funchal / Madeira, Casablanca, Gibraltar and Naples. It was a glorious ten-day voyage. Ingrid's parents picked us up and drove us "home." Home at last!

VIII

Home! *Heimat*? A strangely emotional word in German. Where was this place anyway? Especially when you are sitting on the deck of our house in Lake Wobegon, drinking Cold Spring beer, listening to the singing frogs in the slough behind the house. No, we thought "home" will be Innsbruck, where we had bought a lovely apartment with a glorious view of the Serles. From now on, everything would fall into place: I might retire at some time as a teacher in Tyrol, or as an innkeeper at some mountain hut serving beer and brats to hikers. But I would always lack that genuine Tyrolean accent. How could Tyrol be my *Heimat*? I did not even have a Lesachtal accent as a boy because of my Viennese mother. I never lost my German accent in the U.S., however, so even there it would be difficult to claim being a local guy. One lives between two worlds, familiar with both, but "at home" in neither. To highlight this feeling, I have a framed original manuscript of Guido Zernatto hanging in my study. It is a poem he wrote in exile in New York in 1942, one year before he died, "A last summer bee / flies through my city window / late at night. . . ."

Too bad he could not have come to Minnesota. He would have loved it. They say he died of homesickness. There is no medical condition like that which is known to cause death. But he failed to discover a home in exile. I never suffered the same hardship, but I lived in better times. The 20th century was not an easy time for so many. So much went wrong between Sarajevo in 1914 and Kosovo in 1998. For us, fortunately, it provided a happy ending, with a feeling of being "at home." For that I am grateful.

The story of my roots in the remote Lesachtal must start with my father, a man about whom I know very little. I was only ten when he disappeared during the war somewhere in Yugoslavia in 1944. He left me a document that lists my ancestry, an *Ahnenpass*—document in a brown folder with a swastika on the cover. It states that there are, unfortunately, no Jewish family members in our clan. Not only was my father a country school teacher in the Lesachtal; he was also the court clerk and registered marriages and deaths in Birnbaum. And he issued my *Ahnenpass*. It says that my father, Maximilian Drekonja, was born near Treffen on January 18, 1901. He was raised in a small yellow house with an attached barn for goats. His father, Alois Drekonja, was a railroad worker during the Habsburg monarchy. He was born in 1867. He did not have much to show for his life until he married a local farm girl, a Maria Tengg. That was in 1897. He died in 1940, she in 1955. She was a wonderful woman whom I loved. We spent several summer vacations in their home and admired the closeness to Lake Ossiach and the romantic ruins of Landskron. Grandfather Alois was the son of a lumberjack named Anton Drekonja, born in 1835. He, too, married a local girl, Anna Gamnig from Töbring. That was in 1874. He died in 1888 and she in 1912.

There was also a weaver, Blasius Drekonja. In 1824 he married a Marianne Humer. He is the earliest recorded Drekonja. Before him, there are only Gamnigs and Allmanns. A Margarethe was born in 1787. They were those women, whom the migrating Drekonjas married, hoping to find a home, a piece of land, a cow or some goats. Originally, the Drekonjas came from the Dalmatian coastal area of the k.u.k. (Imperial) Monarchy, the Friuli area, where people spoke either Italian or Slovenian. They went north in search of jobs and stayed near Treffen, where the Zernattos were wealthy farmers and industrialists who produced the fine Pomona fruit juices.

My father and Guido Zernatto went to school together. As teenagers, they experienced the catastrophic outbreak of WW I in 1914. My father, an offspring of Dalmatian ancestors, returned to the Mediterranean shores of Istria in 1916. He faked his age and enlisted as a sailor in the k.k. Imperial Navy. He was stationed in Pula, where the sailors mutinied in 1918 in the waning days of the glorious monarchy. His battleship *Viribus Unitis* was sunk.

One of the officers on that ship was a Hermann Pflüger, a brother of Ingrid's beloved grandmother who died in 1999 at the age of 103. He lost his mind after the sinking and lived as a weird guy in some remote home in the Carinthian hills. As the monarchy crumbled, Yugoslavian troops tried to occupy parts of Carinthia in 1919. Guido Zernatto, then sixteen years old, joined the militias fighting the invading troops. My father did not. He did not even go back home. He left for Vienna and was an unemployed metalworker for many years. For a decade, nobody knew much about him. He lived in a poor section of town in the twelfth district.

Not too far from his basement apartment was the tiny flat of a k.u.k. gendarme, Anton Weghofer. Their daughter, Maria, born in 1907, introduced Max to a Catholic youth organization called *Neuland*. They were a kind of flower-power generation that was religiously traditional, politically conservative and attracted by the simple life in the country rather than the decadent life of big cities. They moved with tents and guitars, Latin chant books and in medieval dress to the lakes and mountains of the dramatically shrunken First Republic of Austria.

The First Republic was a left-leaning social democratic construction rather alien to this pious group of Romantics. It did not do too well. In 1927, there were bloody riots between the Left and the conservative Right. In 1934, there was an even bloodier civil war. In the summer of 1934, there was a Nazi putsch that failed, and in 1938, the annexation of Austria by Nazi Germany.

It was not an easy time for an unemployed ex-sailor from the country. My father kept a diary in the '20s, which told me more about him and his future wife Maria. She was the one who told him that there would be no future for their relationship if they continued to sing Gregorian chants in the mountains and failed to find a regular job. Now, behind each successful man stands a surprised woman. Max did indeed leave Vienna in 1928 and went back to Carinthia, where he enrolled in a one-year teacher training program and became a country school teacher in 1929. Eventually, they both left Vienna and Max decorated his bride with a wreath of freshly picked Edelweiss from the Lesachtal Mountains. Nobody from the Drekonja clan was present when they married romantically at the castle of Wildegg on August 15, 1931.

The bold move was that of my mother. She left the big city and a good job at the *Dorotheum*, where she not only worked well but saved quite a bit of money with which she bought beautiful furniture and expensive household articles. Where would they settle? My father got a job in the most remote corner of the Lesachtal, a valley cut off from the rest of the world in winter and accessible only with horse-drawn carts. For my mother, a child of the city, it was a move into a dreadful isolation. But she hated the depressing poverty of her parents' apartment in Vienna, and she lived with the romantic optimism that life in the country was better than in the city. Unfortunately, it was not. It was a bold and brave move. She was a strong woman. She had to be. And she was happy, at least for a few years before the outbreak of WW II.

What does my *Ahnenpass* say about her family? She was born in 1907 in a two-room apartment in Vienna. The WC and water were shared by others. There was one window to the north, no sun. The father was a macho tyrant and self-centered man; his wife, Maria, an angel of a woman. He was born in 1876, as was she. They were married in 1903. When he died in 1958, she told me, "Now that he is dead, I will have such a good life!" She died in December 1964. They had two children: my mother, born in 1907, and my Uncle Toni, born in 1913. This was still in the "good old times" before all hell broke loose after the ill-fated ultimatum, which aging Emperor Franz Joseph had sent to the Serbs in the summer of 1914. But the days of the Habsburg Empire were numbered. WW I ended in November 1918. So did the monarchy.

What was left was a tiny and shaken Austria. My mother was malnourished and was sent to Denmark for one year, where she learned fluent Danish and gained weight. She was a very intelligent and motivated woman. But her father did not want to waste money on her education, so she went to school secretly while her younger brother, Anton, was sent to the "Wine *Gymnasium*" (a technical high school for the science of growing fruit and producing wine) in Klosterneuburg. He joined the Vienna police force, like his father. The riots of 1927, when a mob burned down the Palace of Justice, saw both police officers in action. There were many killed. Then even more during the civil war in February 1934 and the failed Nazi putsch of July 1934.

Those traumatic events confirmed the staunch conservative Catholic values of that family. They all welcomed the clerical corporate fascist state under Dollfuss. In the eyes of my parents, he was a saint. In the eyes of the Social-Democrats, he was a killer of workers. In 1938, the compromised state vanished after Hitler's annexation in March. The twenty-five-year-old Anton joined the Luftwaffe: Norway, France, ... He was sent to the sports academy of Detmold and thus avoided the Eastern front. In 1944, he kept firing V-2 rockets into London and Antwerp. Then he was a POW in France. In 1947, he was back in Vienna. He died in 1996 after a remarkable career as a sports professor at the University of Vienna. During the Olympics in 1936, he swam against Johnny Weismueller. He became vice-president of the Austrian Olympic Committee. He was a man with wit, charm and luck. His wonderful wife, Tante Anni, is still alive and lives in a home near Thomas in Salzburg. Of Anton's father, she would say, "Poor Mama. He is lucky he did not marry me. I would have killed him."

Maria W., born Blaszezyk, was also a strong woman. Her father was a railroad worker born in 1849. In 1873, he married an Anna Benczka, who was born in Hochstetten in 1846. There was even a homeowner, Andreas Blaszezyk from Wolica in Habsburg Galicia, who married an Anna Floryan in Lack in 1845. Andreas was born in 1824, and if one traces a Franz Benem back, the father of Katharine Benczka, then one finds a reference to a *Woywode*, a free landowner. But there the traces of my grandmother's family in Poland vanish in the *Ahnenpass*. They were part of the Galicia of Joseph Roth and his wonderful *Radetzkymarch*.

The traces of the Weghofers, Max's maternal grandparents, are clearer. The great-grandfather, Anton Weghofer, was born in Eichbühel in 1849. He was the owner of a small house. He married a nineteen-year-old Maria Urban from Katzelsdorf in 1872. Further back, there is another Anton Weghofer listed as "manager of an estate." He was born in 1816. They were all hard-working small people, often going from serfs to estate owners. They were diligent and frugal, working hard and dreaming of moving to Vienna and obtaining a government job. My mother's father and Anton succeeded. But the real success story is that of my Uncle Toni, who was seen in the company of all presidents of the Second Republic.

Would my father, the stranded and unemployed ex-sailor Max, have amounted to anything without the first push from my ambitious mother? She was also grimly determined to break out of the petty oppressiveness of her Viennese confines and move into a middle-class existence, which her brother accomplished so formidably. She did get Max to become a teacher, buy a violin and have a regular job. That this job would take him and her into the remote Lesachtal was one of the ironies she had to get used to. She never did adjust fully. She always remained an alien in a tough world of small farmers, lumberjacks, drunks and barbarians.

For my father, the return to Carinthia was a blessing. He was a man with artistic talents. He enjoyed singing polyphonic songs, acting in lay drama, drawing and reading. He was a quiet and peaceful man. My mother was lively and gregarious. He enjoyed the splendid countryside in the remote village close to the Italian border. He was happy with the Austrian corporate state with the glorified form of country-living. He was blind to the beginning of fascism in Germany and Italy. I remember going with him to church, gathering mushrooms and berries, going on hikes and listening to his stories. It was a wonderful time for me as a young boy, for whom the Lesachtal was paradise. A safe and sacred world, with organ music, Corpus Christi processions, Easter and Christmas rituals and a world filled with majestic mountains. I was the second of four children born in Kornat above Birnbaum. Then this world changed dramatically in 1938 with the Anschluss and in 1939 with the outbreak of WW II.

My father, now almost forty, became a soldier again, this time in the regular grey of infantry rather than the white of the navy. I thought that war was exciting. My parents had a fine radio that could receive the BBC. We were told that this was a secret nobody could know about. Sometimes, my mother took me to a local movie theater where we would see the newsreels from the front. We boys started playing war and built bunkers and weapons out of wood and old pipes. But for the Drekonjas, it was no game. My father became increasingly somber and silent when he came home. I had started elementary school in Kornat, in the meantime. The Lesachtal was a peaceful world—except all the young men disappeared with the draft, and the women prayed for them in church, a fine Gothic structure from the 14th century.

Food was rationed, but the farmers in the village kept us supplied with extra portions of bread and butter, flour and bacon. My mother kept a flock of chickens, so we had our own eggs. On Sundays, we kids did our part for the war effort and collected donations for the WHW, the German relief fund. For that we had neat red metal boxes, and we handed out great collectors' items such as pins with coats of arms, local dress and city emblems. I wish I had preserved some of those goodies!

In the summer of 1942, my father came home in civilian dress. My parents talked a lot until late in the night—serious things, about which they said little. Today, I know more. My father had received an offer to serve his military duties as a civilian administrator and teacher in German-occupied Yugoslavia / Slovenia. There would be a modern schoolhouse with a pool and garden, and he could take his family along. Except that he had to be a reliable German *Übermensch* and become a Nazi Party member. But nobody mentioned that. Nothing was said anymore. Only later did I realize that my father had engaged in that pact with Mephisto, like the great Actor Gustav Gründgens in the movie *Mephisto* by Szabo, Klaus Mann and Karl Maria Brandauer.

Later, my mother always denied that he had become a party member. However, it was painfully clear that he had because after the war she was denied a pension for several years. I also requested my father's party file from the Berlin Archives. The Germans always were good bookkeepers, and they had him on file, of course. I know it must have been a hard decision for my parents, but they did it for reasons with which I cannot argue. Maybe my father thought by having the family near and by being a party member he could protect his two handicapped daughters better. By then there were four of us children. Erika was born in 1932 with both hands handicapped. I came in 1934. Hildegard in 1936, with a heart defect and handicapped hands. Gerhard came in 1939. We boys were lucky. We were normal. Not being genetically perfect in the Third Reich was a dangerous condition to be in.

But now, we would all move together to a wonderful place that was safely occupied by German troops. So they said. In reality it was a brooding cauldron with Germans controlling the day and Tito's partisans the night. There were constant skirmishes on an increasing scale. The schoolhouse was not only comfortable and elegant; it was also a fortress, with a barricaded door and windows netted against hand grenades. In my father's desk were some hand grenades. He also had a gun with two hundred rounds of ammunition.

The many trips from the Lesachtal to Slovenia were exciting for us. In Kötschach we would board a train, and then switch outside Villach to a Balkan-bound train. We often stopped next to supply trains carrying tanks and guns painted in desert colors for Rommel's army in Africa. They would load them onto ships in Greece, and the Brits would sink them before they reached Libya. But I did not know that then. We would leave the train in Skofja Loka and go from there to Zabnica.

The people were friendly. We learned Slovenian, but school was taught in German. We went to church on Sundays; that impressed the locals. Nazis normally did not hang around the altar too much. Instead they went to Wagnerian operas and paraded in uniforms. The local farmers brought white bread, vegetables and *kasha*, a local cereal. Things did not look bad at all. For the first time ever, we had a tiled bathroom. We were already reading books of Nordic background: *Nonni and Manni*, the books by Sven Hedin, fairy tales and books about ships and mountains, which my father loved. Dr. Julius Kugy described the Julian peaks, which we could see from the south. At night, we were allowed to stay up until Lale Andersen would sing the haunting song *"Vor der Kaserne . . . ,"* the signature song of Mr. Goebbels' radio station, which otherwise reported awesome progress of the German Wehrmacht in the East, in Africa, on the Atlantic and in the air.

My parents became much more reserved and cautious about what they said. At night, there were ongoing shootings. During the day, some strafing planes bothered us occasionally on the way to school in Skofja Loka. After the shootings in the night, the bodies of the killed were usually taken to the burial chapel at the cemetery. I became curious and sneaked in one day and saw, for the first time, a pile of riddled bodies—men and women. I was shocked and burst into tears. I ran home, but did not want to say where I had been, so I faked a stomach ache. I was taken to the hospital. Appendix? Nothing was found. Of course not. Eventually, I got used to such sights. Actually, I developed a morbid sense of curiosity, with an almost clinical sense of distance. In February 1942 news reached us that my father's brother Otto had been killed on the Eastern front. With the picture of a soldier's grave in wintry Russia, he was first of the three Drekonjas to die in the war.

In the summer of 1942, Aunt Paula, my father's sister, married to Heinrich Gärtner, a railroad worker, came and pleaded for help. Heinrich was part of a Communist welfare organization that helped families with members in prison. The Gestapo had arrested him and wanted to hear who else was involved. He remained silent and was severely injured during interrogation.

My cousin, Dr. Michael Gärtner, grandson of Aunt Paula and Heinrich Gärtner, eventually requested the Gestapo file. It was meticulously preserved and available. According to the file, he was beaten to death after having been sentenced to serve time on February 23, 1943. The official cause of death was listed as suicide. After the war, the Gestapo officers connected to those cases were put on trial in a people's court, especially a Mr. Johann Stelzl. Although he denied any wrongdoing, "I was only a small officer in a big system and only followed orders from above . . . ," he was sentenced to death on March 3, 1947 in Graz and executed on October 9, 1947. A request for clemency had been turned down. But in 1942, my father, in spite of his party membership, was unable to help or rescue his brother-in-law. It burdened him very much.

In January 1943, it became clear to me that something big had gone wrong: Movie theaters were closed for three days because of Stalingrad.

More troops poured into Yugoslavia and tried to subdue the Tito uprising, once and for all. Troops were also housed overnight in our building before going on missions. It must have been for that reason that one night in spring, partisans broke into the fortress. My father did not shoot back, so they allowed us to get out before they blew up the building. I admired those romantic-looking guys with the red star on their caps. They were calm and professional, not mean or sinister. They took us out, we ducked in a ditch and the building blew up with a massive boom. Some farmers took us in. The next morning, we skimmed through the rubble. We were sworn to secrecy about the fact that my father had handed over his arms to the partisans. That would have been a death verdict if the Germans had found out.

The empty parish house became the new schoolhouse. My parents felt safe now because they believed the partisans saw them as "good Germans." Another pact with Mephisto? It did not last long. On December 6, 1944, Tito's troops broke into the house after a shooting in town. Only my sister Erika and my father were there. My mother and the three of us had left the day before for Christmas break in the safety of the Lesachtal. On the 7th, an officer came and reported to my distraught mother that my father had been taken prisoner the day before. Erika was safe. My father was gone. Nobody ever heard or saw anything from him after that day. Today, his name is on the war memorial in Kornat; the last name on the list. Missing in Yugoslavia as of 1944.

That is all I know about my father. From now on, I have to tell the story of my mother who turned into a heroic person, stronger than the "Mother Courage" of Bertolt Brecht. It was not easy for her from then on. Without her, we would not be where we are today.

IX

My mother did not comprehend on that day in December 1944 that this might be the last thing she would ever hear of her husband, nor did we, the shocked children. We were in the safety of the remote Lesach Valley. Erika, the oldest, was transported home by a military escort. The war was still going on. On clear winter days, the bomber formations from Italy droned north to unload their cargo on German cities, leaving long white vapor trails in the blue sky

It was before Christmas that our mother left with a heavy backpack and winter clothes. The winter of 1944/1945 was particularly harsh with much snow. We would not go back to Yugoslavia, but our mother did. It could have been an opera plot: Florestan and Fidelio. But it was real. She fought her way back to Yugoslavia. The trains were no longer running reliably and were constantly under air attack. When she arrived, she crossed the German lines on foot and entered partisan-controlled country. She was six months pregnant and kept asking where she might find the *utschitel*, the teacher of Sabnica.

She carried warm clothes and good winter boots for her husband. She also had a loaf of dark bread. Nobody took away what she had. She even carried her husband's Luger pistol, but nobody searched her. They even gave her some food and tea, but told her to go back home to her children. Nobody wanted to or could say anything about her husband, who was by then long dead and covered by snow. She did make it back. But she was a pitiful sight. She hitched rides on trucks with retreating German soldiers from General Loehr's Army Group B from Greece, fighting their way north through Yugoslavia. After crossing borders into Austria she was taken to a hospital in Lienz, where she lost her baby. In January, she came back—-with the backpack and the winter clothes, boots and mittens. She saw us again in February. We were so happy. We were not sure she would come back anymore, but she did. She was tough and brave, desperate but hopeful. It was all in vain. He was never heard from again.

The last months of the war in the spring saw German troops move in from Italy and take defensive positions against Tito's advancing troops. We attended school in the two-room schoolhouse. The teachers were young kids from bombed-out cities in the North. On May 8th, the Brits moved in from Italy over the Plöckenpass. The Germans surrendered. So did the Russian Cossack army and the Croatian Ustaschi. Both were soon to be handed over to the Soviets and the Yugoslavs, who executed all of them.

The locals butchered the many horses and smoked sausages in the wood-fired chimneys. The whole valley smelled of salami. But the food got very scarce. Our mother bought two goats, and we had some chickens. That helped. Otherwise, we went to the farmers asking for flour, bread or even butter. On top of that, the local officials, having been informed of my father's Party membership, tried to evict us from the schoolhouse. My mother fought like a tiger and got help from friends in *Neuland*, one of whom had now become the Secretary of Education. That helped, but they still stopped her payments. No pension, no funds. Nothing. Regardless, she felt we had to go to school. Therefore, she looked for people to take us in.

I was the luckiest and moved to the Lamprecht farm above Kötschach, where I attended a wonderful junior high school. Erika went to a farmer in Leisach and Hildegard to friends in the British Zone in Vienna. Gerhard, the youngest, stayed with her until 1949, after which he joined a seminary near Salzburg, for which the parish priest paid. Our family had ceased to exist. In summer, we all came home, and I worked as a sheepherder in the mountains. We took care of our goats and our poor mother. Every evening she would sit in front of the radio and listen to the Red Cross reports of the missing: "Any information on so and so . . . last seen at . . . ." No report ever of our missing father.

It was not until 1948 that my mother accepted the fact that he might be dead. By now the "denazification process" was over and even our mother would qualify for a pension—if she could produce a death certificate for my father. But he was simply "missing." On a mild summer day, my mother and I hitchhiked, catching a ride on a British truck to the Drava Bridge, beyond which was the Yugoslavian-occupied territory of Austria. From the bridge, we hiked to a village in the border region, where we had the address of a partisan officer.

He was friendly and helpful. He typed a sheet on which he said, "It can be assumed that Max Drekonja did not live beyond the date of December 6, 1944 . . . ." To make it official, the Yugoslovian document got a Communist stamp and back we went. She filed the document with the state government and asked for a pension. The post-war laws even suggested that in the case of accident or disease while employed, one could qualify to get a pension for ten extra years. That would have made a big difference. My father had only taught for thirteen years. However, the response was sobering, "Since you have only a rather casual document from a Communist Party organization in Loibl, and since it does not indicate that your husband suffered from a disease or had an accident, the law does not apply, and your request is denied. . . ." But she did get a small pension and a modest amount of life insurance money. Unfortunately, it was shortly before the currency reform, which would devalue money to one-tenth of its previous value. So a friendly farmer sold her precious lumber for the old (and soon worthless) money, and he bought it back for its real value in new money.

For the first time ever, she had a little extra money on hand. She decided to get the family together and buy a small house in the capital of the province, Klagenfurt. That is where the secondary schools and the colleges we would attend were. There was a theater, an opera house, a concert hall, a conservatory and jobs for us kids working at construction sites and railroad yards. One summer I even worked on a dig for Roman ruins on the Magdalensberg and bought a bike with the earnings. Life was starting to get almost normal again. My mother got certified as a teacher for agricultural vocational schools out in the country. We did not have much, but we were together again.

In 1948, I had started at the teachers' training college and at the same time studied music at the conservatory. My younger brother returned from the prep school for priests and went to the Humanist *Gymnasium* (secondary school). Both sisters attended business schools and soon landed jobs in town. I joined the Alpine Club and explored my beloved mountains in Carinthia. It was a good time. Food was no longer rationed. The radio played beautiful music on the American Forces Network. I learned to play jazz. We did a lot of musical productions in school: Mozart operas, Haydn oratorios and Schubert Masses. We went to Vienna to compete in chorus competitions and won first prize. We wore very poor and shabby clothes. We got around on bicycles. We were young and sometimes in love, but mostly shy and insecure. We were the war kids. We were always told, "Shut up. What do you know anyway? We could tell you something, but . . . ."

The war seemed like ancient history. Nobody talked about it. Nobody knew anything about it, let alone Jews, *Untermenschen* or *Übermenschen*. In history, we learned things about the Greeks and the Romans, but not about Nazis, Nuremberg Race Laws or "Arianization." And nobody knew where our fathers had vanished to. Only ruined buildings said, "Yes, there was a war!"

For my mother, the war was never over. The vacuum caused by her missing husband was simply insurmountable. It not only reduced her to a life of great loneliness, but also a life of bitter social degradation and financial humiliation. She was a very intelligent and proud person, but she had to accept the fact that in the end she was sidelined by a post-war society that was more impressed with economic and social achievement, looks and position in society. Above all, there was nobody she could share her grief with except the two daughters who were suffering from rejection at large because of their handicaps. Many a challenge would hit her in her later years in this context. Fortunately, we were at least back from the U.S. after 1964 and, thus, available when the roof was on fire.

In the meantime, she had become a very successful teacher, building her own professional base and adding income to the meager pension she received from a republic that tried to shake as many social and financial responsibilities that were caused by the war as it could. On top of that, Austrians learned to live with a glorious political lie, namely, having been "the first victim of Nazi aggression" rather than a perpetrator of the dismal acts during the Third Reich. The Moscow Declaration of 1943 provided a base for that myth, even though it was essentially intended as a desperate gamble by the hard-pressed Red Army to cause Austrian defections from the Wehrmacht. Even though this never happened on a large scale, the 1955 State Treaty singled out Austria as a "virtuous" state vis-à-vis Germany, which was burdened, divided and unredeemed. Only the GDR, the country of East Germany between 1949 and 1989, was more successful in shaking off any responsibility for German transgressions during the war. They saw themselves as "the better Germany," antifascist, Communist and pacifist. For the Austrians, the redemption came from the pope, who declared that Austria is "the Island of the Blessed." Thus, the country was redeemed by Strauss waltzes, a "who-me?" cult of neutrality and *The Sound of Music*, even though Austrians never saw this great commercial for a sunny place in the mountains.

Nevertheless, our mother was a firm Austrian patriot and saw to it that the flag would fly from her magnificent little house—an Austrian flag, which we have now brought to the U.S. as her legacy of having brought peace and civility to a world out of control. She was indeed the "Mother Courage" Bertolt Brecht envisioned. And she was happy in her small house with a meticulously groomed garden, always eager to have her children close by.

Hildegard, the younger one, married a slime-ball of a con man. He was abusive and a criminal. We helped her with a divorce, after which she married kind and caring Felix. She died young in 1970 at the age of thirty-four.

Erika, the older sister, had a difficult life and few friends. Many of her hardships showed only later when they were catastrophic. Again, we were there when the roof was on fire.

It was all in the time when we had returned from the U.S. and established our residence in the splendid city of Innsbruck. It could have been our most happy time and could have lasted forever. With the savings from our work in the U.S., we had bought a condo, sight unseen. It was a good place for the three of us: Thomas, Ingrid and me. We arrived there on Austrian Air in September 1964. I am still homesick for the place.

X

Innsbruck, Fall 1964. The Fulbright Fellows have returned home. We arrived from Genoa, where we left the SS *Constitution*. In Klagenfurt, where Ingrid's family lived, we boarded an Austrian Airlines Vickers Viscount for Innsbruck. It was a marvelous flight over the mountains to Tyrol, the most beautiful part of Austria. There, we had bought a condo in the Olympic Village and used all the money we had for the down payment. We were rich in experience, high on the notion that we could now accomplish anything and ecstatically happy with our son Thomas, now eighteen months old. But we were also broke. We had no jobs yet.

Ingrid landed one first and started teaching grade school in Wattens, where the Swarovskis produce crystal. The current executives, whom she also taught to play the recorder, were her students then. Getting to work took a daily train ride and two rather lengthy walks to and from the stations. That was hard. I was the house husband and made changes in our fine apartment. Thomas hated it because it was very noisy drilling through cement walls.

In October, they offered me a job teaching English and German at the teachers' training college in Innsbruck. First, I had to find a sitter for Thomas. The Schilling family in the same block took care of that. Then, we bought a tacky old VW in order to make the daily trips easier for Ingrid. That was great because it also helped us to take magnificent excursions around Innsbruck with its splendid mountains all around. In winter, we would put Thomas in a backpack and ski down the runs of Patscherkofel. In summer, we would hike to the peaks above Innsbruck.

By now, Thomas was already attending pre-school with "Aunt" Erika, who would try to keep her opulent chest inside her blouse. He loved to snuggle up to her, getting an erotic high from her baroque build. There was also "Aunt" Paula, who was a bit more stern, but he still had a good time while we were at work trying to pay for our costly purchase.

It would take about ten years of a teacher's income to pay for the apartment. Therefore, we started renting out a room. I took a second job as a lowly assistant at the English Department at the University of Innsbruck. I mostly worked for an American professor, John Hinz, from New York. I did the work while he was often out of town. He was actually back in New York, but I was not supposed to let that be known.

At that time, a former dean of Saint John's University, Fr. Dunstan Tucker, O.S.B., had a severe lung operation in the U.S., and they thought he might recuperate better in sunny Italy. So they sent him to a lovely Benedictine abbey, Abbazia di San Miniato al Monte, on the Piazzale Michelangelo in Florence. Alas, the winters are cold and heating is very poor. He told us in Innsbruck that he was freezing. We all, so he said, should go back to Minnesota, where the houses are warm. He did go back to Minnesota and kept sending us invitations and attractive offers to come back. For a couple of years, we ignored them, but each year, the offers got better, and we felt more and more tempted. But the time was not ripe, yet.

On top of everything else, other difficulties arose. Not financial, we had that under control. Rather unexpectedly, my professor (a man named Thurnher) confided that he had lost interest in my dissertation project on Zernatto—the person I had researched so well in New York—and sent a terse letter telling me that it was over. How about that! I was stunned.

You can only pursue a doctorate if your professor is willing, able and alive. He was virtually dead, as far as I was concerned. It was an unbelievable turn of events that nobody had foreseen. However, there was a silver lining. He was a much detested autocrat, and one of his colleagues, Professor Walter Weiss, left Innsbruck in disgust and moved to the University of Salzburg. He invited me to come with him and do the project there! That was also unbelievable, and nice. Except that in order to be a legitimate Ph.D. candidate there, I had to enroll in four more semesters, even though I had already fulfilled all requirements in Innsbruck. With my gray, tacky VW, I jetted back and forth between Innsbruck and Salzburg and slowly earned the necessary extra credits. I also found a very helpful mentor there, Professor K.H. Rossbacher, without whom I would not have prevailed. It was a very stressful time but with a glimmer of hope on the horizon.

The glimmer of hope was so tangible, that by fall 1965 we thought about having another baby. Ingrid did get pregnant. By now, she had a much more convenient teaching job in the grade school kitty-corner from our apartment. On top of that, Austria has socialized medicine, under which Austrians enjoy maternity benefits that allow the women six weeks off before and six weeks after delivery with full pay and assured return.

We were happy and confident. Everything looked good. The due date was the end of June, but the baby refused to come. Three weeks

overdue, Ingrid was no longer slim, and we decided to boldly challenge fate and do something about it. We took the cable car to the top
of the mountain and began to walk down through the woods. For
hours we were out of sight and out of reach of medical help, should it
become necessary. We thought gravity and bumpy trails would do the
job that Mother Nature had so far refused to do. We came home late
and went to bed, not telling anybody of our crazy *tour de force*.

At 5:00 in the morning, I took Ingrid to the clinic and went to work
at the institute. I was told in the afternoon that our daughter had arrived safely, but I came too late for visitation hours and did not see her
for the next few days. Ingrid was livid. I was sad. The nurses were
grumpy. But we did agree that our fine daughter should be called
Natascha—not exactly a Tyrolean household name. A week later,
both came home, and we were so happy and grateful. She was a stunningly beautiful girl with long hair and fine features. A week later, we
planned a baptism in the modern church next door. We invited Ingrid's Aunt Ilse and her daughter Monika, as well as, my mother and
my sister Erika. Monika and Erika were the godparents. It was a lovely
July day, and the baby Natascha was baptized in glorious Tyrolean sur-
roundings in Innsbruck.

My younger sister Hildegard, a very intelligent and gregarious
young woman who coped formidably with her handicap and who was
very close to our mother, had fallen in love with a handsome but sinister guy. He was in need of support, and Hildegard thought she could
save him from a life of crime, violence and gang ties.

She was not very healthy, but she held a good job. They moved into
a nice apartment. Everything looked suspiciously good. But secretly—
mother must not know—she told us of her life of misery. He used her
money. He pawned off her belongings. He beat her up. We made several "top secret" trips to Klagenfurt and arranged for lawyers and initiated divorce procedures. We equipped her with the things she needed
and supported her as best we could. She escaped from the trap and,
soon thereafter, married the kindest guy on earth, Felix—a fitting
name. A happy ending. Wonderful!

There was a different story with my brother Gerhard. Back from the Fulbright in Cornell, he was at the University of Vienna finishing his Ph.D. in history. Then we got a call in the spring of 1965, "Come to Vienna tomorrow! I need a best man. I am going to marry a wonderful Jewish woman I met at a masked ball. Helene!"

She was born in London. Her Viennese Jewish parents had escaped the Nazis after her father had fought in the International Brigade in the Spanish Civil War. The mother had told him to do so. He survived, came back and divorced her. The mother was a fine Jewish dominant, bossy type. She was suspicious of Gerhard's revolutionary looks and demeanor. Helene studied at the arts academy in Vienna.

It was too short notice, and I could not be there. They married anyway. Gerhard won the prestigious "Renner Award" and accepted a professorship at the Universidad de los Andes in Bogotá, Colombia. Helene should come along. She did. She hated Bogotá. She hated a Third-World lifestyle. She hated Gerhard who had done this to her.

Eventually, Gerhard put her on a KLM plane and shipped her home; airfare to be billed to her mother. The mother was livid. She saw us as the saviors. Would I be able to reform my unruly brother and tell him what to do and take better care of her princess? She showed up in Innsbruck many times. Ingrid got tired of her. I got tired of her. When she came, I found urgent work to do in the Institute. I made one try and went to Vienna to meet with Helene. I knew it was over. A year later, they were divorced *in absentia*. It must have been a wild and passionate affair. But in the end, also a happy ending.

Gerhard came back for a while. At one time, he drove for days and nights on a motorbike from Spain and looked for shelter in Innsbruck. Since he also needed money, I gave him my weekend job of escorting British old folks from London to Venice by bus—a hard job on little sleep. But I slept very little in the Innsbruck years anyway since all the weekends were filled with extra jobs: NEH groups from the U.S. in town to be entertained: school visits, Tyrolean evenings, outings on the Hafele-Kar by cable car . . . .

Then I got a more steady and reputable job. A Swiss Company in Lugano was looking for tour guides for Globus-Gateway. Well, that was the job for me! With U.S. tourists, I traveled from London-Amsterdam-Heidelberg-Zurich-Innsbruck-Venice-Florence-Rome-Cannes-Camonix to Paris. Museums, monuments, music, Folies-Bergères . . . lots of fun! And good money, too. I would fly back to Innsbruck from Paris and see my Natascha, a daughter whom I barely saw during these days. Nor did I bond a lot with Thomas, unfortunately.

For us, it was bad enough. Thomas was bewildered. Natascha demanded attention. I had to work and pursue a degree. It dawned on me that my academic career in Innsbruck might, in the end, suffer from too much tour guiding, skiing and having too many fingers in too many pies. It was getting to be too much, we thought. It was then, in 1967, that we decided to escape for a while and accepted a fine offer from Saint John's University. I was far from having finished my dissertation. I told them I could finish even from a distance and informed them that they could reach me at a U.S. address. But I would also dutifully return each summer to finish my academic work there. My professor was astounded to hear that I would do it while in the U.S., but I booked a flight for September. Tyrol was full of golden colors of fall. With a sad and uneasy feeling, I left for Munich and boarded a Lufthansa jet for Chicago.

What was supposed to be our permanent place in Austria had taken a rather temporary shape. So, on September 6, 1967, I left for the U.S.A., and Ingrid and the two children followed on October 6th. We had left a beautiful place but a difficult one. We deserved a break, we thought. And the Benedictine tranquility of Collegeville would provide it. Minnesota would be the place for us to recover, focus and live again. It felt like running away and abandoning a family in distress, but we had to find our bearings and a more peaceful place. That place was indeed Lake Wobegon, that lovely, legendary place, where "all the women are strong, all the men good-looking and all the children above average." We were made exactly for this place, and we were glad to be back for a while at least.

Sitting in an airplane over the Atlantic gives you that feeling of suspension: You are no longer where you were, and you are not yet where you are supposed to be. You feel free and relieved, weightless and out of reach from anybody and anything. The three years in Innsbruck flew by in my mind. In many ways, they were the most beautiful years of our life so far. We had two healthy and wonderful babies. We had a lovely apartment to come back to. We took so many magnificent walks in the mountains around that glorious city of old Emperor Maximilian I. He loved that city more than any other place in his huge Holy Roman Empire of the German nation. We had good friends there. We had interesting jobs. We even earned enough money to make ends meet, even though it was difficult. We had the tackiest VW in town, but it got us around. Life was hectic, but it was good. It was also the most stressful part of our life.

"Innsbruck, I must leave you. . . ." was the sad song of Heinrich Isaac, a contemporary of Emperor Maximilian I in the 16th century. We felt as sad as he did, when he left for war and work elsewhere in the empire. We were more fortunate. We kept our apartment and would go back many times during vacations.

XI

It was fall 1967. I had arrived at the Saint John's University campus in the glory of those intense fall colors of Minnesota. My arrival had been announced as a kind of celebrity case: the great white hope for a yet to be upgraded language department, fully in line with the National Defense Education Act that hoped to make Americans multilingual. The fact that I arrived without a completed degree made it a bit delicate, but everyone played it down and suggested, "It will come." And that is exactly what I hoped, too.

The acting chair of the department was an elderly French professor, Ms. Dorothy Pettis. She was a bit at odds with a newly-hired young woman in the French Department, who was a bit too assertive for her taste. Classics had been upgraded with a very fine young Ray Larson, also no degree yet in hand. But he was the pride of old dean Fr. Dunstan Tucker, O.S.B. He wrote to us in Innsbruck, "I have also hired a very fine classicist, though Protestant . . . you will like him." We did.

The real chair of the Modern and Classical Languages Department (MCL) was Fr. John Kulas, O.S.B., but he was still at George Washington University in Washington, D.C., working on his German doctorate. So, we were all a bunch of brooding hens sitting on our academic eggs, yet to hatch. We were the department that was "up and coming."

What impressed me most upon my arrival was the charisma of the new president, Fr. Colman Barry, O.S.B., a man with gregarious charm, a quick wit and a bold vision. He was a history professor and wrote the definitive book on the history of Saint John's, as well as a biography on a German cardinal. For the MCL, he arranged a national connection with the Chicago-based Institute of European Studies. This would give our students a better chance to study abroad.

I much enjoyed the yearly meetings of this creative team in Chicago. They even elected me as a member of the curriculum committee, which had the welcomed obligation to travel to Europe every year and inspect centers in Madrid, Paris, Vienna and Freiburg. More importantly, Father Colman empowered one of his former students, Bill Kling, to become the president of a new radio station, Minnesota Public Radio. He sent him to graduate school, and Bill soon took over control of a station that went on the air when we arrived in the fall of 1967.

On two channels, this station would send national and international news, commentary and interactive call-in programs; the other channel had nothing but classical music, selected by Michael Barone in an impeccably professional manner. This station has blossomed beyond anyone's wildest dreams and made the airwaves of Minnesota the envy of the nation. Actually, that station transformed itself into NPR (National Public Radio), and Bill Kling is still at the helm of this enterprise. Life without MPR is unthinkable. And it was the brainchild of Father Colman.

Not his only brainchild though. He also founded the "Chair for Jewish Studies"—the first at a Catholic institution. On the shores of one of their fine lakes (needless to say, the Benedictines always pick the finest real-estate for their earthly missions. In this case, 2,400 acres of untouched land with lakes, hills and woods), he built a center for ecumenical research. Every year it brings a dozen international scholars to pursue work and interact while here.

Most importantly, he was determined to make Saint John's a nationally known university. You do that by hiring the best people you can find. That is why they hired, among others, me. The university already had very respectable departments: History, English, biology, chemistry and, soon, MCL would rank in their category. We would gel into the department with a cosmopolitan flair.

Finally, in the year I came, he introduced a new schedule: the January term. It became the vehicle for my Central European plans and allowed me to do many programs on site in Venice, Prague, Vienna and Budapest. Over the years, we would also touch base with places like Krakow, Auschwitz, Ljubljana, Zagreb, Trieste and, of course, Salzburg and Innsbruck, our emotional home base. This January program, introduced in 1967, would last until my retirement in 2001. It was a wonderful field for experimentation. It also gave me access to students from other colleges in the Midwest through a consortium (UMAIE) e.g., Gustavus, Saint Thomas, Hamline and Macalester.

But one of the most profound innovations of Father Colman was the cooperation with the women's College of St. Benedict. It ended a one hundred-year-old tradition of single-sex education on either campus. As I mentioned before, Ingrid was the first beneficiary of this joint venture by taking French from Fr. Roland Behrendt, O.S.B. He was a lawyer trained in Leipzig and escaped the clutches of the Third Reich in the Benedictine enclave of the abbey in the woods, here at SJU. You would have thought that he would be the ideal German professor. (As were the Berlin Jews Frank Hirschbach and Gerhard Weiss at the University of Minnesota. They first escaped Berlin before the war and returned in the uniform of a G.I. Gerhard stayed there in a slave labor camp and cleared Berlin from rubble after air attacks. Both became splendid ambassadors of the German Heritage of Weimar. They also became fabulous colleagues and mentors of mine. Frank Hirschbach would later open the doors to the GDR for me after a National Endowment for the Humanities (NEH) summer seminar, for which I am most grateful.)

Needless to say, Saint John's was already on the map as an architectural gem because of the bold concrete structures of the Bauhaus architect Marcel Breuer, a Hungarian Jew who left his legacy not only here but also in the Whitney Museum in New York, the UNESCO building in Paris and administrative buildings in Washington, D.C. All that, one might say, was a gift from Adolf to the U.S. because of his grotesque brain-drain, chasing out Jews who were actually the cultural elite of Germany. That included Mrs. Riccarda Zernatto-Weidenhaus, the Jewish wife of my Guido Zernatto, who was now the topic of a dissertation yet to be written.

But back to the visionary Fr. Colman Barry, O.S.B. He was instrumental in that we would indeed stay here. Only a year later, the old university in Memphis, Tennessee (Rhodes College, formerly Southwestern at Memphis) had heard that we were back, and they made a very lucrative offer to join their faculty. So did Stetson University in Orlando, Florida. I sent them my colleague from Innsbruck, Dietmar Larcher. And while I was doing the interview in Memphis, Ingrid drilled a hole in a piece of land near Saint John's and found water. When I heard that, I jumped on the return plane and said sorry to the folks in Memphis. It was that easy to land a job then—if you were as brilliant as they thought I was!

Father Colman certainly did, and I appreciated his support immensely. Why nobody has built a statue on campus for him is a mystery to me. It may be "Benedictine humility," this cult of understatement, which is partly virtuous, partly envy, and by some good portion, an inability to differentiate between good and brilliant. Father Colman was brilliant.

Alas, only three yeas later, he would leave the presidency in turmoil during the Vietnam protests. Students, led by John Thavis (now director of the U.S. news service of the Vatican) built barricades and closed the campus. Black students took over the president's office and drank his good cognac. Strangely, the anti-war movement was led by the very people who were draft-exempt because they were students (much later, during the Iraq War, lower middle-class and under-class students would join the army in order to be able to go to college). Mourning over the disorder, Father Colman resigned and later became a dean at The Catholic University of America in Washington. A great loss for SJU.

But they had us back. We enjoyed living in a lake cottage in Avon. We had to vacate the place in the summer, so we flew home to Innsbruck for three months, which were spent hiking, spending weeks at the campground of Caorle in Italy and seeing our families.

My mother particularly appreciated our extensive visit to our homeland. Erika actually became my coworker, and she typed the early and, later, the final drafts of my dissertation. She deserved my degree as much as I did. We would entertain guests from the U.S. in Innsbruck: the Tapps from Kent State, the not yet Senator Durenberger from Collegeville, and a colorful classicist from the University of Minnesota, Joe Schork, whose young trophy wife drove him nuts when she flirted with the *pappagallos* in Venice. He had rented a Mercedes with a manual transmission he could not handle, and when he failed to return from Italy on time, we were sure he had dropped the car with her in it over a cliff and was now hiding somewhere in the Roman ruins of southern Spain. We had also brought a baby-sitter, Gayle, from Avon. She was mostly tired. Only later did we find out she was pregnant and happy to be away from home.

It was a good summer in 1969. The Americans landed a man on the moon. I made mild progress with my degree pursuit. And our families were happy to have us near again. I continued to run the NEA summer seminars in Innsbruck. That paid for my trip, and it was fun.

In the fall of 1969 we flew back. LH 331 from FRA to ORD became our routine. Sometimes, we switched to Icelandic Air via Reykjavik and Luxembourg. Sometimes, we took stranger charters that should never have taken off, but we always made it.

I started teaching courses where, for the first time, I enjoyed the reading of primary sources rather than secondary literature and short-cuts: the novels of Mann, Roth, Musil, Zweig and Horvath, the plays of Schiller, Brecht, Kleist, Handke and Thomas Bernhard. . . . It was so good to make up all the reading that should have been done and wasn't. The courses had titles like Medieval Literature, The Age of Goethe, Romanticism, German Poetry, Turn of the Century, Weimar Republic, Modern German Literature, GDR Literature, Austrian Literature. I taught them all and became a well-read member of my discipline. I started to attend the year-end meetings of the MLA and learned who was who in my field. I started presenting papers and became known as a rising star. I came across as a very effective teacher, a fact that I owe to the Haselbachs way back in Klagenfurt. My students and I did performances: *Publikumsbeschimpfung* by Handke. *"Faust*: A Puppet Play" in our adaptation, songs of Bertolt Brecht and Kurt Weill. My students were far less inhibited than those in Vienna or Innsbruck and were fine performers. It was so much fun to bring literature to life. For the first time, I felt I was in the right discipline after all.

There were still good friends and colleagues from our first time here, Jack and Rita Lange from mathematics. We always had luncheons in their home when we did the weekly wash in town. There were Gerhard and Michi Track from Vienna. He was a gifted musician, an improviser and a self-promoter. I played in his orchestra. He had his *Wien Show* on MPR. He enjoyed a folksy popularity but would have loved to have been a star conductor. Alas, he never got a position with a first-rate orchestra, even though he conducted the Minneapolis Youth Symphony. In 1969, he left SJU for the Pueblo Symphony. Eventually, he returned to Vienna and became director of the Vienna Conservatory in the Johannesgasse. The best part of Track's record was his work with the SJU Men's Chorus, an ensemble with which he won many international competitions. His wife Michaela was a first-rate pianist. Their two sons are now living in LA, one is a TV actor in *Everybody Loves Raymond* and the other is a pop music producer.

They introduced us to their friends, Dr. Rudi and Gisela Mueller. Gisela became a very close friend of Ingrid's. Gisela was the daughter of a respected, conservative Catholic family in the Saar. She was a most gifted pianist and was about to start at the Paris Conservatory with a scholarship when WW II broke out. She then started to study medicine in Würzburg and met Rudi, a Bavarian farm boy, also studying medicine. He finished quickly and became a very young navy doctor in Königsberg. Shortly before the Soviets took the town, he got out with a transport of patients. He was taken prisoner by the Brits but escaped and made his way home to the Saar, where they married. They became French citizens in the French-occupied Saar. But he had to agree that he would not practice medicine in France, so he worked in the coal mines instead.

In the '50s, they came to the U.S. He went through medical training again and started to work in Minnesota. He was a good doctor but a difficult husband and father for his kids, especially the daughter. Gisela outlived him by some years, and we enjoyed her company and friendship very much.

Back from Innsbruck in 1968, we saw the U.S. slide into much turmoil: the assassinations of Robert Kennedy and Martin Luther King, Jr., the tumultuous Democratic convention in Chicago, the growing unease with the disastrous war in Vietnam, and an economy that went into double-digit inflation. The Peace Movement gained momentum, spearheaded, among others, by the SJU graduate Eugene McCarthy, then a presidential contender. But we got Richard Nixon instead. "I am not a crook!" Well, later it turned out he was.

My brother Gerhard came for a visit and even flirted with a position here at SJU. He noticed my slow progress with my dissertation and volunteered to edit and rewrite sections. I knew I had to finish soon because my future here without a degree was dim. But I enjoyed teaching, and Thomas was by now in elementary school in Albany, where Ingrid taught high school English and German. A stern Mrs. Evelyn Fischer was the baby-sitter when we were busy.

The lake was beautiful. The seasons were glorious. In winter, we ice skated in front of the house. In the spring, we watched the ice crumble in the waves.

In the summer of 1968, we decided that we must have a home that we would not have to vacate in summer. Upon returning, Ingrid went to an auction and bought an old schoolhouse for $100.00, but the bank refused to finance an old house. They would do it with a new one. Matt Zwilling, an old farmer who spoke German, agreed to sell us an acre or two of his farm, a beautiful corner of the Avon Hills. It was within walking distance from SJU. In the fall of 1968, they poured the foundation. They worked inside during the winter. In May 1969, we moved in, only to leave shortly after for Innsbruck, and our neighbors, the Twomeys, who were also building a home, moved in during the summer.

On my last trips to Salzburg to settle the details of my project—I had become, in the meantime, a notorious celebrity: an absentee landlord in pursuit of a doctorate—I collided with a big city bus and knocked out the bus with my old tacky VW. I patched up the VW and decided that it all had to come to an end soon. Besides, the new dean, Fr. Hilary Thimmesh, O.S.B., wondered out loud when it would be. Soon! I kept writing, and Erika kept typing. It started to look good.

In the spring of 1970, I would travel with the IES Academic Committee to Madrid and Vienna. I told Professor Weiss to be ready for my opus: *Guido Zernatto: Poetry and Politics* . PAN/AM was still flying. It was a wonderful time in Madrid. While in Vienna, I took a side trip to Salzburg and delivered my bound copy and followed my group to Paris. I felt happy and relieved and enjoyed the distractions of Paris from the Louvre to the Crazy Horse Saloon.

Well, it had taken me three years to write the dissertation. My committee was in no rush to read it overnight. When we came there that summer, I got a few suggestions for changes. It looked manageable, but I was disappointed. We spent time with our families. My sister Hildegard confided that she felt very ill, and mother should not know about it in detail. When we left Klagenfurt by train, she waved good bye and took some nice shots of us. We left with a heavy heart.

In September 1970, I got a distraught call from my mother; her beloved daughter Hildegard had died. Her heart had given up. Her liver had given up. She was thirty-four years old. The semester had already started, but I hopped on the next Lufthansa plane for FRA and connected to KLU. I tried to console my mother at the funeral. Hildegard's husband Felix was a fine companion for her to the end.

Tired and emotionally spent I hopped on a return TWA flight back to New York. There I got stuck. No flight for Minneapolis until the next morning. One does not sleep well on a seat at the airport. But I made it home and back to work. Three trips in one year: a promising one in March, a disappointing one in summer, and a sad one in September.

Back home in the new house, we spent much time on landscaping and furnishing. The house stood in the midst of a sandpit and urgently needed some green grass, trees, shrubs and bushes. It would take some time. Now, we are living in a green belt full of trees and flowers. It is paradise. Back then, it was not yet so.

I had to change some portions of my dissertation, and I did it with a vengeance. I sent the three bound copies in the winter. In the spring, they said it was okay, and I should arrive in June for the defense. I left already at the end of May and stayed with my mother at her quaint house and garden and prepared for the defense.

I had to be good because I had pushed my luck with my absenteeism beyond what was normal. I knew I had to be shining. I was. It was a hot June day. I showed up in my dark suit and fended most questions with ease, some with luck and a few with bluffing just a little. It was good, they said. Except Professor Erika Weinzierl, the history and political expert on my topic, had forgotten the date and had left for vacation in Yugoslavia. It was discovered that she would stay overnight in Graz. Would I be able to be there the next morning and do my defense with her at breakfast? She was at the *Erzherzog Johann*, a fine five-star outfit. My brother-in-law Felix, recently widowed, drove me there. It was a wonderful breakfast, and we had a most enjoyable, animated discussion about the politics of the '20s and '30s. She gave me an "A," and I thanked her profusely. Then I called Ingrid. I do not know who was happier, she or I.

On the way back we stopped at Peter Handke's home in Griffen. He had been at SJU in May. A novel about the U.S. trip was in the plans. It would come out soon and would be a story of alienation—Kafka in America with a new twist. It was the story of his divorce from the actress Liebgart Schwarz, a woman with a lovely Carinthian accent. She had come to Saint John's, but it was an uneasy relationship. It was even more strained, when I saw them again in Griffen that summer. When the book came out, it was titled, *The Short Letter to the Long Farewell*.

My invitation to Peter Handke to come to SJU made me a kind of local *Wunderkind*. Handke reading in front of the full science hall auditorium was sensational, as was the appearance of Yevtushenko later at Macalester, which then produced a loud anti-Soviet demonstration. None of that here. They loved the beat-generation poet Handke, who was a celebrity in the U.S. ever since his reading at the Group 47 at Princeton in '62.

My decision not to let Kolleritsch, the famous guy from the "Forum Stadtpark" in Graz, introduce Handke was a near debacle. He wanted to give a lecture on Austrian literature. They wanted to hear the poet. They were as eager to hear something about Austrian literature as they would have been to hear an esoteric lecture on Arkansas or Alabama literature. So, I silenced Kolleritsch and introduced Handke on my terms. What an arrogant upstart I was!

My graduation ceremony in Salzburg would not be until December 1971. While 1970 was a stressful year with sadness and uncertainty, 1971 was wonderful. We had moved into our new house. My dean was relieved about the outcome of the degree, and so were we. I got tenure right away and a promotion. Thomas was in school in nearby St. Joseph at Kennedy Elementary. Ingrid had accepted a position as a lecturer at SJU in German, a job she would hold for thirteen years. It was not a permanent position, and it was poorly paid. But she taught well and became a much noted asset to the MCL. Only later did she decide to work for real money and became a nurse. She started making preparations early and took courses in physics, biology and chemistry. She and her friend Eileen Haeg were even flirting with applying for medical school. They actually did so later, but the University of Minnesota did not recognize what stellar candidates they were and declined. Their loss. That is when Ingrid moved into nursing. First, she wanted an M.S. in psychology from St. Cloud State University. That degree she earned in 1973. Nursing on a psychiatric ward came later. She was a brave and resourceful woman.

XII

In December, all four of us hopped on an Icelandic Air flight for Luxembourg. After a very bumpy landing we took a train to Trier, a lovely city at night with Christmas decorations. We caught a connecting train to Koblenz and then to Salzburg. It was a sleepless night. We were all glassy-eyed when we got to Salzburg. Our proud families were already there. After a quick shower we looked and smelled better.

The graduation ceremony started at 11:00—string quartets, speeches, diplomas, handshakes. Then there were photo ops with Professor Weiss, with my stepfather, Herbert Glaunach, with Ingrid and the kids. The splendor of Salzburg was lost on us tired folks. A graduation dinner at the k.u.k. restaurant had the kids sleeping under the table and us celebrating as best we could. There were Ingrid's parents and her grandmother, Dr. Schmidt and his wife who were our mountain climbing friends, my proud mother and Erika.

And there was something else to celebrate. Erika was married in the fall to a wonderful retired librarian named Roman Wernig. It would have been the fourth transatlantic trip that year, had I come for the event, but I did not. I still feel guilty and sorry for that omission. She was also expecting, and we all were keeping our fingers crossed for a healthy baby. It would be a wonderful boy called Martin. After so many hardships, there was now hope and a new happy life for my poor sister and my burdened mother.

Barbara Haselbach, a good friend of Ingrid's, was also at the celebration. We all felt good, but numbingly tired. Christmas "at home" was nice, but we missed our home in Minnesota. Ten days later, we flew back. Again via Reykjavik, into the permafrost of Minnesota winter at its worst. But even when it is cold, the sun shines. Only the horses missed us.

Yes, there were new members in the family, four ponies. We had gotten them from John Gagliardi, the legendary SJU football coach. He could not keep them at his place anymore because the spiritual folks at the Center for Ecumenical Studies did not like the earthy smell of manure. We asked our old Matt Zwilling whether his barn and the one hundred acres of land would be available for our horses, and he invited them most cordially. All we had to do was keep up the fences and buy hay. That we did, and our children were so happy to ride them, as were we.

The year 1971 was also eventful at SJU. The legendary Fr. Colman Barry, O.S.B., had resigned and a young ambitious Fr. Michael Blecker, O.S.B., followed. He dreamed of making SJU the "Harvard of the Midwest." People smiled, but he did his best to attract new good people. Among others were Khalil Nakhleh, an Israeli Palestinian sociologist, and Bill and Carmela Franklin. Bill was a rising star as a church historian. Carmela thought of herself as being the greatest classicist after Winckelmann. He came from southern high-society, and she was the offspring of Albanian immigrants. The Franklins stayed for a while until they landed more lucrative offers in New York.

Add to these folks an interesting Black teacher with overwhelming charm, Norman James in the Psychology Department, and most importantly a new dean, a New York Jew named Bill Perlmutter, who was civil, educated, kind and cosmopolitan. He insisted that we needed a better door to the rest of the world: International Studies.

Our MCL Department was supposed to take the initiative, so we did. Unfortunately, Dr. Perlmutter's vision was a bit bold and scared some of the more conservative colleagues, especially in the science departments. It was there, that a peasant uprising, which almost led to his ouster, started slowly brewing. He died of liver cancer before any of this could happen.

He was married to a Finnish woman who had notions of grandeur. She taught English and looked down upon most of us. Her children, all adopted, were supposedly brilliant. Before Bill Perlmutter died, he said to Ingrid and me, "Our children should grow up together." His wife did not allow that and kept them under her protective umbrella.

For us, 1972 was a good year. Dr. John Hinz from CUNY invited me to teach summer school in New York. After a wonderful vacation at the Outer Banks in North Carolina, Ingrid and the children flew home, and I stayed in the big city on Staten Island. It was a glorious summer. I taught the great novels of German literature from around 1900. At night, I would hop on the Staten Island Ferry and pick up the next day's *NYT*. In the morning, I would admire the incoming ocean liners. In the news there was a trickle of irregularities at the Watergate complex. A third rate burglary? Or the beginning of the end of R. Nixon? Vietnam was still out of control. Kissinger tried his luck with the North Vietnamese. The Middle East was brewing. But New York was wonderful. In the fall, I drove back to Minnesota with Frances Simon, a member of our old host family from Westport. Fall in Minnesota was, as always, great.

With a Perlmutter mandate, I was sent to Europe to establish summer schools for our students. I picked Krems in the Wachau and Chartres in France. For several years, from 1973–1976, those places offered great programs for our students. In Chartres, Malcolm Miller became a legendary mentor and interpreter of the cathedral.

I felt right at home in Krems, where I had been teaching more than ten years ago. I much enjoyed the institutional link with beautiful Austria, which was then also blessed with the wise leadership of Bruno Kreisky, a man I much admired. I would meet him later in the U.S. several times, especially when he came to Minneapolis in 1977 with an Austrian gift to start the "Center for Austrian Studies."

Austria indeed looked good in the early '70s because the U.S. looked so burdened by Vietnam, internal rift, oil crises and financial woes. And there was Austria, "the Island of the Blessed." I became a little sentimental. Sure, we had a fine new house, new friends, horses, plus a magnificent collie named "Playboy," but I decided to submit an application for a job vacancy in Vienna for the position of dean of the Institute for European Studies at the Palais Kinsky. Ed Mowatt had resigned. I was familiar with the IES in Chicago, as I was on their curriculum committee. They knew me, and I knew them. I got on their short list and got an interview in Chicago. Father Colman—reluctantly—wrote me a recommendation. In the end, much to his delight, they picked a German fellow, Harms Kaufmann. He did not last long.

Then one of my very best students, Lonnie Johnson, took the job. He was a student at IES and was a Fulbright Fellow afterwards. Then, he met a blue-blooded Bohemian *contessa* named Monika, and they married. He earned a Ph.D. in philosophy at the University of Vienna and became the dean of IES. Soon, some of his books on Austria came out and were duly noted. Later, he wrote the definitive book on Central Europe at Oxford University Press, now in its second edition, *Central Europe: Enemies, Neighbors, Friends*. It is a splendid book by a great author, who is now the executive secretary of the Austrian Fulbright Commission and president of the European Fulbright Consortium. Well, I stayed at Saint John's and followed the deconstruction of R.M. Nixon in the Watergate scandal with fascination. It was democracy at work. The bad guys get ousted in a lawful manner. That is the way it should be. I was consoled with America.

At Saint John's, I got firmly integrated into the administrative process. I joined the Rank and Tenure Committee and became chair. It is the most important body for making personnel decisions. Nothing matters more in academe. However, it exposes you to legal matters, accusations and lawsuits—never a boring moment. I had fine colleagues on that body: Fr. Martin Schirber, O.S.B., a Harvard-trained economist; Joe Friedrich, an in-house future hope in economics; and Ray Larson, the fine classicist. Aside from that, Dr. Perlmutter wanted me to oversee the study abroad activities, which I had been doing for a while already as an unpaid extra load.

The cooperation with CSB was ongoing, but at times delicate. Overseas programs were still separate. When I tried for a merger of our summer programs in Chartres and Krems, a furious CSB president, an ex-navy guy, barked into the phone of my secretary Rolf Anderson, "Tell that Central European I will piss on his grave!" I did not know until then that being Central European was such a shameful stigma.

Fr. Jerome Tupa, O.S.B., a most enterprising monk, fell so much in love with Chartres that he tried to buy a formidable medieval nunnery for our program. He almost did it, but it heightened problems for Dr. Perlmutter, who was seen as reckless. It would have been a good buy, though!

The Department of Modern and Classical Languages (MCL) was now chaired by one of the finest and fairest monks, Fr. John Kulas, O.S.B. He returned from Washington, where he had studied at George Washington and had taken care of the liturgical needs of the JFK family. He was a very good chair of a still separated department between CSB and SJU. He actually finished his doctorate at the University of Minnesota under Gerhard Weiss, out of which came a fine book on *Der Wanderer*, a German paper from the 19th century. There was always a bit of jealousy between the two branches, the Modern and the Classical, which was at times rather ridiculous. Eventually, Dr. Sy Theisen saw to it that we were "legally married" rather than living in sin, and John became the first chair of the joint department.

Sy was a Minnesota farm boy turned sophisticated intellectual. A sociologist by training, he also worked for the U.N. World Food Organization in Rome and, after the war, for the U.S. Bishops' Relief Agency in Germany. At that time in 1948 or so, he met a young Italian woman at a *Wurststand* eating brats. He thought he could help a lonely and hungry woman and befriended her.

She was Vera, daughter of Italian high society. Her father owned shipping and insurance empires. When the war broke out, she was with him in New York on one of his liners. She stayed there and grew up in New York. After the war, as a teenager, she returned to Italy. The family in Milan had disintegrated during the war years. They sent her to Germany to learn German. In comes Sy. Before she introduced the farm boy to her family, he had to get a new wardrobe—white gloves and flowers. It was an exotic mix, the princess and the pauper, or so.

Sy and Vera married, and she came to Minnesota. They have nine children. Vera became a member of the MCL Department and is still teaching French. But she is equally fluent in Spanish, Italian, and good enough in German to order brats, I am sure.

Vera's father died much later, quite lonely. The family enterprise split and turned to navigational instruments produced in Milan and Lugano, Switzerland. Sy and Vera have a lake home near Ely. Sy is retired and reads a lot. Vera is teaching, because, she says, "What else would I do? I would go nuts."

XIII

The year 1974 was wonderful for us. On May 7th, our third child was born, a healthy boy named Dimitri. When Ingrid was eight months pregnant, we were at a concert of the Solisti di Zagreb. On the program were all the musicians' exotic first names: Branko, Stanko, Mirko, Dimitri. That is it! The delivery was hard; Ingrid was thirty-six. But it went well, fortunately. We were so relieved and happy. Our luxury baby! We now had a home, time, money, flexibility, and three is a good number!

I decided to apply for a sabbatical for the next year and go to Marbella, Spain, where we would rent a villa on the Mediterranean. We took Spanish lessons from Violeta de Pintado, a fabulous professor from Cuba. Soon, we were able to handle the essentials. First, we would go to Austria at the end of 1975, take our children to ski school on the Gerlitze and then drive a car we would buy to Spain via Italy and France. That was the plan. It worked magnificently. But first, we had work to finish here, and Ingrid had to recover from the delivery. And of course, we had to enjoy our new baby!

It was the winter of 1974. Dr. Perlmutter had been diagnosed with liver cancer and would die soon. Joe Ebacher, a magnificent French professor, had just died while shoveling snow. Father John's father had died, and John could not go to the MLA convention in New York. We had vacancies in French and German, so he asked me to go and find new talent. I always enjoyed going to New York.

The Modern Language Association combines the scholarly activities with the job market. I took great delight in interviewing young colleagues. In the end, we hired a promising young Jew from New York, Nathaniel Dubin. He was multi-lingual, well-read, sophisticated, aggressive and witty. His wife played a good viola. I thought it would be good to add Jewish salt to the Benedictine mildness.

In German, I found an equally assertive woman, Judith Scheidt. Judith left us soon after for Wisconsin.

At that time, I got a call from my mother. Erika's husband, Roman, had died. Martin was only three. I was heartbroken. It had been bliss for Erika. Now, she was a widow with a young boy. She would visit us at times. Martin would eventually spend a year and two summers with us. There was thought that he might stay here with us. He would have been more than welcome. But in the end, Erika needed him back, and that was good.

XIV

Our children were now attending the fabulous Lab School of St. Cloud State University. It was the best grade school possible, and they were happy there. As they became more and more integrated into the web of American life, dreams of relocating back to Austria vanished.

They loved their horses. On the 4th of July, they would celebrate the American holiday by riding the ponies or driving a wagon hitched to them in the St. Joseph, Minnesota, parade. In the year of the oil crisis, they rode with a banner, "Save gas, go pony!"

We discovered America on trips with them to Lake Superior, Canada and the East, to New York, Williamsburg and Washington, to the Smithsonian, the Lincoln Memorial and to the Outer Banks in North Carolina. Thomas so enjoyed riding the Staten Island Ferry, discovering unspent quarters in the viewers.

And they had wonderful neighbor kids to play with. Up the hill were the Twomeys, who all but adopted Dimitri later on. They had three children: Joe, who became a fine lawyer; Jon, who turned prosthodontist; and Lisa, who married a Madrileño pharmacist. She earned a Ph.D. in Madrid but would eventually come back home—much to our delight—and teach at Concordia College in Moorhead. Judy, the mother, is one of the best nurses, a fact from which Dimitri would later benefit greatly because it was she who first diagnosed his celiac condition, which he keeps under control well. Mark, a calm and serious man with a great sense of humor and warmth, is the editorial director of the Liturgical Press, the publishing house at Saint John's.

Then, there are the Farrys. Joe, a lively Irishman with a knack for local politics, was a fine colleague in political science. Jill, his wife, works with students who do internships in the corporate world and, thus, connects the ivory tower of academe with the real world. Their son John—Natascha would always call him "Hohn"—is a corporate lawyer for Deutsche Bank in New York. He is married to Brooke who works for the *Washington Post*. Their daughter Catherine is a gifted woman who lives with her husband Chris and their two children in Madison, Wisconsin, and works as a conference manager. She is bright and interesting, with a degree from Carleton and fluent in German, thanks to her parents' sabbatical in Innsbruck, where they lived in our apartment. The youngest is Michael, who lives in the Berkeley counter-culture, and may one day be one of the finest English professors.

We took many trips together to the Grand Tetons, to the Badlands, to the Twin Cities, to Cape Hatteras, and to the lakes. They have a cottage on Woman Lake, where we love to visit.

Then, there are the Haegs. Eileen, a nurse and PA by profession, is the director of the SJU Health Service. She is married to a man with almost too may talents. To finish all his plans, he would have to age like Methuselah. He built his own homes, raised cows, chicken, sheep, a llama and ducks. He does fine woodwork and became immortal as a glass painter by putting his name on the huge glass window of the Saint John's Abbey Church by Breuer, together with Bruno Bach.

They have six children, two of whom (Tim and Greg) became our good neighbors on the old Zwilling farm. Tim found gold in building septic systems, and Greg is a universal talent doing delicate projects like hanging huge projection screens for movie theaters, stage designs, remodeling homes in a most professional manner, and fishing in Alaska.

Greg has a lovely wife from Alaska, Megan McNair. She is a beautiful woman with a Mediterranean look. Rumor has it that they had fallen hopelessly in love in sixth grade. Then fate parted them, but she kept waiting for him. Then they were married in Alaska. I may not have all the facts, but Greg is a reticent guy, calm, quiet and competent. We were at their wedding, which was a magnificent feast in a stunning environment. Have you ever flown up and around Denali Mountain on K2 Airlines? It is a must! Well, Greg and Megan are great!

Ben is a doctor in Sauk Centre, which is the home of Sinclair Lewis. Marietta is a chemistry professor at Boston University, and Dan is dreaming of becoming the Nobel Prize winner in cosmic sciences. It may take a while, but never give up hope. Chris is the most romantic, looking for his fortune on the West Coast.

Dick is a generous friend, and Eileen is one of Ingrid's most understanding and supportive friends. She and Ingrid paint cards, ornaments ("Balls R Us"), eggs and dishes. And they help each other whenever life is tough, as they enjoy each other when life is good.

Our most spontaneous close friends are the McKeons. Mark is a fine lawyer in Cold Spring, and Susie is easily the best teacher Avon has ever had, even though a hysterical principal, a former cheerleader, tries to ignore it. Their three children are very close to our three. Dan is a great outdoors guy and a mesmerizing teacher in a charter school. Meghan is a radiologist, and Bridget is married in Ohio and left law for which she was trained, as did most characters in John Grisham's novels. Mark and Susie are at our home often and bring with them a touch of kindness and care we much appreciate, which we also do when John Kulas, the Farrys or the Haegs come visiting.

I must not forget our neighbor across the road on a "Century Farm" from 1864, Al and Bertha Eich. They let us share their spectacular land with the Gator and the dogs. They bring us berries and fish, and they love to see our children come home.

We are indeed blessed with the very best neighbors imaginable. That is why we are still here and not in Memphis, Innsbruck, Vienna or Ötz in Tyrol. All were options, but here we are happy.

Needless to say, it was my life at Saint John's that made the decision to stay easy. They appreciated my work and promoted me to full professor promptly. In Innsbruck, under Professor Kuehnelt or even Thurnher, it might never have happened. All my colleagues from way back then at the University of Innsbruck left or vanished. Klaus Lanzinger ended up at Notre Dame, Dietmar Larcher in Klagenfurt, Arno Heller in Graz. Christoph Zecha became a *Gymnasium* teacher; Lumpi vanished completely, and the great Sonja Bahm from South Africa stayed but was never promoted. Maybe I would have become a *Hüttenwirt* at some Alpine chalet in the Tyrolean Mountains where the deep-frozen Ötzi from five thousand years ago was found with an arrow in his chest and a Stone Age wardrobe.

There were some rather fascinating colleagues at SJU. The director of the Honors Program was an inscrutable Korean, Fr. Chrysostom Kim, O.S.B. He was a man from a military dynasty in North Korea, educated in Moscow, fluent in Chinese and Japanese, well read in Western thought and familiar with all the heavyweights at the Chicago School of Social Thought; he was in charge of the "best and the brightest" here at SJU. He easily intimidated people with his cold

Asian stare, but he was quite approachable and curious. He brought to campus many of his friends from Chicago: the Nobel Laureate Saul Bellow, Hannah Arendt and David Green.

It was an unforgettable event, when Saul Bellow would read in an overflowing science hall auditorium. He was open to questions and shared his insights. But when someone had the audacity to ask a "stupid" question, Chrysostom Kim would shoot up from his podium, point his finger like God on the ceiling of the Sistine Chapel and demand that the questioner, "Stand up, you, yes you! You are disgraced!" Saul Bellow would handle that a bit more humanely. When a question not fully thought out came up, he would say, "Ask that question again later." When that poor guy would try to rephrase it, he would interrupt and say, "No, not now, in a few years, when you have read more." Just to show that this was never easy entertainment but rigid intellectual discourse.

There was that magnificent master of manuscripts at the Hill Monastic Manuscript Library, Dr. Julian Plante. The library, too, was a creation of that great Fr. Colman Barry, O.S.B. In this bunker, one would have at his fingertips the four complete manuscripts of the Nibelungen MS and the twenty-one fragments. It was so exciting to teach the course on medieval literature with those treasures so accessible via microfilm. The project was started many years ago, and by now, every hand-written page in Austria, Ethiopia, Malta, Poland, Sweden is on file here.

There were also the good colleagues in MCL. Ray Larson, the lively classicist, Thorpe Running, the profound Latin America scholar with roots in Argentina; Violeta de Pintado from Cuba, a stellar master teacher and Fr. John Kulas, O.S.B., our great and fair chair.

What I enjoyed especially in those early years was the fact that I was in charge of scheduling the in-house professional discourse, the Faculty Colloquium. Together with Frank Rioux, a chemistry professor, we scheduled events and papers would then be published in a magazine of the same name, *Faculty Colloquium*. We did the introduc-

School photo Grades 5–8. Spring 1945.
Otmar in the third row on the right.

Birnbaum in the Lesachtal.

Drekonja family portrait 1940.
Front: Hildegard, Maria, Gerhard.
Back: Otmar, Max, Erika.

Otmar's class of the St. Philippen Grade School in Spring of 1956.
Otmar as school teacher on the right.

Otmar 5 years old, drinking from
a fountain.

The 14th-century church in
Birnbaum in the Lesachtal with the
Alps in the background.

Otmar and his father Max in the summer 1940.

Otmar and Ingrid's wedding in Klagenfurt on October 9, 1961.

Family photo in Birnbaum 1941. Otmar on the right.

Maria and Max on their honeymoon in Venice 1930.

Otmar welcoming Salzburg Governor Wilfried Hasslauer to Saint John's University in 1978.

Studio photo of Otmar as a Fullbright Fellow at Kent State University in 1962.

Otmar receiving his Ph.D. at the University of Salzburg.

Reception at the University of Minnesota in 1977. Otmar and Ingrid are greeted by the Austrian Chancellor, Dr. Bruno Kreisky.

Otmar recieves the Austrian Medal First Class for Arts and Sciences at Saint John's University in 1991.
Left to right: Dr. Julian Plante, Fr. Oliver Kapsner, O.S.B. SJU President Fr. Hilary Thimmesh O.S.B., Dr. Otmar M. Drekonja.

Otmar in 1958   Otmar climbing 1958

Ceremony at Saint John's University in 1991. Otmar received the Austrian Medal
First Class for Arts and Sciences from the Austrian Consul General.

Ceremony at the Musil Institute in Klagenfurt, Austria.
Otmar transfers the papers of Guido Zernatto from Saint John's University to Klagenfurt as a gift to the Musil Literary Institute.

From left to right: Vice President Dr. Martin Hitz, Dr. Otmar M. Drekonja, Dr. Klaus Amann, Director of the Musil Institute.

"The Abbey in the Woods." Artist's rendition of the Saint John's Abbey Church by Marcel Breuer and the Great Hall, 1974. Courtesy of Saint John's Abbey Archives, Collegeville, Minnesota.

tions and presented the colleagues in a very lively forum. I did a number of presentations in this forum, on Karl Kraus, on Bertolt Brecht, and on the disintegration of Yugoslavia. It was a good place for us, and we were happy.

XV

But a fountain cannot provide abundant clean water all the time. There are droughts. That is when the flow turns into a trickle and eventually a drip. That is why in academe, there are sabbaticals. The assumption is that after seven years of teaching there is nothing left in your heart and mind, let alone in the brain. That is why one takes time off and tries to recharge and wait for the next downpour of heavenly insight, creative energy and communicable wisdom. I was not in my seventh year. In 1975, I was already in my eighth, which was ample time for me to be silent for a while and be elsewhere—like on the Costa del Sol in southern Spain!

I had applied for a sabbatical and planned to prepare for a book on my man, Guido Zernatto. It was only natural to start in Treffen near Villach, where one of his poems, "The Sun Dial," is on the steeple of the church. Treffen is the village where Zernatto came from. It was around Christmas of '75. Ingrid's Aunt Ilse had an apartment at the ski resort on the Gerlitze. A steep, windy street led up to it.

We were there before in 1973 with the Farrys. It is a place with a stunning view of the Italian and Slovenian Julian Alps—steep, wild, romantic. There was an indoor pool and a fine ski school for Thomas and Natascha. We would take them there in the morning and ski the rest of the day to our heart's delight. The sunsets were spectacular, and we were happy up there. I am always happy in thin air, somewhere up high.

We had bought an old but reliable VW station wagon. In January, we set out for Tarvisio in Italy and then down to Venice, where we stayed in a fine hotel and showed our children the splendor of the Venetian doges, the seafarers of Marco Polo's time. Venice in winter is so nice—empty and melancholic; pure beauty undisturbed by crowds. The next day we drove on to Florence, and stayed at an even nicer hotel there. We enjoyed the fine works of Michelangelo, his *David* and the *Pietà*, the Uffizi Gallery, and the majestic marble *duomo*. From there we went on to the Ligurian Coast past Genoa and spent another night in Italy. The next day, we would be in France on the Riviera—Cannes, Mentone and Montpellier. Then it was time for a stop for French food and wine.

The next day we crossed the border into Spain. The country was in motion and in a mood of uncertainty; Generalisimo Franco had died. Finally. Many Spaniards thought the country would fall apart. Everything was *se vende*, for sale. But we did not want to buy; we wanted to enjoy Spain. We found a hotel near Benidorm with only saltwater in the bathroom. The next day, we turned inland and reached the Moorish paradise of Granada, where we stayed in the most opulent hotel we ever set foot in, the Parador Nacional. A five-star place filled with the amenities of Arabian princes. It was majestic!

Finally, the next day would be the last leg to our destination in Marbella. There, we had rented a villa right on the ocean. It had a roof terrace from which you could see the snow-covered Atlas Mountains in Morocco and the little spike of Gibraltar. Behind the house were the hills of the Cruz de Juanar, a fine mountain we would climb eventually. There were orange groves (*se vende*), villas (*se vende*), orchards (*se vende*), and palaces (*se vende*).

We enrolled our children in the local Spanish school. Natascha got her blue and white school uniform that she loved dearly. We had all learned some Spanish, but not enough. They had a fine teacher, Señor Rivera, who helped them so much.

We simply enjoyed the days. Stroll through the sand, shop in town, read, and watch the *últimas noticias* on TV at night. It was four months of luxury and leisure. In the afternoon, Thomas would swim out to the boat of Paco, the fisherman, and help him rake clams. They were so good with garlic and *zanahorias* or *Carrottas*, as the German tourists would say without blinking an eye.

It was an interesting time in Spain. We always believed that no chaos would result just because an old fascist dictator had died. But it is a society with long memories. And they would still talk about *los Rojos*, who did this and who did that. Yes, it was Franco country down there.

The *Guardia Civil* with their funny hats would look sternly at every-body. It was not good to ask where García Lorca might be buried near Granada. We would read Michener's *Iberia* and get a feel for the place. Or Hemingway. Or mail from the U.S. or Austria. Or the new daily paper with a Republican twist. The king and queen, rather than Franco, were on the postage stamps. They looked much better anyway.

Winter was mild and sunny but too cold to swim. Spring came early, and the slopes turned green and colorful. Unfortunately, most of the trees were gone. They had all been turned into charcoal for the grills in homes. Burros would haul big loads of thin wood down from the mountains. On the slopes there were many empty homes, finished, but without water. The view of the sea from up there was spectacular. In Marbella, we would frequent the excellent *Café El Greco*. Dimitri would crawl in the sand at the beach. Natascha would see her friend at the snack bar, and Thomas would be out on the clam boat with Paco.

While in Spain, we had visitors. At Easter, Ingrid's mother and step-father came, flying into Malaga. Easter is a big and spooky-looking feast in Spain. After Easter, Thomas, Natascha and I hopped on a ferry in Algeciras and crossed over to Morocco. We drove into the hinter-land and camped on beautifully clean beaches, then rode camels until we finally reached the Spanish colony of Ceuta.

After close scrutiny by the Spanish police, we hopped back on the ship and sailed home. It was a real African safari. Actually, there was an-other one in Spain with African animals out in the open. We drove through, and in no time we had an extra passenger in the car, a monkey!

Then Sy and Vera Theisen came in. Their son Paul became a good friend of Thomas. It was at that time, early in May, that it warmed up and Thomas spent quite a bit of time in the water on his way to reach Paco. He had also built himself a fine raft from eucalyptus trees, on which he would sit in a chair and read while rolling in the surf. Then he caught a cold, a real bad one. The doctors thought it might be tu-berculosis. Our German landlord freaked out when he heard about it. We could have bought his lovely place for little money had we con-firmed TB. Alas, it was only pneumonia. But Thomas was weak and recovered very slowly.

Jill's parents also came and asked, "And what do you know about Joe and Jill?" Well, we had mail and stories. They were a delightful couple, and we much enjoyed their visit.

At the end of May, we were supposed to move back. I was supposed to direct the Krems Program in the summer. However, Thomas was in no condition for a long car ride. Ingrid and the two boys flew from Malaga to Munich, while Natascha and I started the long trip home by car.

First, we camped in a tent outside Granada in a poppy field. From there it was back to the Costa Brava near Barcelona, where we stayed at a noisy campground full of drunken Germans. Then we reached the French Riviera and slept in a lavender field. In Italy, we stopped in Riva on Lake Garda, and Natascha pleaded for a hotel. But we stayed the course and camped again. The next day would be the last one. It was a glorious drive through the Dolomite Mountains. We were back home after almost a week on the road. We looked like happy gypsies. Ingrid was glad to have us back. The car was fine the whole time. We sold it in Klagenfurt, and I hopped on a train to Paris to pick up the Krems students. After a nice day in Paris, a night train took us to St. Pölten and Krems. While I was working, Ingrid and the children stayed for a while with the relatives. My mother was especially fond of Natascha. She was now ten and loved her *Omi's* cats.

We were again back in the familiar ambience of Austria—family, friends and colleagues. But our summer programs in Krems had awakened my curiosity in the greater Austria. That of the past with the Kakanian traces in the imperial city of Vienna, the splendor of Prague, the haunting beauty of Venice, the flair of the port of Trieste, and the lure of Budapest. Excursions to these places supplemented our eight-week study sequence. Add the baroque luster of the abbeys of Göttweig, Melk and Klosterneuburg, and the charm of the Wachau in the romantic Danube Valley with the traces of the Nibelungen, and you have a cultural mix that is hard not to get addicted to. I did.

Back at Saint John's in the fall of 1976, a number of things changed. I proposed offering January-term courses in Central Europe with the UMAIE Consortium. This suggestion was enthusiastically supported and kept me there for the next two decades or so, mostly every other year, in all some fifteen times. U.S. students, I thought, could learn much from Central Europe: the aesthetic values of six hundred years of Habsburg presence, the lure of power, the hubris of power, and the danger of power and the notion that civilization does not prevent barbaric behavior. That less could be more, and that small is beautiful. What a lesson for a superpower to contemplate!

The 20th century, in particular, left so many scars in this region. It all started in Sarajevo in 1914 and ended there in 1995. But life goes on and the music survives, as do the narratives, the monuments and the people. Besides, getting away from Minnesota is not so bad either! Poor Ingrid who had to shovel snow during those weeks while I sent postcards from the Castle of Miramare, the Charles Bridge or the ski slopes of the Lizum near Innsbruck.

The relative success of our summer programs had the effect that the administration wanted more and longer programs, semester programs. Where? When? How? That became part of my agenda.

Most importantly, after the great success with school in Marbella, Thomas, now thirteen, was determined not to continue at St. Cloud's North Junior High, a place he detested. Could he go to Saint John's Preparatory? He wrote a letter to that effect from Marbella and was told he might be able to do so if he scored way above the norm and better than most fourteen-year-olds. Well, Señor Rivera saw to it that his test was done as a "joint venture" and helped him to produce scores that put him in the range of a young Einstein. The guy, who barely survived breaking through the ice on Lake Wörther with his grandfather in December, now sailed into the future as the great white hope and was admitted to Saint John's Prep. Somehow, they always wondered why he would not live up fully to his intellectual potential. Well, he was an understating guy. He became the photo editor and a fine prep student, not caving in to any peer pressure and retaining his strong sense of individualism. Four years later, he and his friend Paul Theisen would enroll at the University of San Diego and lay the foundation for a great career to come. He owes it in no small part to Señor Rivera in Marbella.

Ingrid also had to rethink her career. As an adjunct lecturer at SJU, she did a very fine job, but for little money and no future. She could, of course, finish her Ph.D. in German and stay in the field. Or do something new. She planned to apply for medical school. When that did not work three years later, she decided to go into nursing instead. She became a nurse on the psychiatric floor of the St. Cloud Hospital, and she enjoyed her work.

But she would do well everywhere. Let me share some things about her as she was just about to make a monumental career change. She has made bold moves before. I remember when I was still in Ferlach, and we were at a formal dance all night long. We had (stupidly) agreed to go skiing the next morning. Oh, well, Ingrid was at the bus stop. I was not. She called my home. My mother picked up and told her, "Let him sleep. You know he was at a dance last night!" I would invite her to climb a tough peak in the Koschuta; she would come along. I persuaded her to go on glacial hikes on the Grossglockner or the Wildspitze in the Ötztal, and she did it. When I was in Vienna missing crucial lectures because of my work schedule, she took notes and filled me in as we sat in the purple seats of the *Café Votiv*. I asked if she would go skiing on a Thursday and skip lectures, and she would. We ran into a sheepish prof, and all smiled forgivingly.

I was in Innsbruck during the summer working on Petersen Exhibit Tents—big structures and dangerous, hard work. It was hot. Ingrid was in southern Tyrol and sent me a crate of fresh fruit. The year was 1959. I decided I would marry her if she would take me. Two years later, we were married. Ever since, she has been at my side—and even followed me to the U.S.! Maybe there were a few Austrian girls lusting after me, but not many would have had the guts to follow me to Lake Wobegon and an uncertain future. She did.

It helped that her family was a bit difficult. Marrying me was not in their master plan. Ingrid came from an upper-class family. Her father, a judge, died in Greece during WW II. Her stepfather was an engineer. He was pedantic, controlling and miserly ("One thing is clear," he said when we bought the condo in Innsbruck, "help, we cannot!"). Her grandmother, who lived to be nearly 103, was a wonderful, gracious woman, whom Ingrid loved dearly. Her mother was always more impressed with her sons and people who made more money than I did. Ingrid's brother Wolfi is a former advertisement executive who has seen better days. He now roams the Mediterranean on his yacht. His life was rough. His wife shot herself. His daughter Rose killed herself. One daughter is now an architect in London, the other married in Berlin. Wolfi has very little contact with Ingrid. Her two stepbrothers are Alfred, the man who transformed the Glaunach firm into a global venture. His wife died young of cancer. Now he enjoys his yacht in Croatia as an escape. The other, Peter, is a bit scurrilous and could be out of a *Grillparzer* plot.

Her half-brother Uli is the star in her mother's eyes. He's an executive for a French cement firm, and he has real-estate in Vienna, Paris, Carinthia and Frankfurt. You see, he is the fulfillment of her yearnings. We are humble and remote. But I must admit, my mother-in-law really likes me now, and I can do no wrong anymore. I am "Herr Professor," and I treat her daughter well. So, we are at peace.

Needless to say, we always visit Austria, every year. The children know the larger family. We have not gotten lost in the "New World." But they are sad we are here and not there.

The year 1976 ended nicely at SJU. The nation was now two hundred years old. Later on, when we read the books on John Adams by Mc-Cullough or on Hamilton by Chemow, we would better understand the monumental venture of the founding fathers two hundred years back. Bruno Kreisky also celebrated the birthday and collected money in Austria for an Austrian Studies Center in the U.S. A year later he came to Minneapolis in person and handed over a million dollar gift to the University of Minnesota. Since then, we have a fine connection with Austria, not only in Stanford but also in Minnesota.

There is another connection with Austria: our Salzburg semester. It was before Easter in 1977 that VP Gunther Rolfson, O.S.B., came to our home and said, "Beware of vice presidents bringing flowers. . . . Would you come with me and found a semester program at the University of Munich?" he asked. I knew of some rumors that said this was being talked about. I also knew there was a Benedictine place in Munich, St. Boniface, but I also knew that the semester calendar of the University of Munich was not the same as ours. I made a few calls to my friends in Salzburg, my alma mater after all, and said that we might end up there should Munich fail.

The next evening, we were sitting on a Lufthansa jet and were welcomed in the morning by the friendly monks of St. Boniface. (By the way, their Andechs beer is superb!) It took only a few meetings, and we were on a train to Salzburg, where the hospitable monks of St. Peter housed and fed us. We shared with them the Easter liturgies, and in between we met with the dean, the president, my Professor Weiss, and K.H. Rossbacher. Within days, we had a legal document, a charter for cooperation, sealed and signed. It was my most successful diplomatic mission, and I was ably assisted by Father Gunther.

Somehow, we also met a Mrs. Wächter, who owned a hotel and would have liked to house our students. She was a sophisticated lady, a bit cagy, though. She took us to a cemetery in Tyrol, where her husband, Dr. Otto Wächter, was buried in an unmarked grave in Fieberbrunn. There, she owned a wonderful old farm house. In a frame was the picture of her husband, in the uniform of a high-ranking SS officer.

She was a very religious woman and hoped to become an oblate of Saint John's Abbey, she said. I somehow remembered the name from my studies with Professor Weinzierl. Sure, he was one of those lawyers, who tried a Nazi putsch and killed Chancellor Dollfuss in July 1934. A relative of my wife, Dr. Friedl Rainer, also was involved. Later, Dr. Wächter became military governor of the province of Krakow. Within his jurisdiction was nearby Auschwitz. After the War he escaped to the Vatican, which protected him from the Nuremberg War Crimes Court. He died there in 1948 and was brought home on mules by his sons over mountain paths and buried in Fieberbrunn in an unmarked grave. But his life is well known in the history of the Holocaust. So is that of Dr. Rainer, who became proconsul of Italian-occupied Dalmatia and Krain after the Italian surrender. There he implemented—late, but nevertheless—the "final solution" for Italian and Yugoslavian Jews. He was handed over to Tito by the Brits and was executed. See *The Past in the Present*, a book by Lonnie Johnson. And a day in Salzburg with Mrs. Wächter, born Schöller Bleckmann (steel dynasty).

We did not sign a contract for housing with her. The Salzburg Program is now in its 28th year and doing well. It is a splendid opportunity for our students to study in the city of Amadeus and see Central Europe from the site of *The Sound of Music*, reading Erich Kästner's

Kleiner Grenzverkehr. Bela Petheo was the first director. I came in '78. I know that Father Gunther is very proud and thankful for what I helped him with. It was a good move.

In April '77, I went to Washington University in St. Louis, the place where I had met Chancellor Kurt von Schuschnigg in 1963, and presented a paper on "Aristocracy as a Role Model for Upper-Class Modern Society in the Republic of Austria." All I had to do was look at the family I had married into. They had never quite forgiven me the fact that I would greet them with a simple *"Grüss* Gott" instead of *"Küss die Hand."*

Back in Minnesota in May, the inauguration of the Center for Austrian Studies was celebrated at the University of Minnesota. Bruno Kreisky met with all of us, and I enjoyed meeting him very much. From now on in May, there would be the traditional symposium on Austrian affairs. I was there often as a listener, sometimes as a speaker. Always welcome. Always grateful for this fine link to our intellectual and emotional roots.

The year was 1978 when in more than one way our ties with the Old World were strengthened. Thomas, now fifteen years old and a student at Saint John's Preparatory, announced that he would like to go back to Spain and fish during the summer with his friend Paco in Marbella. It was a bold move, but we knew he could do it, and he did. Subsequently, a friend of Ingrid's, who runs a hotel in Berg, let it be known that they are always in search of waiters, mountain guides, sailing guides and tour guides. From then on, Natascha and Thomas found frequent summer employment there and served Schnitzel in Dirndl and stitched vest. There were also three daughters with considerable sex appeal, and Thomas must have learned a few lessons from them, to the point that he ultimately decided to follow one of the *Putz Frauen* to Vienna and study medicine there, rather than in the U.S. But that was far from clear way back then.

Ingrid taught full-time at CSB, while I left with Natascha for Salzburg. Arriving in Munich, I met the suntanned Thomas stepping off an Iberia plane from Malaga. I was so happy to see him back and in good shape after his summer in Spain. Then, the three of us settled in Salzburg, in the apartment of the Rossbachers.

It was a splendid semester. The two children attended the local *Gymnasium*. We were met by the governor. We toured Central Europe ranging from Prague to Trieste and Venice. My brother Gerhard, still looking for a permanent job in Austrian academe, came with his friend Patricia from Pittsburgh. With their Berlin connection, they introduced me to an interesting man from the GDR, who would eventually come to SJU for a while, do a U.S. tour arranged by us and make SJU immortal with his story, "The Abbey in the Woods."

At Christmas, Ingrid, Dimitri and Father John came. We all went skiing at the Reisseck, way up high. It was too high for Father John, who ended up in the Spittal Clinic. But he recovered nicely. We were joined for skiing by Monika and Bernd Felderer and my old climbing partner Erich Grolitsch, who did not fail to notice that Natascha was a very attractive young lady. Later she would work for him at his Hotel Felshof. She became even more beautiful later, and, unfortunately, Erich crossed a few lines of propriety, which ended our contact.

After a few initial problems, the Salzburg semester was now in good standing and allowed me to return several times as a guest professor to my alma mater in the future. It was nice to see that our children felt quite "at home" in the old country, in its schools, institutions and workplaces. My mother and Ingrid's family were especially happy with their fine grandchildren nearby.

For me, two intellectual horizons opened: curiosity with the GDR, East Germany, and my interest in contemporary Austrian literature. The latter I pursued increasingly at the University of California at Riverside, where Donald Daviau held his yearly symposium in the spring. I presented a number of papers there, on Thomas Bernhard, on Peter Rosegger, on the issue of nationalities in Central Europe, and on Zernatto. It was a great place to listen to colleagues in the field and listen to Austrian writers read from their books. As a fringe benefit, one could escape the gray never-ending winter in Minnesota and see the colors of abundant flowers in California, inhale the aroma of orange groves and drive over the St. Anna Mountains to the Pacific Coast near San Juan Capistrano and Dana Point. Sometimes we would have dinner at the old Mission Inn in Riverside. We always met with our old friends from Kent, Norene and Don Hokett.

XVI

In 1978, we started a cooperative program with the *Technische Universität* in Berlin, where Friedrich Knilli, a professor of media and communication, assisted us in video exchanges. We taped and sent him U.S. videos, and we received German tapes. It was the time of the U.S. *Holocaust* series, and the Germans were very interested in the reception here and there. In August 1978, I was invited to a *Mediothek* forum discussion on the Holocaust at the TU in Berlin. Subsequently, we invited Knilli to SJU.

Every summer, we would meet with suitcases of three-quarter-inch tapes somewhere between Graz (where he is from) and Klagenfurt on the Pack Pass and exchange our pirated tapes. The U.S. customs people always thought we smuggled pornography. The FBI probably knew we were dealing in Communist propaganda. I thought he was joking when Marc Catudal, my colleague here at SJU, wondered out loud, whether I was a *Stasi* agent myself. But I cared more for Bach and M. Luther in the GDR.

The Berlin connection with the GDR in the background became of interest because of the presence of a brilliant colleague in political science at SJU, Honore Marc Catudal. Married to a Berlin woman, Renate, he taught here and wrote many books at breathtaking speed: in 1971 the *Steinstücken Deal in Berlin*, in 1979 the *Exclave Problem in Europe*, in 1977 the *Diplomacy of the Quadripartite Agreement on Berlin*, in1989 the *Kennedy and the Berlin Wall Crisis*, in 1985 the *Nuclear Deterrence: Does it Deter?*, in 1988 the *Soviet Nuclear Strategy from Stalin to Gorbachev*. However, his most sensational book came out in 1991 on the taboo topic of *Israel's Nuclear Weaponry*.

Marc and I met in Berlin several times. He earned prestigious awards, and I was fascinated by his work. Unfortunately, he was quite manic and would write substantive books in a short time and then crash. Soon, he became rather vulnerable emotionally. In Berlin, he saw me as a spy and at SJU as a friend. He underwent a strong religious conversion. Some time in the summer, Ingrid and the boys were still in Austria, he came to my house and wanted to stay here. He had strained relations with Renate. He would not eat. He wanted the Lord to call him via starvation. I told him he could stay here and eat, but not if he does not. So he went to the basement of the Breuer church. I called the abbot who became quite concerned about him. He met with him and suggested treatment. Marc refused. We went to court, and after two days of hearings he was forced to undergo treatment at the veterans hospital. In court he felt I had stabbed him in the back as a friend. But he did get better over time. Alas, the medication took the spunk out of him. He left the university and went on disability. A sad end to a great man.

His wife divorced him and went back to Berlin, and so did his two children. I knew his son as a very good student here at SJU. Marc then married a nurse, who takes good care of him here. The side effects of medication have turned him into a shaking and disoriented man. It breaks my heart when I see him, especially, when he shows up in church. Religion is like poison to him. Or maybe the only consolation left to him? A drug? There is too much religion in U.S. society these days. One has to be careful with Bush and Co.

I became more curious about that other Germany behind the Berlin Wall. Very few people in my field, especially in the U.S., addressed the topic of GDR literature from Bertolt Brecht to Christa Wolf, Ulrich Plenzdorf, Becher, Fries or Irmtraud Morgner. I put those texts on my reading lists and suggested to install a permanent course on GDR literature. But I knew too little about it, so I applied for an NEH Seminar at the University of Minnesota taught by Frank Hirschbach. I was accepted for the 1979 seminar.

Frank Hirschbach was a Berlin Jew who had been able to emigrate in 1939. He came to Yale, corresponded with Thomas Mann, joined the U.S. Army, landed in Italy and came back to Berlin after the war. He was a stellar product of the Weimar Republic: left, liberal, democratic, anti-fascist and proud to be German. He became a professor at the University of Minnesota, together with the equally brilliant Gerhard Weiss who, as I mentioned before, was another Berlin Jew who survived the war in a forced labor camp and cleaned up Berlin after air raids. He came here after the war. Both became wonderful cultural ambassadors for the German heritage in its most noble shape: Weimar, its dreams and manifestations. Sure, Weimar lies near Buchenwald, but they knew how to transmit the noble side of Germany while fully and painfully aware of its sinister undertow.

I loved them both, and they became very good mentors of mine. At that summer seminar, I met with like-minded colleagues: John Reynolds and Brigitte Scheer. We were a good team, the "Hirschbach Brigade." I am sure the FBI kept an eye on us, especially since we all were eager to spend time in the GDR afterwards. We got much encouragement from the GDR and its *Liga für Voelkerfreundschaft*, which offered stipends and seminars for students and colleagues of mine.

My first experience with the "First German Workers and Farmers State" was in 1980. I traveled to Weimar, where the University of Jena held an eight-week seminar. There were few Americans, many Soviet colleagues and many Poles, who behaved rather outspokenly at the very start of the *Solidarnoz* Movement, the first thaw in the cohesive Eastern block after the futile uprising of 1953 in Berlin, 1956 in Budapest and 1968 in Prague. Little did I know nor did anybody dream of events to come in 1989!

For me, Weimar was a pilgrimage into the German past, better than any course at a university. To see the roots of German Romanticism and Classicism around Jena in the Harz Mountains and in the Ilm Park, where Goethe's garden house still stands, to visit the homes of Goethe and Schiller, to make the pilgrimage to Buchenwald—all was of breathtaking novelty to me.

I shared a room with a colleague from North Vietnam. There were also some Italian and French colleagues. The French were mostly true Communism believers, the Poles the skeptics, and the Italians the realists. No West German colleagues. There were a few Romanians and the four of us from the U.S. "Hirschbach Brigrade." On a weekend trip to Berlin, I met Fritz Rudolf Fries for the first time in the opera café, *Unter den Linden*. I extended the invitation for him to come to the U.S. He accepted, as long as we financed the deal. I thought we would find the money, and we did. The fact that he could travel did not surprise me too much then. Only after 1998 did it become clear why he could: He was a *Stasi* informant, an IMF, an "informal coworker with enemy contact." He is a wonderful man. I love him, and I am grateful for the fact that he introduced me into German literature as Dr. D. in "The Abbey in the Woods." Now I am immortal!

One of the most attractive academic rituals was the yearly conferences on The Fantastic in the Arts at Atlantic University in Boca Raton, Florida. I presented a number of papers there, while enjoying a hotel right on the Atlantic. I met the Nobel Laureate Bashevis Singer there. I introduced Fritz Rudolf Fries there and gave a paper on the dream world he created in a world of jazz, escapism and fantasy. His early fame came with his book *Road to Oobliadoh*, a lovely, romantic book for modern dreamers and jazz lovers.

Yes, academics are gypsies, always on the move, always looking for new feeding grounds. How did academe function before the invention of the jet plane? Maybe Germanists had more time to think, to read and to write without the pressure of "publish or perish." I find that lifestyle rather attractive and much fun: walking through Goethe's library, talking with the Nobel Laureate Saul Bellow, seeing a play by Brecht at the Theater am Schiffbauerdamm near the Spree, reading poems by Rilke and Goethe, Schiller's plays and Schnitzler's dramas.

One of the pleasures of being a German professor with American students is the fact they can be inspired so genuinely when introduced to primary texts. The European obsession with secondary sources and the pretense of having read a source, when in fact it had not been read, is alien to American students. I am very fond of literary heavyweights like Marcel Reich Ranicki, who never studied German literature but loved it and can transmit this fascination to readers and listeners. I am not a Marcel Ranicki, but I was a rather good teacher. Many of my students attest to that and are in the process of collecting money for a Drekonja scholarship at SJU—another form of immortality bestowed upon me by my students, to whom I am grateful.

Some of my stellar students should be mentioned. There was Mark Thamert. He took my course "The Age of Goethe" and became convinced that German was his calling. He was madly in love with an actress who dropped him. Later he became a monk, Fr. Mark Thamert,

O.S.B. He earned a Ph.D. in German at Princeton and came back to be my most inspirational colleague in the German section. He is a great teacher and a pillar of the department. He also teaches in the Honors Program, where he was director for some time. He also took some time off to be president of Saint John's Preparatory where he transformed the institution with the help of an equally sublime teacher, Sarah Pruett. But fortunately, he came back and now delights students with German poetry. *"Herr, es ist Zeit, der Sommer war sehr gross. . . ."* He is the greatest.

Then there is Lonnie Johnson, an unobtrusive Midwesterner, who enrolled in the IES Vienna Program (formerly chaired by our deceased Dr. Perlmutter). Then, he obtained a Fulbright Fellowship, married his lovely Monika from Bohemia and studied at the University of Vienna, where he earned a Ph.D. Now he is the secretary general of the Austrian Fulbright Commission and president of the European Fulbright Commission. He got many of our graduates into the Fulbright Program. I acted for many years as the SJU Fulbright Advisor, and Lonnie became a trusted and enthusiastic co-worker, helping me to place some three dozen fellows over the years.

There is also the understating Rolf Anderson. He studied at the University of Innsbruck for a year and came back to study architecture at the University of Minnesota. He is a known architectural historian and does fine work. He loved the period of the '20s and '30s; thus, he is a friend of Elisabeth Close, the Austrian architect in Minneapolis. I wrote about her mother, Helene Scheu-Riesz, in a biography. She was an important woman during the First Republic in Red Vienna. Being Jewish, she escaped to the U.S.; her brother Friedrich Scheu escaped to London. He was, and became again after the war, chief editor of the *Arbeiterzeitung*, a social democratic daily, unfortunately no longer in existence.

There is fiery Kathleen Fluegel, an outspoken and energetic red-headed woman. Some of the nuns at CSB thought she did not fit in here and dropped her from CSB while she was studying at the University of Vienna. I got her back in with the help of Sr. Kristin Malloy, O.S.B., who deviated from the party line. Kathleen also became a Fulbright Fellow and returned to the U.S. to pursue a Ph.D. in German from New York University. As a New Yorker, she found her way into the MOMA, and there she edited the German papers of Mies Van der Rohe. Then she became the development director for the Bronx Zoo, the Bronx Children's Museum and back home to Minnesota at the Walker Art Museum, the modern gallery. After a few sparks there, she left and became development director of the magnificent Weisman Museum at the University of Minnesota, a steel building by Frank Gehry, the architect of the Bilbao Museum.

Then there is John Thavis, the instigator of the anti-Vietnam campus blockade in 1970. Today, they would send him to Guantanamo Bay. He studied Goethe's *Faust* with me. The great blind Argentinean poet (Jorge Luis Borges) called it "the most overrated German drama." Has anybody ever seen a *Faust II* production on any German stage recently? I never did. I always was amused by the way in which God saves Faust in the end: by the inability of the super smart Mephisto to differentiate between *conjunctivus irrealis* and *conjunctivus potentialis*. "If such activity would go on . . . I would say to the moment . . . *Verweile doch, du bist so schön* . . . ." Faust drops dead. Mephisto thinks he has won the bet from *Vorspiel im Himmel*. Not so, says the voice from above. "Whoever strives, we can save . . . ." Mephisto has yet to take a course in advanced German grammar. Yes, John Thavis strived. He is now director of the Catholic News Service for the Vatican. He travels with the pope and enjoys life in Rome. He also has a nice country house in Umbria. He is married to Lori O'Connell, daughter of Joe O'Connell, the great print maker and sculptor in Collegeville, who chiseled on marble while listening to old-fashioned Chicago jazz.

Leo Riegert is just finishing a Ph.D. in German at the University of Minnesota on a Jewish Austrian writer from around 1900—a name unknown to me, but I will learn it soon.

Bob Acker wrote a dissertation on Uwe Johnson at Texas A and M and is teaching German in Missoula, Montana.

Mike Crouser became a great photographer and produced the fine SJU picture book with the introduction by Jon Hassler, including my portrait as a master teacher.

Brooke Kreitinger pursues a graduate degree in German at George-town University.

Tom Linnemann, turned football star, later became a sales execu-tive. His father, John Linnemann, also one of my German majors, be-came one of the best Minnesota high school teachers and spun a fine network with German schools for his students.

Timothy Scott wanted to become a monk but turned to law, which he now practices in Wisconsin.

There are many more I am proud of. They all made the most out of our department, the Fulbright connection, the GDR connection and the Salzburg Program.

There is also a number of great colleagues from whom I benefited much over the years:

Violeta de Pintado came from Cuba. She was the grand dame of the department. She was a fine teacher who taught me Spanish—and how to teach. Now she is retired back in Miami.

Dean Robert Spaeth was a maverick intellectual. With little formal training, he became the intellectual inspiration of the faculty. Im-mensely well read (he would even read while driving), he encouraged our research, was curious and supportive. He died young. We miss him.

He had a knack for cutting through insignificant trivia by looking into your eyes and saying with that sober tone of his, "Life is too short." And that was the end of that. Only once did I have an issue with him. In 1967, the year we came, SJU offered January-term courses. The fac-ulty workload was seven courses a year. Before it had been six. Many wondered how nice it would be to go back to six and dump J-term. Es-pecially Carmela Franklin and her valiant women colleagues pushed that line—while never ever teaching a J-term.

Dean Spaeth saw that imbalance in the workload and became em-phatic. But rather than addressing the guilty ones, he issued a decree to all, reminding us of the duty of working during J-term. I had just arrived from a J-term in Central Europe, tired, pale and jet-lagged. And Dean Spaeth always returned suntanned and energized from San Diego, where he did his writing. In an angry impulse, I wrote an in-house article mocking those who did not work while coming back with a suntan of undisclosed nature. He gave me a forgiving smile and said, "Don't worry."

However, soon, I got a bristling letter from the new academic vice-president, Sr. Eva Hooker, C.S.C. She is a Nicaraguan, with partly Black background, and a feminist and minority advocate with a powerful following among women colleagues, especially Carmela Franklin, Annette Atkins and others. She read my missive as an attack on someone Black. Well, I was in trouble for a long time. Eventually, we made peace, and I convinced her that she was not the target of my indignation. She gave me a copy of *Beloved* by the Black Nobel Laureate Tony Morrison, and we celebrated a cross-cultural peace treaty. Sister Eva is still with us. Bob Spaeth is dead. We all miss him. He was an inspirational man and a fine dean.

Two writers of distinction came to SJU because of Bob Spaeth: the Irish novelist J.F. Powers and Jon Hassler, the "Minnesota Dickens" (F.R. Fries). J.F. Powers, married to Betty Wahl, a writer and sister of Fr. Tom Wahl, O.S.B, is one of the great and underrated storytellers of U.S. literature. He has a fine sense of sardonic humor, biting wit, great sense of dialogue and a deep insight into the minds of priests, who are his actors. *Morte d'Urban* and *Wheat That Springeth Green*, plus collections of stories are his major opus. He wrote slowly but with impeccable perfection. Even my mother, who knew Catholic writers well, had his German translations in her collection.

He had a terse exterior. He was not sociable. But he had an astute observing eye, with which he measured everybody around him. During Mass on Sundays, he would sit alone up in the balcony in order to avoid shaking hands with others during the Sign of Peace. Later, his friend Joe O'Connell, the sculptor, joined him. They were good friends, and Garrison Keillor would tell many a story about them on MPR in the "News from Lake Wobegon."

Powers taught "Creative Writing," until he confessed that he could no longer read poor writing samples and quit teaching. He lived in a simple house and walked to church every day. His office was high up in Engel Hall, a place later taken over by Joe Farry, a very fine political science professor and a good friend of ours. J.F. Powers is dead now.

Unfortunately, there is no marker on campus mentioning his distinguished presence here over the years. I guess it's another sign of Benedictine humility, but sad nevertheless.

Jon Hassler is also a very introspective man. He is a very private and low key guy, kind and curious. He writes a lot and fast and well—a novel a year, no problem. *The Love Hunter* is an American classic. He is a graduate of SJU and taught for a while in northern Minnesota. Bob Spaeth brought him back to SJU.

One J-term he and his wife, Gretchen Fandel, joined me on a journey to Central Europe. He kept a diary, as did the students. At night, we would read from them and compare how we responded differently to the same things we saw or experienced. It was "creative writing" in progress.

He is a very kind man. Unfortunately, he fights an illness that disables him slowly. But he keeps on writing, either in his home in Minneapolis, or at his winter home in Florida. He translated the Midwestern world into a human comedy with divine inspiration. Ordinary characters with a great gift for making moments memorable are his creations. He is a very successful man, maybe not of the magnitude of John Grisham from Memphis—but close. Every airport bookstore carries some of his titles. I always recommend him strongly. I am fortunate to be among his friends, for which I am grateful.

Another colleague is Raymond Larson, the classicist I have mentioned before. Father Dunstan brought him here in 1967. His office was next to mine the whole time. He was a great conversationalist, fond of gossip, well versed in the world of antiquity. His hearty laughter would fill the classrooms and the office. He was adored by students, whom he treated with infinite patience, love and care. He was a Minnesota farm boy. He still owns his parents' farm in southern Minnesota, even though he retired to the desert at Borrego Springs near San Diego.

He published excellent translations of Plato. He was also a student of German at the University of Minnesota, where he met his wife, Lucy, a fine pianist turned public accountant. She taught accounting here for many years and is now also in Borrego Springs, where they volunteer as park attendants. We miss them much.

Robert Weber in political science keeps looking after me. He is a man from Montana and a man with a caring heart. He also has a knack for politics and a very fine sense of predicting political outcomes in the tumultuous American scene. I love chatting with him.

I enjoy networking with Richard Ice in Media and Communication. He is a DFL party secretary in Minnesota and fiercely active for the Democratic cause. He is a young and aggressive colleague with a firm voice in the faculty, feared by some and cherished by others. He is certainly much appreciated by me, who also had a knack for being outspoken in the faculty forum.

Joe Farry, one of our best friends, is from the Political Science Department. He was a reliable pillar for me over the years; a man with a fine sense of propriety and professional ethos. Much more cautious and fair than I am at times, he speaks and teaches with a passion that is controlled by reason. Students loved him and cherish his memory as a professor. There is even a "Joe Farry Chair" carrying his legacy. He is an unobtrusive gentleman with a great voice at SJU, even though he is now retired.

Thorpe Running was another fine colleague next to my office. He is a great Latin America scholar with many books and contributions to his field. He feels most at home in Argentina, where he knows the literary elite, and they know him. He was there several times, on a Fulbright and otherwise. A most understating Norwegian from Concordia College, he marks the Protestant presence at this Benedictine place, together with Ray Larson and the outspoken theologian John Helgeland, who is now a dean of the School of Theology at North Dakota State University in Fargo. Thorpe is still teaching, and even though he fell off his bike four years ago and is now paralyzed from the neck down, he moves and works!

Those were my stellar colleagues at Saint John's. Add in the great English professor Steve Humphrey, the Vatican theologian Fr. Godfrey Dieckmann, O.S.B. , the super musicians Axel Theimer, Fr. Robert Koopmann, O.S.B., and my great clarinet mentor Bruce Thornton. They all add luster to this place and enjoyment to those living here.

Had I had Bruce Thornton fifty years ago, God only knows what a great clarinet player I could be now!

One colleague who contributed so much to the aesthetic dimension of our home and our visual world is, of course, Bela Petheo, from Budapest. He left Hungary in the turmoil of 1956, came to Vienna and then Chicago, until Father Dunstan brought him here. He is a painter from the school of Kokoschka, a man who influenced him, whom he appreciated and about whom Bela wrote a fine book.

There are a number of his works in our home: a Venice view of Santa Maria della Salute, a Salzburg *aquarelle*, portraits of Ingrid, Natascha, Thomas, Dimitri and me, a street scene from southern France, a view of our lake, a view of our slough, several lithographs and a sumptuous nude á la Titian with a CSB model giving me moral support in a tempting pose. We are lucky to have so many works of this fine and vastly underrated artist.

Yes, there were a few more scurrilous ones too. Dr. Gabriele Winkler—a German woman with an iron will and an obsession for being right. Father William of Holdingford found her in Rome, where she was a fashion designer, and brought her here as a liturgist. Her personal life remained shrouded in secrecy. She became the one and only expert on baptismal rights in Syriac in the first half of the third century. She knew all the old languages that no longer exist: Coptic, Urdu . . . . She traveled in circles of wise men to the Middle East and southern Russia. She published in papers most do not even know of.

She watched jealously over what she published. When a friendly monk referenced her work in a paraphrased footnote rather than in a documented quotation, she sued him for plagiarism. That split the School of Theology into a schism it barely survived.

Ultimately peace returned, because she took a call to fill a chair at the University of Tübingen, where she now pontificates. How much of baptismal rights can you take without feeling overwhelmed? She became a legend. Nobody misses her much, though.

A man I do miss is Dr. Julian Plante, splendidly immortalized by Bela Petheo in a stunning portrait. He left the Hill Monastic Microfilm

Library under a cloud of mystery. No better director has ever been found after him. He was indeed the "Magister Ludi," the man from the medieval world with all its splendor. I miss him very much.

Maybe I am getting a bit involved with the university. Life goes on outside, as well, especially in the family. Let me take you back to 1977, the year I became full professor, the year we started the Salzburg connection, the year after we had returned from Andalusia in Spain.

Dimitri was by now three, Natascha eleven, and Thomas a prep student at fourteen. Ingrid had earned her M.S. in psychology, and we were ready to discover a portion of the New World. We set out on a three-week trip in our VW bus, following the trails of Lewis and Clark. We invited Father John to come along, and he did. The Farrys also came along for a while.

First, one travels endlessly through the flat grasslands of South Dakota, stopping at the Indian museum of Pipestone. Crossing the Missouri River, the farmland turns into wide open ranch land. Then it's hundreds of miles of open landscape and skies, until one reaches the bizarre sandstone formations of the Badlands. A stop at Wall Drug is mandatory. Then come the wonderful Black Hills—Indian country, buffalo country. Leaving the Dakotas, we moved into Wyoming and stayed in the Big Horn Mountains. I climbed Cloud Peak, over fourteen thousand feet high—a two-day hike. We fished and enjoyed the abundance of wild flowers in the highlands. Our target, however, was the Grand Tetons, the Dolomites of the U.S. We found a spot at the Jenny Lake campground and shared our fried eggs with the bears that came to breakfast.

There were some Californians with fine climbing gear. I had none, so I took my pup tent and camped above them on the Lower Saddle. I had forgotten to pack my sleeping bag. Ingrid, like Fidelio in the opera, came and brought it up to me. What a valiant woman! What a stupid climber! The next day, I connected with the Californians and led them on the route to the Grand Teton. Rappelling, we returned and Ingrid had a great meal for all of us.

The Farrys left us, and we continued on to Idaho, where we camped at Craters of the Moon. Then on to Oregon, which is full of vegetation, trees and flowers. The Three Sisters Pass leads past volcanic peaks to the coastal area at the windy Pacific. Fog, mist, lighthouses, sea lions, birds, berries and flowers—it's a cool coast with ice-cold water. But Thomas tried his diving gear he had bought with the money earned from distributing newspapers. (All American millionaires start that way.) He came out like a crab, red and frozen. We enjoyed a splendid campground and having all the children with us the whole time.

The return trip took us north to the Columbia River into Canada and over the mountains of Glacier National Park. Then we drove across the endless flats of northern Montana and North Dakota. After three weeks, we passed through Avon and turned off I-94 into St. John's, where Dimitri cried out, "Daddy, you did find the way home!"

Yes, I did, and we were happy. It took Lewis and Clark three years. We did it in three weeks. But in 1803, it was a less hospitable country, more Indians, harsher weather and greater uncertainties. No maps, campgrounds or markets helped them when they explored the full dimension of the Louisiana Purchase, the greatest deal America ever made besides the purchase of Alaska from the Russians. Our children certainly had a grasp of the vastness of the country and the feeling of comfort when staying together.

In later years, we would do more expeditions. We traveled along the Great Lakes to New York and down to Cape Hatteras with visits to Washington, D.C., and Williamsburg. Several times we would take the children to Yellowstone National Park, the Karl May playground. We would go back to the Tetons several times, and Dimitri would become an expert guide. We explored the East from New York to the whaling port of Mystic in Connecticut. Moby Dick was there! Thomas even looked into the Coast Guard Academy at Groton, the U.S. Navy's submarine port, but he was ruled ineligible because of pimples. So, he continued with prep school and kept his options open. We also showed them Florida, Grand Cayman and San Diego.

The discovery of the New World was always done as a family venture. Several glorious weeks together with the children allowed us all to experience the awesome dimensions of this great country. Later, our children became rather resourceful explorers on their own. Dimitri turned into an expert canoe guide in Voyageurs National Park. He is also quite at home in the mountains of Wyoming and Colorado.

Natascha learned to explore the hinterland of Denver with those lovely peaks of the Indian Mountains, Mt. Audubon, Mt. Elbert, Long's Peak, and the ski slopes up there as well. She also moved to Boston later to attend Boston College and got a taste of the East Coast.

Thomas was the most daring. First, he went to San Diego by Greyhound to inspect the University there. He loved it, loved the Pacific and the sailing. He is a Californian at heart. At some point, he sat with a girl friend in a NW Airlines plane bound for Miami. There, they announced that the passengers for Grand Cayman should remain seated for take-off. Well, they were not booked for the Caymans, but they remained seated and landed at the island paradise of Grand Cayman. It could have been the island right out of *Treasure Island*.

They had to improvise, since their funds were finite. Their visa had zero credit. But they met Ms. Lillian Ohl, a motherly New Yorker with a few cabins. Instead of paying rent, Thomas cleaned her boats, her home and her garden. She took them in and was hospitable, understanding and supportive. This place became our favorite escape in later years. It was a splendid discovery!

XVII

The year was 1980. Dimitri was now six, and we had learned how to control his celiac condition, thanks to our friend and neighbor Judy Twomey. We had been very concerned, and at one point even panicked when he almost drowned in Woman Lake. But I got him out in time. Too much adrenaline!

There was the time Thomas went through the ice on Lake Wörther. And then Dimitri also swallowed water up north. We must have been inattentive parents.

It was the year after my NEH Seminar on the GDR, and I had received the scholarship to go to Weimar in East Germany. Thomas was seventeen and graduated from prep school. He left home for San Diego after a "last supper" at a railroad diner with the McKeons and the Twomeys. It was a sad day to see him leave home. Natascha, now fourteen, followed in his footsteps and became a prep student, a good runner and a wonderful looking young woman.

That summer we all went to Europe. Thomas and Natascha worked at the Putz Hotel in Berg. I invited my sister Erika for some hikes but noticed that she would get totally exhausted on the way to Wolayer Lake in the Lesachtal. Something was not right. We suggested she come to Mayo for a check-up, and she did. They said she had MS. It was quite a shock to her and to us.

Her son Martin was eight. Could he come to us for a while, so she could have a break? He did and spent a year and two summers with us and attended the fine lab school in St. Cloud, learned to play the trumpet and became part of our family. Later on, the question did come up whether he would want to stay here or go back. It was a hard decision for all, but he went back because my mother could not see her daughter without him. Erika struggled bravely with her condition for over twenty years and was a good mother to Martin.

There were other children of the clan that we provided shelter for. Christoph, son of Aunt Jutta and Uncle Herbert, came here from Canada, hungry and penniless. He stayed with us until Interpol wanted to see him back home. He and his friend had eloped with a black Mercedes belonging to the friend's dad. The car was reported missing and showed up in the investigation about the assassination of Hans-Martin Schleyer, a banker in the Red Brigades in Germany. Christoph and his friend had sold the car in Morocco and flew from there to Canada.

When he needed help, he called us. We sent him a Greyhound ticket, and he enjoyed a leisurely summer at our place. He was about to continue his vagabondage in Latin America, when his parents told him in no uncertain terms to come home now. He did.

There was also Rosie Luger, one of the three daughters of Ingrid's brother Wolfgang, then an advertisement executive. She was sixteen going on twenty-one and immensely enjoyed the sense of freedom of being away from home. After the summer, she was supposed to go home but had fallen in love with a German exchange student. So she stayed for the year and went to Apollo High, took flute lessons and discovered the lure of her femininity. She was bold, brash and provocative, but hard to reign in. Ingrid had many a headache.

In the middle of the year, the German playboy left for home, and she wanted me to find her a seat next to him on the same plane. I did, and she went home. A year later, her mother shot herself. A few years later Rosie committed suicide herself by jumping from a scaffold. Her friends had been wild guys from the drug scene of Vienna. Maybe she would have been better here and would have lived longer?

We also had Martin Hitz here, the brilliant offspring of Aunt Ilse and Uncle Konrad. He was a very fine student at Apollo and a lovely kid. He became a great academician at Klagenfurt University, where he rose to vice-president later. Of course, all the kids are above average here!

Our "day-care" operation for gifted or troubled children was quite something. Eventually, we decided that we had to concentrate on our own children, especially at a time when they would start leaving home in the near future. We always felt America was too big for family. The distances between San Diego, Boston, Denver or even the University of Minnesota, are too far for frequent get-togethers.

In order to be together with "runaway kids," I suggested that my next J-term in Central Europe in 1981 should be co-directed by Thomas, who was at that time a sophomore in San Diego. He had already earned diplomatic experience and cross-cultural refinement by being part of a group of U.S. students invited to come to Austria for the 25th anniversary of the Austrian State Treaty, which marked Austrian neutrality and Austrian independence. He met with Chancellor Bruno Kreisky, the mayor of Vienna, CEOs of Austrian industry and VIPs of the cultural scene. It was a great honor. However, his chemistry professor in San Diego did not take his participation in this mission as a sign of commitment to his discipline. He missed two weeks of the fall semester. Yes, but . . . . In January of '81, he would not miss classes, though.

We took off with over thirty students and visited Munich, Salzburg, Vienna, Prague, Budapest, Zagreb . . . . Everything went splendidly. Then in Ljubljana, Yugoslavia, it happened. Robbers broke into our hotel room. They drugged us and robbed us. Our trip seemed to be finished, but we improvised splendidly and moved on to Trieste, Venice and Innsbruck. We pulled through, in spite of everything, but it was a close call! It was so good to overnight in Frankfurt before flying back to the States. UMAIE officials welcomed us as heroes and were happy to see the program succeed after all.

On the plus side, while in Vienna, my mother introduced me to her old hometown sweetheart Willy Kowarz, a retired country doctor. It was a wonderful love affair for the elderly couple in their second youth. I took them to the opera, and we saw Richard Strauss's *Salome*. My mother was so happy. It was a fairy tale come true, at least for a while.

Two years later Willy died trying to scrape the icy window of his car in front of her house. It left her heartbroken and devastated. Her will to live was gone. We tried to lure her to come to Minnesota and be in our midst. We already had a visa, a ticket and Thomas ready for the transfer in October 1985. She died on September 20th that year.

But 1981 also had a special significance. In this year, a small book came out in Leipzig, GDR, by Fritz Rudolf Fries, *Leipzig am Herzen und die Welt dazu*. In this book is the story of "The Abbey in the Woods." It made our place and the characters therein immortal. Fries, with a touch of sardonic humor and a keen sense of observation, saw through all of us.

We had invited him to come to the U.S. and do a lecture tour. We found the money and had made arrangements here, in California, in Florida, at Cornell and at the University of Minnesota. He also taught a semester course on East German literature. He was a wonderful guest, but a bit cryptic and unpredictable. When he did not show up for his lecture at Cornell, they called here and asked where he might be. Well, he was in California, but where? God knows. A victim of crime? An accident? He was a very fragile man.

I called the GDR Embassy. No, they had no information. Did he defect? That would have been terrible for us. Little did we know then, that he was a trusted *Stasi* informant with a travel option in non-socialist "enemy countries." He duly spied on us, but said nothing bad about me, as I could see many years later when I got a copy of my *Stasi* file. It was a human comedy of sorts, a bittersweet human comedy. I do love this learned man with the sly smile.

Over the years I had invited many writers and scholars to SJU and the U.S.: my professor Walter Weiss, writers from the Graz Forum, colleagues from East and West Berlin, the Austrian economist Bernd Felderer, and the poet Peter Handke. It was very exciting, but always a bit stressful to find money and to schedule events. We also translated Brandstetter's *Die Abtei* into English and made a radio production of a Handke play.

But Fries was special. He lived with his second wife from Leipzig, east of Berlin near Straussberg. I visited him there often in his home filled with jazz and Spanish memorabilia. His first wife was a ballet dancer and lived in Rostock. He survived the stress of the German unification and his outing as a *Stasi* agent. He is writing again. May he see many more successes in the wonderful world of literature.

The best way to do justice to this scurrilous man is to let the text speak for itself. Here is his story of our "The Abbey in the Woods." The translation is mine. It appeared here in the SJU publication *Symposium* and in other places. His only other work in English is his first novel, *Road to Oobliadooh*, a sentimental story about his youth when the Americans were in Leipzig before the Russians in 1945. He deserves more translations, and they will come eventually.

XVIII

"The Abbey in the Woods" by F.R. Fries
Translated from the German by O.M. Drekonja

When I heard the term "collect call," I was reminded of the collection in church where one drops the pious penny or even the not so piously— maybe even sinfully—earned mark on the collection plate. . . . Calling collect was the beginning of my venture to reach the monks in Minnesota at Saint John's University, not far from a place called St. Cloud. A bit further up north, as I recall the geography of this area, is the Canadian cities of Winnipeg and a bit further down, the Siamese twin city of Minneapolis-St. Paul, where I happen to be right now. At one of those airports to be exact, on the way from Chicago. Everything is quite simple—if they pick you up, you can rest your travel-weary head on that proverbially friendly and hospitable shoulder providing American hospitality, which is one of the virtues surviving from the days of the pioneers. There always was and still is a friendly neighbor providing encouragement to a weary stranger whose waning go-West optimism is in desperate need of an encouraging and comforting smile. Oh yes, I have heard of some recent stories about some long-haired weirdos that have been shot at from a passing car. But perhaps they had stolen some eggs at a remote farm, or some flowers. And vigilantes are as alert today as they were in those pioneer days.

A patient and helpful telephone operator provides access to the Saint John's switchboard, but nobody is willing to accept the charges for my collect call and that resourceful and eager Austrian docent Dr. D., who had arranged my whole trip, is nowhere to be found. He put my arrival time on his desk calendar, but on the wrong page. The secretary, probably a young monk, whose vow of poverty must have produced a sense of rigid frugality, refuses to listen to the concerned voice of the operator suggesting that there is obviously a stranger in need, who does not know his way through the woods and would benefit from some help. No, sorry, he cannot accept. That's it.

My first attempts to locate Saint John's University geographically lead nowhere. Nobody knows the habitat of those monks in the woods or the university which they allegedly sponsor. I do not have enough dollars for a taxi to get there. Could it be that Dr. D. had invented a *fata morgana*, in a hallucinating *deja vu*, had created a legend worthy of Stifter: the Abbey in the Woods, one of those utopias envisioned by the Bavarian King Ludwig I (his mad son adored Wagner and dreams of mythical castles) who thought he could create in Minnesota a colony as an oasis of justice and virtue? Soon pilgrims followed that call and endured the hardships of perilous journeys, they cleared a patch in the woods, fought the Indians, were defeated and scalped, managed to fight another war against the savages with more success and chased the Indians out into the cold. Then they returned to their chores and tried to make a living in the woods. Soon there were fields as far as the eye could see, cattle, abundant fish from those ten thousand lakes in Minnesota. Brutal winters and dusty summers undermined their health. The survivors married the immigrating Finns,

Swedes, Poles, even Germans. The abbey disintegrated, and in its crumbling library I suspect that Dr. D., who is probably sitting there right now reading a Salutation by John E. Eidenschink, O.S.B., has completely forgotten to meet me here and pick me up.

I try some stale coffee in a paper cup and stare through glass panels of the gate area with its slick plastic floor in the direction from which I came. There is a constant line of airplanes landing and taking off. Everything seems to move according to some well-thought-out plan. I am struck by the image of the ugly American: wearing a large checkered jacket and a sort of paramilitary cap and displaying contemptuous arrogance in the constantly chewing jaws. Here he is, to be studied in person. I ask him for the whereabouts of Saint John's University. All of a sudden the ugly American changes. The contemptuous ice melts from his face and drops from his jaws. My comrade is all ears, accepts me as his "buddy" and calls me by my first name—as if the English language had not already made the distinction between the formal and familiar "you" impossible. No, he says, no, he has never heard of such a place. Maybe someone at the bus stop knows more. The driver of the next bus does. With a glimmer in his eyes that reveals a sudden enlightenment, he confides to me that I should first go to St. Cloud. The ticket is four dollars. From then on the mini-bus follows endless interstate highways, endless highways passing the kind of farms that the early Bob Dylan would sing about,

"I never want to work on Maggie's farm no more." Endless flat landscapes with evergreens on the horizon, billboards, towering silos and walls with large lettering of some sort; occasionally typical water towers, pregnant-looking bulging bellies on thin long stilts.

All of a sudden I find myself back in a familiar America. Not a touch of alienation or exotic strangeness, even though I have never been here before. I recognize it as part of myself, the whole trip from Florida to Minnesota, as if I was paging through familiar books by Jules Verne, Karl May, Hans Dominik, Sienkiewicz and somewhere further up north the Canadian Winnipeg with the animal stories from Ernest Seton-Thompson. While traveling on the so-called planet of the future, I return to my past days as a reader in the public library of the Georg Schwarz Street in Leipzig.

My fellow travelers in the bus doze along. To my left a woman, one of those ageless American women, with whom it is virtually impossible to flirt—not because she is so old, but because her artificiality makes you as insecure as if you were walking on ice. The woman has a grandson, who is studying with the monks at Saint John's. He is waiting for her at the Holiday Inn in St. Cloud. They cordially invite me to join them on their ride to Saint John's. I put my whole European charm into a most appreciative "Oh, thank you, madam." Hasn't America always been the country where God sends a kind soul to show the right way to the just? This is especially true for Minnesota, which according to my neighbor, has no problems with Blacks, since there are hardly any; nor with the Indians, because there are hardly any left except on some reservations; no problems with environmental hazards. The state is, after all, rather large—217,736 km.? (The GDR is only 108,178.)

There are really no problems with crime, at least in comparison with New York or even Minneapolis with all its rich grain and commodity brokers, for whom virtually nothing is too expensive, not even Alfred Brendel for an all-Liszt concert; in one word: a clean state with clean lakes, uncontaminated fish and children, and open doors all over. There are no fences around homes, which seems to suggest that most neighbors are equally well off with no discernible difference in middle-class standards. Bob Dylan[1] has never been in Minnesota. My curiosity tries to imagine what sins the monks of Saint John's could possibly pray for in such a proper state. If it were not for the TV antennas on the roofs of the faculty homes, to which the monks are occasionally invited for dinner and entertainment, their prayers could still be concerned with hopes for a good harvest, against the draughts or the never-ending winters, like way back then in the days of the quaint King of Bavaria.

An exit road takes us to the campus, a Latin word which means "field" or wide open area. There is gray grass and cold gray-blue lakes (it is only the middle of April), woods and a wide road, which leads right up to the bell tower of Marcel Breuer's modernist church with some colorful stained glass windows. Jogging young men pass the small car. Sparta in Minnesota. The setting winter sun is reflected in the windows of the student dormitories. These are for the male population; the women students sleep in different buildings at a separate college four miles away. No problem for a well-trained runner. All the classrooms and public places are in a 19th-century brick building. Between

---

1. Bob Dylan, alias Bob Zimmerman, is from Hibbing, Minnesota, after all.

the old structure and the church is a flat sort of bungalow, narrow and with quite a bit of glass: the abbey and its guest wing. The whole thing seems well-planned: On cold winter days you can avoid the blizzards and frozen faces while walking from church to the cafeteria. The same is true for going to the lecture halls. "Cafeteria" is the term for *mensa*, except one does not pronounced it the Spanish way, but rather with this peculiar idiosyncrasy with which Anglo Saxons also handle the Latin language: "Caefeitierja."

Thanks to a pass issued for the guest by Father K., I shall receive all my meals and drinks here for the next few weeks. I shall get myself soft drinks from all those dispensers of coffee, tea and milk with different fat-levels, Coca- and Pepsi Cola and root beer, which tastes like some kind of fermented root juice.

They will put on my plate the most beloved cakes of the American nation—pancakes, which have no similarity with our egg omelets but are useful for virtually everything——most courses are in pancake form, too! There is a salad bar with raw vegetables of the rawest kind, then those fried potatoes to be eaten with their peelings and above all ice cream *ad infinitum* . . . . A kind of wonderland, where everything has some kind of sweet taste. "Are you sure you are eating enough?" ask the concerned wives of the hospitable faculty at night, while putting more pancakes with syrup on my plate and pouring more healthy milk into my cup. I have given up asking for some kind of alcoholic drink. All I would get would be that okay California wine, which resembles, at least in color, Italian or French wine. I know, I am exaggerating mischievously. In the homes of the professors the cuisine has retained a distinct European flavor: Oh, that Irish whiskey poured from a sheepishly concealed bottle in the hands of the writer P., who also works here at the university as a professor and is hailed as the greatest Catholic writer in America. Oh, those seafood dishes in the House of Austria of Dr. D. and his wife. Oh, those Norwegian entrées in the house of Professor Th., who is a Borges specialist. His two rosy-cheeked daughters aged nine and eleven devour for dessert the most grisly comics I have ever seen, full of sarcastic cruelty and monsters with ugly features, which put to shame the quaint eeriness of Grimm's fairytales, which could well pass as pious reading for nuns by comparison. But lo and behold, the girls, according to their parents, display a mental equilibrium ever since becoming hooked on this kind of literary diet. They have such a good attitude towards school and home that one is tempted to believe those psychologists who claim that comics are really a mental purification device. Obviously Americans don't read enough such books.

The attempted assassination of President Reagan dominates the conversation for days. Also in the cafeteria. "What does the guest make of such news?" ask the well-fed girls and boys, and the guest fails to understand why every citizen can have the right to have a Colt or a machine gun under his bed. The turgid topic of violence follows us in the classrooms and seminars, which the guest has come to conduct.

I am not entirely sure what kind of instruction is offered here. Certainly it is not the traditional sequence approach. The doors to the seminar rooms remain wide open. So do the doors to the offices. I stick out because I am always extending my hand for a shake and closing doors behind me. Europeans are that way. The students of German of Professor D. do not study German in order to pursue a job related to German. Where is the familiar notion of periods: one semester of Faust, one semester of Brecht, a survey of literature during the Thirty Years War? Here the likings of the professor seem to dictate the curriculum, or the recent readings of the professor correspond with the interests expressed by the students. It seems as if every seminar is the last class where the professor serves a portion of Theodor Storm or Strittmatter. Career plans seem to be quite vague. Wait and see. In any case one does well in taking a semester of business or two. A manager makes more money than a teacher or editor in a publishing house. And no editor or teacher can do without business. Is it a coincidence or not: The two professors of business administration are the unruly part in this solemn quadrumvirate with their Mephistophelian brilliance? Their wicked wit is the spice of every conversation. I can't help but think that some institution tired of their venomous rhetoric punished them by shipping them to Saint John's. Not so they claim! With the monks they enjoy the greatest degree of freedom to corrupt their students.

The campus with the fresh snow from last night looks cheerfully naive. People try to catch their frisbees like in a slow-motion ballet. Nobody smokes. Nobody is noisy, except those stereos at night. The monks stroll past in their long robes and with umbrellas and those paramilitary hats. They nod in response to greetings, with heaven and the earth fully at peace.

The abbey in the woods as a kind of Castalia? As the guest drops this thought in a careless moment an awesome silence takes over. The nuns stare embarrassed at their black shoes. The padres shake their heads as if they had not heard right. The German professors snicker: Hermann Hesse, *The Glass Bead Game*. The writer H. grins sardonically. He too earns his living by teaching at Saint John's, even though he is well on his way to being transformed from a Minnesota Dickens to one of the great writers in America. I admit my suggestion seems a bit unfounded. The abbey in the woods is quite open-minded, after all. The library carries a good assortment of daily papers in several languages. The students talk about Nicaragua, Catholicism, and Marxism; they discuss the Berlin Wall with the guest and the situation in Poland. The university-sponsored radio station invites the guest to an interview and asks about his works. The pretty girl in front of the microphone quickly interrupts with the question, "Which part of Germany do you come from? The East or the West? Oh yes, the East, I see. And what part are the Communists in?"

Castalia? The one most likely to claim this term is the librarian of the huge microfilm library. He fits the mold: a superb player of the Glass Bead Game, a Magister Ludi, in whose library the treasures of the monastic libraries all over the world are stored. Truly, if our world would perish, this monastic library in the woods would preserve its mental image, at least as long as projectors could be fed with electricity or batteries. The library, also a design by Marcel Breuer, resembles a bunker sunk half into the ground.

My cell in the monastery guest wing looks like a motel room in brown and beige. A crucifix on the wall. On the table some brochures with the history of the Benedictine Order. Dr. D. has provided a bottle of California wine and a portable radio for the long evenings. While sipping from the wine, I read a pornographic story by Anais Nin, which makes me doubly frustrated. While listening to the radio, I read James A. Michener, one of those highly intelligent authors completely ignored by our publishing houses—America versus America, a study about the revolution of petit bourgeoisie values in America. The radio remains a reliable companion through the night. Like most other states, Minnesota, too has its Public Radio free of advertisement and with commercial-free programming, which is financed by contributions from listeners. The result is a never-ending flow of music from Mozart to jazz and Bartok (whose birthday is being celebrated during the whole week). A Castalian program including news from campus and commentary of harmonious ambivalence.

After my lectures in the afternoon, I stroll along the lakes with the Indian names. The color of the water, the trees and the size of the lake remind me of a lake at home not far from my house. There is a path connecting the monastery with a beach reserved for monks. A Madonna watches from a grotto up the hill. On the other bend of the road on the west side of the lake is a small graveyard, trimmed lawn and white stones, little ones with children's names. The family names sound like long forgotten German and Polish families.

I felt I should do something about my theological ignorance. Alas, to no avail. The lectures of Father B. indulge in the issue of hunger in the Third World and the views of the Pope—reduced to the common denominator of an active social consciousness. In the evenings, while sitting in front of the fireplace in Dr. D.'s home—his wife, a kind and lively lady, who teaches German classes during the day, is serving beer and pizza—I try to engage Father K. in a conversation. He is a daily guest in this home and a man of insightful kindness. He is wearing a blue wool jacket over his habit and makes a call to his elderly mother. I carefully collect all my terms available and try a shy question like a child at confession, "How do you see a man like Teilhard de Chardin today?" In the end, I found his vision of a growing noosphere, of an increasing closeness of all people due to an expanding pool of information over the years of truly revolutionary impact . . . . Father K., who speaks a flawless German, only slightly spoiled by his Austrian friends, smiles and remains evasive. I try again, "What about Thomism?" even though I do not have the faintest idea what I am getting into. Father K., I know, would have also seriously considered this question. Dr. D. talks about his small farm, his pasture and his horses. A cat sneaks in, a prehistoric monster. Probably a descendant of that cat which King Ludwig I had given as a present to his emigrating pilgrims and that very cat then fell in love with a lynx in the Minnesotan woods.

Dr. D. misses his mountains, which is why he goes to Austria once a year. For his children he is a stranger, who mispronounces the simplest words, even those from the TV.

Later on we are leaving for a party given by the dean in honor of the guest. The dean of the philosophical faculty (probably, they call it something different here), who had learned about the musical tastes of the guest, has selected some of his finest jazz records. And even though we are both the same age, I experience this remarkable return to the artificial paradise of the post-war years, when the announcers of

AFN (American Forces Network) conjured up a kind of America which probably never existed and never will, but which survives nevertheless in jazz, this carefree melancholy, this bankrupt optimism, those metaphors of love written in lipstick by Billie Holliday. Bob, as they call the dean, fills the glasses. His wife refuses to serve from the kitchen as long as Billie Holliday sings—for all the others we turn into a still-life, the liturgical custodians engaged in a religious act and recognizing each other in the magic of the music recreating the American dream for one single night.

Translated and published with the permission of the Aufbau Verlag. The text is from F.R. Fries, *Leipzig am Herzen, und die Welt dazu*. Berlin/ Weimar: Aufbau Verlag, 1983, pp. 122–30.

XIX

I know I am no Fries, but I have to continue my story. *The time is the early '80s.* Thomas has graduated from Saint John's Prep and has decided to go to the University of San Diego. This city, for him, became paradise. Natascha graduated from SJP in 1983, but decided to spend a year in Aix en Provence and in Spain to find herself. In 1984, she enrolled at Boston College. We made many a visit to San Diego or Boston, two of the finest cities in the U.S.—New York, of course, being the best! Maxi (Dimitri) is by now in the St. Cloud State Lab School, a good cello student and a fine runner. We continued to take vacations with the children at Cape Hatteras in North Carolina, in Boca Raton in Florida, in Wyoming and Montana. In between, we always found time for trips to Austria to cultivate the connections with family and the old country. We hiked in the Koschuta and the Julian Alps in Slovenia. We showed our children the imperial city of Vienna, Salzburg, and our old home, Innsbruck. And Ingrid was about to graduate from nursing school. Nineteen hundred and eighty-four was the last year of her poorly paid but splendidly performed job as an instructor at Saint John's University. In 1985, she graduated with an additional degree and became a nurse at the psychiatric ward of the St. Cloud Hospital. For the first time, she developed an understanding of my idiosyncrasies.

My professional interests during this time spanned over four areas: East Germany in summer, Central Europe in January, teaching opera workshops or medieval literature for Elderhostel, a Boston-based program for retired people with interest in this area, and teaching my courses at SJU, which I enjoyed more and more. My heart was especially in the courses entitled Introduction to Literature, Turn of the Century, Weimar Republic, Age of Goethe, Medieval Literature, Romanticism and GDR Studies. Add some language courses, for which we were by now using the best textbook ever written, *German: A Structural Approach* by Strothmann/Lohnes. What lovely soap operas came with the grammar and structural concept from Tante Amalie, Schmidt-Ingelheim and Gisela! Who would ever forget the subjunctive mood after Ingelheim's compliment, *"Ohne deinen Kaffee, Gisela, wäre das Leben nur halb so schön!"* Except, that absent-minded womanizer had forgotten that this time it was not Gisela after all. Shucks!

The January terms were fine-tuned by now to a great success story. How to cope with the loss of imperial power, how to enjoy a great past, how to overcome barbarity by civility and how to learn that less is more and small is beautiful. Are Americans under Bush ready to contemplate those lessons? As usual, we would start in Salzburg and explore the ethos of Biedermeier after the imperial collapse after Napoleon, move on to Innsbruck and discover the days of Habsburg glory under Maximilian I around 1500. Vienna! What can I say?

On to Venice, where power is gone but beauty prevails. Then Trieste with the memory of Maximilian II, the one killed in Mexico, and the demise of the Habsburgs in the 19th century. From there, we would cross into Communist Yugoslavia and visit lovely Ljubljana or Agram—sinister memories of Sarajevo, WW I and WW II, which plunged Europe into unimaginable catastrophes. Budapest would be the place to remember the Nibelungen; see *Siegfried* at the opera, and remember the Turks, the Double Monarchy, 1918, 1944, 1956 . . . how many tragedies—and yet, a city with a splendid vitality and warm spas! A last train ride to Prague, the city of Kafka, Kundera, Dvorak and Alfons Mucha! Sometimes, we went as far as Krakow in Poland and paid a silent visit to the haunting site of Auschwitz. Is it hard to believe that in the end civility survives? In Central Europe it does! And that is a wonderful lesson to contemplate. Hope in the cold of January! Beauty everywhere! Ah!

In the summer of 1982, I was back in that other part of Central Europe, behind the Iron Curtain, in the GDR. I was invited to a seminar in Leipzig, that fine city of books, Bach and Auerbachs Keller, where Goethe's *Faust* was invented. A Faust to be saved, because Mephisto did not know the subjunctive mood!

The train ride from Munich crosses the Iron Curtain in the Thuringian Woods. Jena, Naumburg and finally Leipzig. This time, I stayed with a family named Büchner, whose son served in the *Volkspolizei*. At times, we would go to the *Voelkerschlacht* Memorial of the Napoleonic Wars together and talk freely without worries about delicate subjects.

The German scholars from all over the East, ranging from the Soviet Union to Korea, were good and competent. I was scheduled to give a speech on Fries, which was well received, and the son of F.R. came to greet me. He is a ballet dancer. A Czech colleague, Maria Muchova, related to the great Alfons Mucha, was eager to invite me back to Prague. Most importantly, we visited all the sites connected to Bach around Leipzig, and also those of Martin Luther. The German heritage is indeed kept alive and in good shape in the GDR.

I caused a bit of a stir in the Herder Institute when I wondered out loud why they always have to "fight" for peace. How about "work, strive or plead" for peace? The audience applauded. A Soviet colleague got indignant. I was invited to the inner circles, and they suggested that offending Soviet scholars was not polite.

I enjoyed the weeks at the Karl Marx University, the music at the Gewandhaus Hall and the treasures of the German National Library. Most of all, everybody enjoyed the gutsy Polish colleagues with their irreverent humor after the *Solidarnoz* Movement from two years ago. They spoke up more freely than I did and came up with all the jokes that got under the skin of the Soviet brothers or friends. For example: What is the COMECON, the Eastern economic block? Answer: It is paradise. It combines the German sense of humor, Polish precision, Czech honesty, Romanian intelligence, Hungarian obedience and Bulgarian courage. Or: What makes the GDR economy blossom? Answer: They pretend to pay us, and we pretend to work.

On a more serious note, Timothy Garton Ash, the great British journalist, an expert on Eastern Europe, had already come out with his book *Und willst du nicht mein Bruder sein,* banned in the GDR, but eagerly smuggled in and read. I sold my copy to the Volkspolizist Büchner for East German currency, with which I got a small set of Meissen dishes. How bourgeois could one get in the land of real existing socialism?

The stability and permanence of the GDR seemed to be taken for granted for generations to come. Who would have thought then, that in less than seven years, right after the fortieth birthday of the First German Farmer and Worker State, the Wall would fall, the GDR cease to exist, the Soviet Union implode and German unification happen? I certainly did not think so. Nor did the CIA or anybody else.

Back at Saint John's at the end of the summer, I offered one of my several Elderhostels, this time on opera. Five operas in one week: *Cosi fan Tutte, Porgy and Bess, Don Carlos, Tristan* and *The Ring of the Nibelung.* My special fan was Mrs. Dubin, mother of my French colleague Nathaniel. She is a Jewish woman from New York with Central European roots and a great opera fan. One could not wish for a better disciple!

In January 1984, I did another J-term on *Habsburg Heritage.* At the end, I sent the students home and went back to Austria to see my mother, age seventy-eight, in a retirement home. She was lonely and losing strength, but she was elated to see me. In the summer, Ingrid and I took her to the lake, church and a coffee house. She looked okay, but she died on September 20th,.1985.

The phone call from my brother reached me in my office. I booked a flight the same night. On the plane, I composed the few words I would say at the grave site:

> She was a brave, strong and selfless person. She fought like a tiger for her four children. She raised us under the most trying and difficult conditions, with a husband missing, with no income, with an uncertain future. The woman from the big city had followed her husband to a most remote Alpine village without any infrastructure. It was a beautiful but harsh reality. And then the war! Yugoslavia—the blown-up house, the captured husband. It was a desperate attempt to find him behind enemy lines in the

midst of winter. An undertaking so bold that it bordered sheer lunacy. She survived and came back, her heart full of hope, belief and love.

After the war, we were all reduced to a begging existence at the mercy of hardhearted locals. She raised goats. She sent us to school, far away from home. She was alone, never desperate but always pained. She had a difficult life. She was a fighter, a bright and proud woman. Eventually, she bought a house in Klagenfurt and brought the family together again. She took the blows of fate with astounding resiliency, but there were the scars.

An old Latin saying at the cathedral of Maria Saal says, *Horas omnes vulnerant–ultima caecat.* ("Every hour wounds you. The last strikes you down.") She stood in the ring of life for many years. She was good to us. Generous, proud and loving. Yes, Bertolt Brecht's "Mother Courage" comes to mind. My mother was even greater. She was indestructible and loving, in an Old Testament way, a love that would cause pain at times. She was the symbol of life triumphing over adversity.

The funeral was two days later. She loved flowers, so I provided two big buckets of long-stemmed roses, and every guest took one home. It was a fine memorial for a wonderful woman.

The plans had been different. After the months in the retirement home, Ingrid suggested she should come to Minnesota and be with us. No, she said, she belonged here. A week before we left her, she said all of a sudden, "I will come!" We arranged for her U.S. visa. Thomas booked the flight for October 7th. (He was already a med student in Vienna.) But she took a different trip—further away and to a place without pain. She deserves all the glory of heaven, where I am sure she is waiting for us.

Right after the funeral, I hopped on a plane for Frankfurt and caught a connection to New York. It was too late for a plane to Minneapolis, but I was so tired that I even slept in the uncomfortable chairs at the airport. The next day I was back at work, pale and spent. Teaching about another formidable woman in medieval literature, Krimhild, the queen of the Nibelungen, and her attempt to restore her honor—at a terrible cost. My mother was of a more humble kind and saw life as more important than a strange concept of honor.

Hitler loved the Nibelungen myth and the opera. And he did not care how many people would have to be killed to achieve his objectives. Some of the many were my father, my Uncle Otto, my Uncle Gärtner, Ingrid's father, Ingrid's uncle and millions of others. My mother defied the cataclysmic upheaval and clung to life for her children. We can only say thank you. I keep her in my mind and learned more about her when I went through over a thousand of her letters. They are documents of courage, love and civility. Her impeccable style and handwriting are uplifting. I took the letters to my brother, the historian. She left a magnificent legacy.

XX

It is time to go back to teaching at SJU. I was finishing writing a book on Lion Feuchtwanger. The Feuchtwanger project started years earlier when Fritz Knilli from the TU in West Berlin invited me to a conference on Feuchtwanger at the Akademie der Wissenschaften. Feuchtwanger was a kind of a saint, considering his purity of solidarity with the Soviet Union. But the West German Fischer Publishing Company bought back the rights from his widow in California and prepared a complete edition. Because of the volatility of this emotionally and ideologically charged project between the GDR and West Germany, it was a closely watched event. Only later, when I got a copy of my *Stasi* file, did I realize that the *Stasi* had sent an agent to West Berlin in order to find out whether my ideological leanings were kosher. They attested that my presentation was "not hostile to the GDR." And why should it have been? I love this splendid story-teller. *The Oppermans* was always a hit on my reading lists. And the GDR was extremely hospitable to me, my students and my colleagues. They provided stipends and scholarships for us, and we were able to discover on site the roots of German heritage in the romantic and classical era: Herder, Bach, Luther, Schiller, Goethe, Kleist, Fontane, Brecht, Weill and all the contemporary writers, of whom we met many.

It was the time when the *Holocaust* series ran on U.S. TV. Germany picked up the topic, long taboo, and invited me to a public forum discussing the series in Berlin. The GDR had its own angle on that, "We did not do it. We are the clean, pacifist, anti-fascist Germans." The Holocaust was the brainchild of the West Germans, Austrians and whatever other fascists. The GDR was innocent and pure. It was an interesting general absolution delivered from above by Honecker and Co. A form of national schizophrenia?

The fact that Buchenwald lies near Weimar is one of those idiosyncrasies of history; the noblest next to the nefarious. On top of that, Buchenwald was in the GDR and used after the war by the Soviets as another concentration camp. But the reparations for Israel were paid exclusively by West Germany. The GDR did not even cultivate ties with Israel. They were considered part of the U.S.-capitalist-imperialist military power. Well, the Palestinians on the West Bank and Gaza would agree—with some justification.

In the summer of 1986, I was back in the GDR, this time in the capital, in Berlin. "East Berlin" would be a forbidden misnomer in the GDR, as would be the term "Wall." It was, instead, the "anti-imperialist protection system." Mr. Sharon has a similar escape in linguistic evasion when addressing the Wall on Palestinian land. Control of language is control of reality. It helps to have some military force. The GDR had its *Volksarmee* and the protection of the big brother, the Soviet Union. The question inside the GDR, whether the Soviets were our brothers or friends, was answered categorically: Our brothers. Friends we would pick.

I was housed in an apartment with an Iraqi colleague from Baghdad. He was a very nice guy with a rare collection of teas, which was hard to come by in the GDR. Aside from the official events, I splurged on the many splendors of Berlin: the concert hall on the Gendarmenplatz, the magnificent theater in the Palast der Republik, the legendary Theater am Schiffbauerdamm, which did Brecht. In the former Gestapo headquarters, there was an exhibit commemorating the 25th anniversary of the German attack on the Soviet Union. I still enjoy the comprehensive catalogue with an abundance of information, pictures and data.

The museums are all on the Museumsinsel, an island containing the Bode, the Deutsches Museum and the National Gallery. In the old Zeughaus was the Museum of German History, seen from a GDR point of view. Right across from the Deutsche Oper was the baroque palace of Humboldt University, where our workshops were held. I gave two lectures and enjoyed the discussions. Not knowing that my chest pain was coming from gallstones, I was admitted to the *Charitee*, which treated me very well and for free.

On weekends, I tried to be independent and would hop on a train. The excursion to the Baltic to see Stralsund and the Island of Rügen with its white limestone was very nice. Forget about finding a hotel that was not booked solidly two years in advance by unions and party organizations. Meeting with Mr. Fries in Petershagen was always pleasant. Strolling *Unter den Linden* up to *Friedrichstrasse* was a real treat, always under the eyes of Frederick the Great of Prussia on horseback. We toured the magnificent palaces of San Souci of Frederick of Prussia in Potsdam, and the film capital of UFA at Babelsberg. It was one of my best summers in the GDR, and Berlin made a fine impression, that of a lively capital of a nation to be there for the long haul. Little did anybody know that three years from then it would all be over and the GDR would implode, as would the Soviet Union.

Going out by Austrian Air from Vienna leaves many GDR citizens nostalgic and sad. Travel outside the Socialist block is not an option they had. I felt spoiled, privileged and happy.

Two years later, I would be invited again on a personal basis and meet with party officials. It was then that they made a move to suggest forming a cooperation with them, e.g., sharing news about the U.S. peace movement. Well, I did not need a negative FBI file on top of a dubious *Stasi* file. So I played a coy and cautious game, while enjoying the perks of high-level party functionaries. What good would such news do them if they could pick up better from U.S. newspapers anyway? It is a strange world, and I knew I would have to retain a purely professional, that means a Germanistic interest in the GDR.

I was housed in Köpenick, where that legendary character of the captain in Zuckmayer's play is from, the man who bluffs anybody in a fine Prussian uniform. The GDR was also taking great pride in demonstrating a Prussian pride in uniforms strangely similar to the Third Reich. At the *Grosse Wache* next to Humboldt University, the guard would goose-step. And at the end of the tree-lined boulevard

Unter den Linden would be the Brandenburg Gate—and the Wall. It was the end of the horizon for GDR citizens. I left several times via the *Friedrichstrasse S-Bahn* or Check-Point Charlie on foot. I visited with the Catudals and witnessed then the beginning of his schizophrenia and paranoia. He took me for a *Stasi* agent trailing him!

Leaving Berlin for Vienna, either by air or by train via Prague, made it possible to see our son Thomas, the medical student, there. He worked weekends at the American Express and lived in an apartment with nice guys who did para-gliding, mountain-climbing and biking. Thomas had bought an old red VW Beetle, which took us to the mountains in Slovenia and Carinthia, to the Rax and to Italy. When the engine gave out, we drove to Spittal and removed an engine from a wreck, put it in, and drove on. It was the beginning of the display of surgical skills Thomas had early on. He even worked during the summers in Alfred Glaunach's factory for industrial filters. He is a wonderfully resourceful guy!

Flying home, I tried to make it via Boston, where Natascha was an undergraduate at Boston College, visit her and move on with a load of fresh lobsters.

Ingrid was by then already working full time at her new job at the St. Cloud Hospital on the mental health unit. Since then, she understands much better all our peculiar hang-ups: my gypsy-life, Thomas's fixation on certain women, Natascha's impulsivity and Maxi's drive. He is the most focused, Thomas the most resourceful and Natascha the most spontaneous.

Yes, I have become a literary person, thanks to F.R. Fries. Besides, we have become true Minnesotans. We even talk like the guys in the movie *Fargo*. But most of all, our children made us rooted near Lake Wobegon.

Our children had sunk roots into Minnesota clay, where sumac, poison ivy, oaks, elms, ash, maple and fir trees grow in abundance. They felt "at home" here, so did we. We had found a fine place when we asked old Matt Zwilling whether he would sell us some land near Saint John's. As you know, he did, and he housed our four horses on his one hundred-acre-farm. They took shelter in his barn, which Ingrid barely saved after lightning had struck and flames flickered under the roof. But she took care of that, called the fire-fighters and with only minutes to waste, they were able to save the old structure that I had painted in a watercolor. Our children loved the horses—and surprisingly, no one ever got hurt. A miracle!

We had bought a corner on Lake Achmann, our "Lake Wobegon." It is an untouched lake with woods all around, our Austrian cabin on the shore and a dock in the water. We go there in summer to cool down and in fall to enjoy the clear air and the colors. In winter we marvel at the snow drifting towards the shore on the ice, and in spring, when the ice cracks around mid-April. It is a good place to escape to with the *New York Times* or the *New Yorker* and forget the daily chores.

Those chores consisted essentially of teaching good courses as far as I am concerned, and for Ingrid to retain a touch of sanity on the mental health ward at the St. Cloud Hospital. Both of us did a decent enough job. We were decently paid and provided good work in return.

My teaching went increasingly well. As I mentioned before, I had learned the ropes way back from Harald and Volkmar Haselbach at the teachers' training college in Klagenfurt. I honed my skills at Austrian grade schools and high schools, at technical colleges for gunsmiths, engravers and architects. . . . I even taught special ed. for retarded children. I should have been prepared for virtually anything, but none of my teaching experiences turned out to be so pleasant as teaching American undergraduates. They can be inspired. They are curious. They are intellectually honest. They ask real questions, "Why do you say that? What do you mean by that? How can a grown-up Don Carlos be so hopelessly romantic and adolescent? Why is *Faust II* so boring?" They keep you honest and on your toes that way.

We read such magnificent primary texts together. I was starved from my student years in Austria, where digging through secondary sources seemed to matter more But here in the U.S., I started reading Thomas Mann, Stefan Zweig, Wolfgang Bauer, Peter Handke, Peter Turrini, Bertolt Brecht, Ödön von Horváth, Büchner, Kleist, Fontane, Peter Rosegger, Lion Feuchtwanger . . . . I felt so good finally overcoming the phony intellectual pretense of our student years in Vienna and was happy to really know the texts ranging from the *Nibelungenlied* to *Des Knaben Wunderhorn*. With my students, I memorized texts including the Faust monologue, Goethe, Rilke, Trakl, Brecht songs and medieval love songs *"Unter der linden auf der heiden."*

Teaching German was fun and exciting for me and my students. I can say that honestly, because they told me then, and they tell me so now. In appreciation, old students are now collecting funds for a "Drekonja Scholarship" here at SJU. Small donations—and big ones, like $5,000.00! It will add up. The driving force is Lonnie Johnson in Vienna, and Leo Riegert and Kathleen Fluegel here. They are reputable Ph.D.s in their field and good friends of mine. I am a lucky man! A fella could have done worse! Yep.

Whom do they remember anyway? Me? Max Birnbaum? An above-average prof?

I so enjoy mail and visits from former students. I get mail from Argentina and from Vienna, from Tokyo and Mexico City. Former students really bond with their profs., which is an almost unthinkable thing to suggest between European students and professors, who are separated by social barriers the magnitude of the Grand Canyon.

I love to listen to what they do, what they have done and what they want to do. Recently, Mike Zumwinkle and his family came to visit. His wife Lori is an energetic woman with great ambition and ability. Their three daughters are full of life, especially the middle one, Gracy. Mike was a great football star under John Gagliardi, and he also took some German. He made the most of it. He accepted a scholarship from the East Germans and honed his skills there as a political science major.

While I was with a student group in Prague during January in Central Europe, he came from Leipzig and told me stories from that other Germany. Later, he became a staff member of the U.S. Embassy on Klara Zetkin Street in East Berlin. His German was excellent, and he became a useful agent for the State Department. He returned from Berlin to Washington and worked his way up in that department but left it later for a career in the corporate world. Now he does government relations for Cargill in Minneapolis. He is a good—albeit Republican—man of fine qualities. He, too, is helping raise money for the Drekonja Scholarship at SJU, together with Kathleen Fluegel, Lonnie Johnson, Leo Riegert and Bob Acker. All of them hold fine Ph.Ds. by now, and I was the one who lured them into the world of the humanities with a German accent.

Another one who made the most of the GDR connection is Tom Chambers. He married a woman from East Germany, and now they teach German in Wisconsin.

East Germany was generous to us. Why? Were we so promising as future *Stasi* agents? They certainly kept good files on all of us. I got mine some time ago. Mike Z. showed me his recently. They kept better diaries and notes on us than we did. They even knew my Avon State Bank account number—but they never made a deposit! Maybe I was not very useful as an "informer."

But we all, colleagues and students, even my daughter Natascha appreciated those grants and discovered the best of the German heritage on site: Weimar, Jena, Leipzig, Potsdam, Dresden, Wittenberg, Wartburg. Goethe, Bach, Martin Luther, Schiller, Herder, but also Marx and Lenin, Brecht and Christa Wolf. Those sites were impeccably preserved. So was the heritage of Brecht in the Theater am Schiftbauerdamm, on the stages in the splendid Palast der Republik, which is unfortunately being torn down now. The great museums in war-ravaged Berlin and the rebirth of the bombed-out gem of a city, Dresden. Yes, Weimar lies near Buchenwald. There is no guarantee that a civil nation will always behave in a civil fashion.

I enjoyed my work in the GDR. Nobody would have believed that on November 9, 1989, it would implode, as would the U.S.S.R. only one year later. In the '80s, the Wall in Berlin looked as permanent as the granite cliffs on Lake Superior. They are still there. The Wall is not.

XXI

"I would like to confuse my readers with the truth."—F.R Fries. The confusion is inevitable. Who is Max Birnbaum? Who is Otmar D.? Who is Dr. D.? Could they be the same? Or similar characters? Maybe Lonnie Johnson, one of my great students from the '70s, now director general of the Austrian Fulbright Commission and the president of the European Fulbright Programs in Vienna, can shed light on this person? Here is an old letter I found from him to me, whoever that may be.

Sehr geehrter Herr Professor!
Lieber Max,

. . . My decision to study the humanities as an undergraduate student was simple enough. Becoming a student of Max B. was a relatively straightforward operation, too. One of the "field of concentration requirements" for humanities majors at the time was "twenty-four credits of a foreign language or its equivalent." I had had four years of high school German which was equivalent to sixteen credits, if (and only if) I could get into the two-semester upper-division sequence of "Conversation and Composition" which, if completed successfully, would put me just four credits short of the thirty credits required for a German minor. What a deal!

My only problem was that I did not know much German. I sought out my academic advisor, a certain Prof. Ray L. from the waning Classics Department. I remember the first time I saw him at freshman orientation in the gym. He was tall, gangly, and wore a patterned shirt open at the neck that clashed with his purple—perhaps even fuchsia—sport coat. Although I had no faith in his taste in clothes, I had great faith in his ability as my advisor to provide me with sage guidance. He encouraged me to talk to Prof. B., and I did.

Whether I missed the German placement test for "Co/Co" as a matter of calculation or as a result of freshman disorientation, I cannot recall. I went to Max B.'s office in the quadrangle, full of apprehension and good intentions and armed with a vital connection. My last high school German teacher, Lordell E., and Max B. knew each other. We had a brief conversation partially in English and partially in German, and Max B. encouraged me to give it a try. I was in!

I found out immediately that I had gotten in over my head. First of all, there was one characteristic that distinguished the other students in the class from me. They actually knew German. Some of them even had been to Germany or Austria before, either as participants in high school exchange or collegiate study abroad programs. Max B. was an engaging teacher. He sought lots of eye contact with his students. He moved around the classroom and gesticulated a lot. His body language reflected what it was like to struggle with a German sentence. I could barely decipher his handwriting on the blackboard. He spoke German. I observed the other students in the class. They understood him. Their heads nodded as a sign of acknowledgement. And when they nodded, they did not mean "yes"; they meant "*Jawohl.*"

I was in trouble. Let's face it. If you do not know the strong verb forms, you are in no position to even start worrying about what all of the abstract nouns mean. I really had only one thing going for me. I looked like I knew German (as Rick Sch., a classmate and a bright kid from Stearns County later intimated to me). I was tall and blond and self-confident and gave people the impression that I knew much more than I did. I looked like an "Aryan" as Rick Sch. observed, and he was intimidated by the fact that someone straight out of a Leni Riefenstahl film was in his German class. There I was. A Hitler youth, a future Nazi paratrooper, under deep cover in Collegeville, Minnesota. I barely knew what was going on and made sure that I got the assignments right by double-checking with my colleagues.

Max B. was a good teacher. He took German seriously. He took us seriously. He was good humored and affirmative and encouraging. He worked hard, and he expected us to work hard, too. He laughed and enjoyed and wanted us to laugh and enjoy, too.

There was something due every day. He expected us to keep a *Tagebuch* in German, due on Mondays. Class only met four times a week, but his idea of a good time on Wednesdays—nominally our day off—was to go to the language lab. There were regular grammar exercises to be handed in from *German in Review* and a very sophisticated book on some of the peculiarities of German as a language, things I only learned to appreciate much later, such as the reliance on the passive voice, the reflexive nature of the verb structures, and the language's facility for abstraction.

These were all structural issues related to the mechanics of the language. However, Max B. wanted us to think, too. Among our weekly regime of assignments was an essay. He gave us a topic, and we were supposed to come up with a little *Aufsatz auf Deutsch*. I remember one assignment in particular. Max B. wanted us to write something about the difference between *Zivilisation und Kultur*. This is pretty heady stuff. Prof. B. brought the young Peter Handke to Saint John's and organized a program on KSJN radio about *Publikumsbeschimpfung*—a play entitled "Berating the Audience." At Handke's public lecture I showboated a bit by asking a question in German: "Ob das alles so schlimm sei, wie er meine." Please note the *Konjunktiv* l.

Max B. was a very good teacher. Unfortunately, although I learned a tremendous amount from him, I was not really a very good student. I hate to admit that there were many more talented students of German in Co/Co at SJU during the 1970–1971 academic year, and all of them knew more German than I did. I think I did about sixteen credits of work for those two four-credit courses during my freshman year. I benefited from this tremendously at a later date, because I had developed an appreciation for the structure of German, but my oral ability and vocabulary were severely limited. This is one of the reasons I did not take the momentum I had developed in my first year of serious language study into the second year by enrolling in an upper-division literature course. My lack of confidence reflected a lack of vocabulary. Sophomore sloth also certainly played a role in this decision, too.

Studying art history as a sophomore, with the Hungarian artist Bela P., one of Max B.'s friends on the faculty and a fellow Central European, was easier than studying German with Max B. as a freshman. Although Bela P. taught with enthusiasm, I do not think that he ever had the same feeling for his undergraduate clientele that Max B. did. Bela P. was obviously physically uncomfortable in the presence of large athletes, and he disliked it when they would fall asleep in his class: a large, warm, and dark room in the basement of Alcuin Library. As a Central European artist and intellectual, he was not too sure which larger frame of reference his less talented students from the Midwest had—if any at all—and noted one day, perhaps in desperation, that it would be "important for us to recognize that the slides projected in class are all the same size: about 12 feet by 12 feet. In real life, pictures are different sizes. This one, for example," he said, pointing to a reclining nude, "is around 18 by 12 inches."

I never did get around to taking that final German class that would have given me a minor in German in the course of my undergraduate career, but I saw Max B. regularly on campus in the subsequent course of his undergraduate career. He kept abreast of his students' interests and activities. He was an institutional presence. He was one of the regulars at cultural and intellectual events.

I told my advisor Prof. Ray L. that I was interested in the Honors Program, and he was amused by the idea. I was an above average student, and I think he nominated me to participate. The program was directed by a cryptic sadist, Father Chr., who was well connected with a lot of Big Names from the House of Reason and brought them all the way up from Chicago to Collegeville. Living in a small community—monastic or otherwise and Collegeville is both—is based on discretion. Max B. has been a good member of that community.

Max B. had encouraged me to think about studying abroad on a number of occasions, and as a humanities major I was intrigued about seeing the "real thing," finding out for myself how large or small the pictures really were. As a junior, I turned to Father Chr. with the idea about studying abroad my senior year; something that would be an aberration from the standard junior year abroad scheme but would also deprive me of the capstone experience of the Senior Honors Seminar with Father Chr. He responded to a serious undergraduate question with a familiar combination of amusement and impatience bordering on contempt by making an inscrutable remark, "Mr. J., Europe will be there long after you and I are gone. . . ." I did not know what the point of this insight was and was tempted to tell him that I did not think that waiting until I would be dead would be a good idea, but I suppressed that urge. However, Father Chr. was clear. The whole idea was sheer folly. He felt that the privilege of being abused by him for two more semesters in the Honors Program would be an infinitely more valuable experience than a year in Europe.

As a junior at SJU, I thought that life ended after senior year, and I did not want to miss this Europe thing. I had to make a choice between forgoing the alleged prestige that would go along with graduating from the Honors Program and the opportunity of studying in Europe. I went to Max B. to talk to him about this study abroad thing and to seek his advice. He acknowledged the Honors Program but was obviously much more excited about the idea of studying abroad.

Saint John's was associated with the Institute of European Studies—a Chicago-based not-for-profit organization that serviced a number of colleges and universities and had centers at a handful of European sites—and Max B. was some kind of campus representative for this organization. He noted that IES had centers in Freiburg im Breisgau, Germany, and in Vienna, Austria. Being a genuine Minnesotan, almost my entire life experience had been confined to the Land of 10,000 Lakes. My first visit to a "foreign country" had been on a family vacation as a child. My parents took a station wagon full of kids (six) and a camping trailer to the Black Hills, and I was impressed by the exoticism of South Dakota. All other foreign experiences in my life to date had been exhausted on a second trip a few years later that was more heroic. My parents took a station wagon full of kids (six) and a camping trailer to California and back. They must have been temporarily insane.

In light of my genuine lack of sophistication and the absence of any real experience with any place that was not Minnesota, I asked Max B. what the differences between Freiburg im Breisgau and Vienna were. He explained to me with an unusual combination of patience and excitement that Freiburg was in the Black Forest and a classic German university city. Maybe thirty thousand inhabitants. Cobblestones. Gabled roofs on the houses. Quaint. I could imagine that. Vienna was a whole different affair. Imperial. A big university. A big city. Big Time. Everything started with capital letters. Art. Music. Opera. Museums. Max B. was enthusiastic about the whole idea. He discussed the different curricula with me. He encouraged me to seriously consider this as a real opportunity. And he had boundless faith in my ability to speak German.

I had more trouble imagining what Vienna might be like than Freiburg, but, as a Minnesotan, I figured that the differences between Freiburg and Vienna were somehow analogous to the ones between St. Cloud and Minneapolis. With that in mind, the choice was easy. Saint John's was quaint. Freiburg was quaint. I was going to a German speaking counterpart of the Twin Cities: Vienna. I did not have the vaguest idea what I was getting into. I had never been farther east than the St. Croix River. I had never been in an airplane. And I was going to Vienna.

My parents, who had been in airplanes and got to know the United States by attending the professional conventions of my father, a dentist, were great believers in a liberal arts education and, hence, open to the idea. During a campus visit they talked to Max B. about the entire scheme, and he managed to dispel any misgivings they had. A talk with the dean of the college, Bill P., a fancy East Coast Jewish intellectual type who had previously been associated with the Institute of European Studies, sealed the deal. He praised the program and Vienna lavishly. I was on my way.

My friends at SJU greeted my decision with a combination of skepticism and concern. Did I really know what I was doing? I was going to miss my senior year on campus. It was going to be the Best-Year-in-Our-Lives. Perhaps I should reconsider. I did not, and within a year or so, four of my college classmates were in Italy, recent SJU graduates, being humanists, and trying to make ends meet.

So I went to Vienna. The German that Max B. had taught me provided an excellent matrix for the German I learned in Vienna. I merely had to pour the vocabulary into the mold. I met a lovely Viennese girl and married her. My relatives in Minnesota still mispronounce her first name by turning the long "o" in Monika to a long, drawn out soft "a"—"Maaanika." And they refer to her as a nice German girl. This confusion is an insult for any Austrian patriot. I wish I could say that she bears it with dignity, but that would be a hopeless exaggeration. She gave up on correcting people a long time ago and otherwise does not care about the issue too much.

I wrote a dissertation in philosophy at the University of Vienna in German and have worked in international education in Austria since then. I wrote a couple of books in English after that, too. One of them was published by a big university press, reviewed in lots of professional journals, and of some distinction.

Judged by the standards of the academy, I am Max B.'s most famous student. This undoubtedly may lead him to think that I was one of his best German students. Unfortunately, I was not. But Max B. did teach me German, and he did get me to Europe. Good undergraduate teaching and good advice and good intentions go a long way.

So the other night at the Fulbright event Dr. Peter K. thought it was somehow a big deal to get from Austria to San Diego. I don't think so, if you know what I mean. Getting from Minnesota to Vienna was harder, I think. But with the right help at the right time, the wildest things are possible.

My warmest regards,
Lonnie
Wien. 12 März 2004

XXII

The decade of the '80s marked significant changes in our daily lives. It was the time of the phony optimism of the Reagan years. It was the end of the glorious years of Kreisky in Austria. Reagan was the most successful facade. Kreisky was the most substantive politician. The rhetoric of the Cold War prevailed. The "Evil Empire" lurked in the East. America boasted to be the defender of freedom and civility. Little did we know then that the baroque language of Reagan—a man similar to my Uncle Toni in Vienna: jovial, engaging and disarmingly charming—was a mild prelude to the aggressive language of the crusader George Bush a decade later.

We had become well-integrated into the social fabric of our wonderful friends in Minnesota and many colleagues at SJU. Our children grew up in a wonderfully peaceful ambience. Dimitri became a great runner and cello player. He stayed with us through the '80s and graduated from Apollo High School in 1992. But Thomas left home for San Diego in 1980 and for Vienna in 1984. Natascha left Saint John's Prep School a bit young and went to France and Spain in 1983 and to Boston in 1984 My mother died in 1985. Matt Zwilling, our wonderful neighbor, died in 1988, and we had to sell our horses he had housed on his farm for twenty-one years. It was a very sad day when they left.

Most importantly, Ingrid had quit her job as a lecturer at SJU, a job she had done well for thirteen years, and she finished nursing school in 1985. That fall she became a registered nurse at the mental health unit at the St. Cloud Hospital. She worked there for over fifteen years and enjoyed her work. She was now earning good money, and we needed it for our children who were attending private colleges in the East and the West. Only Dimitri stayed sober and attended a fine public high school and later went on to Gustavus in Minnesota, where he would graduate without a cent of debt and with high honors. By 1992, all had left home, and we started a new life with large phone bills, wonderful visits to St. Peter, Boston and San Diego and many lonely evenings at home in an empty house. Fortunately, we had collies and cats.

But the most spectacular event was initiated by Gorbachev: the opening of the Soviet Union—and subsequently the breakdown of the "Evil Empire." It happened without a shot, without any bloodshed, without any dramatic upheaval. On November 9, 1989, the Berlin Wall fell in a moment of confusion and uncertainty. It was the biggest party Germany had ever celebrated since the invention of beer by the Germanic barbarians. The GDR started to implode. The Soviet Union started to implode after the bloodless overthrow of Gorbachev, and in 1990, the Soviet Union ceased to exist, and Germany was united under Chancellor Kohl.

The states formerly under Soviet dominance established a life of their own: Poland, Latvia, Estonia, Lithuania, White-Russia, the Ukraine, Hungary, Bulgaria, Romania, Czechoslovakia—still combined—moved back into the European orbit. It looked like a dream by Václav Havel come true. A century that started so belligerently and threw Europe into a barbaric cataclysm with millions of people dead, tortured and/or displaced for half a century saw a happy ending marked by peace and openness dawn at the end of the 20th century! Who would have thought it possible? Maybe the 21st century will be a more civil and peaceful one?

My January seminars in Central Europe became an exercise in witnessing the opening of the East. It was a splendid time to be in Prague, Budapest, Krakow or Ljubljana. A miracle?

Before it happened, there were signs on the Wall. Irreverent jokes multiplied in Stalinist backyards. The economy was stuttering. The internal pressure on people who were being observed and could not travel became unbearable. But never did I or the CIA or the Pentagon dream that it simply would go away without much of a fuss. It did. It was an extension of the Prague "Velvet Revolution."

I was still in East Berlin in the summer of 1989, and it did not look like a change was about to happen as we looked down into the no man's land along the Wall on the old Potsdamer Platz with the remnants of Hitler's bunkers still collecting weeds. However, President Reagan did come to Berlin and called on Mr. Gorbachev, "Tear down this Wall!" Soon, this wish became reality. Yes, a miracle indeed.

In the meantime, the MCL Department in its collective wisdom had elected me as the next chair. A department with over thirty colleagues and many cultural rifts was not an easy one to take over. Thorpe Running turned over the keys to the multi-linguistic double monarchy, the SJU and CSB sections. I was with him at the MLA Convention in San Francisco after Christmas, and my son Thomas came to visit from Vienna. It was really at the next MLA Convention in Washington, D.C., that I was fully in charge and could hire wonderful new colleagues in French, German, Spanish and Classics. And I had that opportunity every year at the same time after Christmas in New York, in Chicago, in Vancouver and in Toronto.

Ingrid came along to Vancouver, where we had a wonderful time whale watching and sailing to Vancouver Island, where everything explodes in flowers and vegetation. I built a strong department over the years, and I received a large national grant from ACE to upgrade our program. We had sessions in Washington, D.C. It was the last year of Con Hamel. He was a great colleague. Ingrid joined us, and we met with John Farry and Brooke Masters.

At home, I had a wonderful secretary in Pam Parsons, to whom I could dictate letters, memoranda, minutes and messages, papers and essays. I became known as the "dictator." It saved me from drafting and rewriting. It worked wonderfully. Being the department chair was fun; it was constructive and entertaining.

In January, I kept doing my Central European seminars in "Kakania" and introduced my students to Milan Kundera, Václav Havel, Joseph Roth, Claudio Magris and Musil. And also to the operas of Dvorak, Mozart, Wagner, Johann Strauss, Richard Strauss, Verdi and Puccini. It was always a wonderful pilgrimage with an electrifying sense of excitement I would not have wanted to miss. Not that life in Minnesota was so drab. Oh no! There is always Minnesota Public Radio—thanks to Fr. Colman Barry, O.S.B.. There is the storyteller Garrison Keillor, the Avon Hills, the lakes and trees, the architecture of Breuer and the bells of SJU.

In 2000, I would be able to retire as a relatively affluent man. I credit it to Mr. Clinton. My grandchildren built a big aircraft carrier in his name at Lake Achmann, and he wrote a very kind note to them on stationery with the Presidential seal. He is a great man. His biography, *My Life*, is one of the finest documents relating to the flourishing '90s.

The '90s were also a good time for our family. In 1992, our son Dimitri graduated from Apollo High School as a National Merit Scholar. He worked during the summer on a research grant at the University of Minnesota and was accepted into Stanford and Northwestern. He ended up enrolling at Gustavus Adolphus in Minnesota and stayed in our area. He thrived there and was wonderfully supported as a scientist, a musician, a long-distance runner and an "above average Lake Wobegon kid." He played a fine cello with the St. Cloud Symphony and the Opera Company. At Gustavus, he would meet a lovely woman, Kara, whom I call "Carissima." They were married at SJU in July of 2000.

Thomas had married a Salzburg woman in 1990 and finished medical school in Vienna in 1991. He started a fine career as a promising doctor. It was an elegant wedding in Salzburg, where the father of the bride, the retired president of the Austrian Supreme Court, said, "We had given up hope that she would bring a man into the house. Now we are blessed with this man from the other world. . . ." Well, if an urbane, good-looking professional woman finds no partner in Austria, and it takes a trusting American to step in and fill the void, one asks why? Two children and four years later, the marriage ended in divorce.

We heard from Thomas while we were on Grand Cayman Island—that paradise he had discovered. Shortly before the end of the marriage, I had met with him and the boys in Cologne, Germany, and he dreamed of taking the boys he loved to someplace where nobody would ever find him. He was desperate, and we were heartbroken. To add insult to injury, that very appreciative retired judge from the supreme court wrote to Ingrid's father, "We became so concerned that his 'American' ways would stand in the way of his boys on their way to becoming educated Central Europeans. . . ." Well, he should not have worried. They have become magnificent young men everybody can be justly proud of.

Natascha finished law school in St. Paul in 1992 and moved to Denver. She married Glenn O'Flaherty in Aspen in December of 2000 and is expecting a baby in February of 2005. She is a very successful and assertive professional woman.

In the '90s, we finished payments on our home and became more financially stable as a result. We had no more children at home, but we took care of their student loans and helped them launch their professional careers as doctors and lawyers.

Shortly before 2000, I gave Thomas the house that had belonged to my mother. We helped Dimitri and Kara to buy a condo in St. Paul, and we had helped Natascha with her house in Denver and her loans. They are on their own now, and we are glad we were able to help. Education in America is costly. Only getting ill is more costly. If President Clinton were still in office, both problems would be a lot more manageable. But Americans turned viciously vitriolic against Bill and Hillary Clinton. Nothing good ever seems to come from them in spite of their splendid accomplishments. It was not just because of Monika Lewinsky. It was sheer spite, envy and malicious effort to derail any and all efforts on their part, sadly.

The department was indeed flourishing. I hired a new office manager, Mary Niedenfuer. She was intelligent, focused, attractive and caring. She added luster to our outfit. She was also politically involved and a reliable agent for Democratic and anti-Bush activities in years to come.

In German, the pillars are Fr. Mark Thamert, O.S.B., one of my former students who went on to earn a Ph.D. at Princeton. He is an inspirational teacher and much involved in the Honors Program, where he defends the traditional canon against all trendy fads. Fr. John Kulas, O.S.B., is a wise, kind and highly intelligent man—the great old man in the section. And a fine friend on top of it. Wendy Sterba from Texas is talented and demanding, just a bit chaotic and disorganized at times. A very lively person. Add my newcomers: Ruth Cape, Gale Wise and Patricia McBride. Nothing but the best. Alas, they left us later. This after years of placing Fulbright Fellows, years of winning scholarships in the GDR and years of producing fine graduate students pursuing Ph.D.s in German! Now, those good guys of better days in the past are collecting resources for the "Drekonja German Scholarship." It may be too late. It will keep the memories of those good years alive for a while. It will keep the fascination with Central Europe active. In the long run, the humanities will succumb to gender studies, gay and lesbian studies, post-colonial studies, anti-dominant culture campaigns and anti-Europe sentiments that will thrive under Bush a decade later.

XXIII

The '90s, on the other hand, promised so much: the fall of the Wall, the end of the Cold War, the bloodless changes in the East, my chairmanship and the rise of the greatest U.S. President in recent history, Mr. Bill Clinton in 1992.

Alas, there was turbulent weather nobody had expected. After the bloodless changes in the "Evil Empire," so well documented by David Remnick, the author of the definitive book on those changes, *Lenin's*

Tomb, and Timothy Garton Ash's narrative on Poland, the GDR and Central Europe on its way back to Europe, a backlash into barbarity erupted in the Balkans. I was back in West Berlin in Grünewald at the European Institute, when the news broke of the crackdown of the Yugoslav army against secessionist Slovenia and, later, Croatia. It was a new war in the Balkans which exploded in full force in Bosnia. By 1995, NATO started to intervene and put an end to butchery, ethnic cleansing and mass murder.

What had started the 20th century so badly in Sarajevo on June 28, 1914 and the outbreak of WW I, finished the century again in Sarajevo, where Milosevic tried to fight centrifugal ethnic, religious and national forces in Yugoslavia ten years after Mr. Tito had died in 1980. He had succeeded where Mr. Milosevic failed. It started the sinister vision of "Wars between Cultures" as a Harvard-based pessimist described it. It soaked the Balkans in blood and soon would spill even more blood in the Middle East.

President Clinton made a valiant effort to contain the situation on the Balkans, and he succeeded. He tried even more desperately to pacify the Middle East, and he failed. He brought the U.S. economy to a magnificent solidity, which fattened my retirement accounts. The rise of the Clintons after the bumpy '80s with Reaganomics and Cold War hyperbole was a real blessing for the nation and the world.

There was one more blessing in family events. In 1989, my brother Gerhard was appointed to the endowed chair of history with a Latin America focus at the University of Vienna. He was fifty years old by then and had spent decades vagabonding between Austrian universities, the Berlin Center for Industrial Development at the Villa Borsig, between the prestigious Cornell University and the Universidad de los Andes in Colombia. He was a prolific researcher and sought-after journalist, but never landed a tenured position until then. He was a kind of Humboldt of the Third World, visiting every country from Cuba and Mexico to Argentina and Ecuador. He felt quite at home there and loved the Spanish-speaking Americas.

The chair in Vienna was really founded and funded in the '70s by Chancellor Bruno Kreisky with the intent to lure back Professor Katz, a Viennese Jewish emigrant of 1938. He had been at the University of Chicago, but, in the end, did not return to Vienna. My brother had applied several times, but the position was kept vacant. In all likelihood, it would be dropped from the budget. But it was not, and he got the appointment. The University of Vienna went so far as to offer Professor Katz the "Golden Doctor Diploma." But their funds were finite, and they planned to send it by mail instead of bringing him home for the event at the place that had kicked him out so shabbily after the *Kristallnacht* in 1938. Gerhard had connections and found the money. There was a glorious ceremony in the *Rathhaus* and my brother gave a splendid speech. It was a high point for both Gerhard and Professor Katz. And justly so.

In 1991, the Austrian President Waldheim even remembered me in the U.S. and awarded me the *Das Österreichische Ehrenkreuz für Wissenschaft und Kunst Erster Klasse*, a decorative order with which Bela Petheo painted me in the early '90s. I could even wear it at the opera ball should I feel tempted to go there.

What pleased me the most, however, was the "Teacher of the Year Award" for excellence in teaching at SJU. It came with a certificate, money and congratulations in 1991. What more could I achieve in my line of work? More of the same! My students expected and appreciated that.

My chairmanship lasted until 1995, two terms of running a multi-cultured, multi-linguistic, multi-ethnic and multi-opinionated outfit. What was left for me to do? Two more Salzburg semesters and three more January terms. Finally, I took up my old instrument and took serious lessons with the brilliant clarinet teacher Bruce Thornton. I became quite good again after so many years of neglect. I played in the opera pit and played jazz again. It was wonderful! It was time to quit. One must do it while one is good at it, and I was.

XXIV

In January 2001, I went into retirement after forty-seven years of teaching. I never was the great musician I once dreamed I would be. I was a poor organist, a bad pianist, a decent woodwind player and an okay choral conductor. I did some good watercolor work, but I was no Bela Petheo. I enjoyed writing, but I was no John Grisham. However, as a teacher I was as good as they get. My old mentor in Klagenfurt, Volkmar Haselbach, would nod in appreciation of my efforts. He always said, "If you love your students, and if you love and master your discipline, you will be a good teacher." He was right. I must say thank you!

Then came the "end of the century." *It was the 31ˢᵗ of December 1999.* We were all in Salzburg with our students, just back from Metten in Bavaria, where our Saint John's monks came from. We had also visited Prague, Krakow and Auschwitz. We had seen the splendor and the agony which this ill-fated century had bestowed upon Central Europe. The New Year's concert had the Czech Philharmonic play in the Great Festival Hall. The program was Gershwin's *Piano Concerto in F* and Dvorak's *"New World" Symphony.* It was a fitting program with a tribute to America. After all, the 20ᵗʰ century was by all standards the "American Century."

We were up on the Mönchsberg and had watched splendid fireworks illuminate the beautiful city of Amadeus, Stefan Zweig, Trakl and Max Reinhardt. Of the four, only Mozart lived without tragedy—unless one considers his early death in 1791 a great tragedy. Stefan Zweig, a Jew, committed suicide in Brazil in 1942. Trakl killed himself on the eastern front during WW I after he ran out of morphine while tending to too many wounded and maimed. Max Reinhardt, one of the founders of the Salzburg Festivals in 1920, was chased into exile because he was a Jew. How many hardships? How many tragedies in one century?

America intervened three times militarily and helped to establish a degree of order: in WW I under Woodrow Wilson, in WW II and afterwards with the Marshall Plan and in the '90s under Clinton when the Balkans exploded again. America was the stable force and a ray of hope in this time. It was at the *Amerika Haus* after WW II where we read all the exiled and forbidden authors of our own language for the first time: Zweig, Freud, Schnitzler, Heinrich Heine, Karl Kraus,

Thomas Mann, Heinrich Mann, Bertold Brecht (although he was held under suspicion by the House Committee on Un-American Activities for his "pink" voice). It was a wonderful place for young readers who had known no contemporary literature at all. We had been fed diets of Ganghofer, Rosegger and Perkonig instead. Now we could even plunge into new terrain with names like Hemingway, Steinbeck, Dreiser and Faulkner. It was splendid! Add to this the lure of Fulbright grants, which helped so many of us to take a step into a new world. We were so lucky in 1962, as was my brother Gerhard.

Most glorious, however, was the new sound of music; *Porgy and Bess* by Gershwin, and the sounds of Louis Armstrong, Dave Brubeck, Stan Getz, Billie Holiday, Ella Fitzgerald and Barbra Streisand! What a sound! Many others and I turned to jazz and became fair players in little bands in Klagenfurt and Krems. As I mentioned before, I was a modest clarinetist, but others, like my comrade Jürgen Bockelmann from the conservatory, transformed into Udo Bolan and later into Udo Jürgens. He was a brilliantly gifted singer and performer who remained on stage for the next half century. He is still playing his soft jazz tunes with a romantic flair and published his memoirs, *The Man with the Bassoon* in 2004. I have a copy with a dedication from him. For us, America was wonderful and exciting. We listened to the tunes from AFN radio, and Gerhard Bronner celebrated *Schlager für Fortgeschrittene* on the Austrian Radio. We did not have much, but we had the books and melodies of the New World. One could even hear Gustav Mahler and Kurt Weill again. All had been *verboten* before.

The opening of a new window happened only after half a century of tragedies ranging from Sarajevo to Auschwitz. My father, first a sailor in the Habsburg navy in WW I, became a member of Hitler's Wehrmacht, and then a teacher in occupied territories and was killed on December 6, 1944. Our home in Slovenia was dynamited by Tito's troops in 1943, but they were kind and let us out before igniting the fuse. My father's brother, Uncle Otto, was killed on the Russian front in February 1942. Uncle Heinrich was killed by the Gestapo during interrogation. He belonged to the Communist cell. Ingrid's father died in Greece. The house of her parents was bombed in 1944. In 1945, the dance of death ended.

What a century it was! It started so nicely in 1901 with the birth of my father to a family of railroad workers who raised goats and chickens. That was also the year when Thomas Mann wrote his first book, *The Buddenbrooks*. Glorious empires seemed to last forever: the Habsburgs, the Ottomans, the Czars and the Wilhelminians—Austria, Turkey, Russia and Germany. By November 1917 and 1918 , they were all history and cursed.

Adolf of Braunau could have been a decent art student at the Vienna Arts Academy, but he was rejected and discovered his love for Wagner and *Götterdämmerung*. He staged it all from Stalingrad to his bunker in Berlin. Would the century have been a different one without him? Would the assimilated Jewish elites in Central Europe have survived to grace Prague, Berlin, Vienna and Budapest? How does one cope with the loss of such a generation that was persecuted, burned, gassed and exiled? Sure, Warsaw, Rotterdam, Dresden, Hamburg, Hiroshima and Nagasaki are rebuilt. But what scars remain!

If 1901 was the beginning of that century with the doom-filled story *Leutnant Gustl* by Schnitzler, it ended with the last installment of the great TV documentary *Heimat* by Edgar Reitz. The chronicle of an era, it is a moving portrait of a shaken nation with a German accent and one of the finer TV productions ever to be done by Germans. But the suffering is by no means confined to the nation of Goethe. There were greater tragedies suffered by the Poles, the Yugoslavs, the Russians and especially the Jews. All that has to be kept in mind when I ponder where my father might be buried, or my wife's father, or my uncles. There is a brotherhood of the dead. They are all silent and without accusing fingers pointed towards anybody. Only we, the living, can reflect, remember, analyze and bear the consequences. One way of doing it is by writing down what one remembers about a century in Europe, about which the Polish Jew Jan Mazower wrote his powerful book *Dark Continent*. By that he does not mean Africa but essentially Central Europe.

At the end of the century, I still confess that I love the place of my roots. I feel at home here in Minnesota, but in my dreams I find myself on those mountain paths in the Lesachtal, that grandiose landscape near the Italian border. I still know all the places where the lingonberries, the raspberries and the blueberries, the mushrooms and the hazelnuts grow. I remember the wonderful nights at the art deco Hotel Central in Prague, the fine Hotel Wandl in Vienna, and the view from the hill of San Giusto in Trieste. I love the memories of foggy January days in Venice. I love to lounge in memory at the warm Szecheny baths in Budapest and the marble bridges of Ljubljana. In my mind I can still stroll through the familiar streets in Klagenfurt and Innsbruck. I can still hear the bells of the church in Kornat and in Salzburg. I love the sounds of the opera houses in Prague, Budapest and Vienna—but especially in Prague with those fine Bohemian musicians! I love to see myself in front of the war memorial in Kornat with the name of my father on it, even though he is buried God knows where.

I still know the trails leading to the mountains I so love: Cebru and Ortler in Italy, the Dom in the Mischabel group and the Matterhorn in Switzerland, the Mont Blanc and the Aiguille de Bionnassay in France, the Hochalm and the Koschuta in Carinthia, the Triglav and Grintouc in Slovenia. . . . It is a wonderful world which has not been touched by historic misfortunes. The cathedrals of Chartres, of St. Vitus in Prague, of St. Stephen's in Vienna, Santa Maria de la Salute and San Marco in Venice defy the very thought of the destruction of civility by barbaric hordes. In the end, such hordes fail, but at what cost?

Considering the turmoil of the first half of the century, the second half of the century sounds more like a happy ending out of *The Sound of Music* as they walk away over a scenic glacier and end up in a cozy world that is content with little, expects even less, and works hard to make ends meet. That was my upbringing, and the upbringing of my generation.

I was lucky; I left the narrow confines of being a country school teacher in some remote valley and ended up in America, like a hero out of Kafka's novel *America*. I married a wonderful and brave woman, who was willing to follow me through all the obstacle courses and adjustments from her home to beautiful Tyrol, to Kent, Ohio, to Memphis, Tennessee, and finally to Minnesota. We were so fortunate to have three wonderful children who feel at home here, as do we.

Sure, those who stayed home also made their way in life. Ingrid's stepbrother Alfred built an industrial silencer firm to global reputation. Her half brother Uli became an executive in a French cement firm dealing with roofing materials globally. Her brother Wolfgang had much talent. He worked in advertisement. The suicide of his wife, and later of his daughter, made him a recluse, and he is now sailing his yacht in the Mediterranean. Her stepbrother Peter was a pedantic administrator in the patent office and has become a bit of a *Grillparzer* figure, lonely, erratic and consumed by his hobby of genealogy.

Aunt Ilse's children did fine mostly. Wonderful Monika married the great Bernd Felderer, the Austrian Alan Greenspan, and they are living in Cologne, Germany, except for the many times when they come to Austria and hike mountains. The older son Konrad inherited a construction firm, but it went bankrupt, much to the distress of his wife. The youngest, Martin, became a fine professor and vice president at Klagenfurt University, and Helmut, after several marriages bemoans the fact that he is living in poverty, about which he does nothing.

Then there are Aunt Jutta's boys. One is an attorney, one is a heating and plumbing specialist, and Christoph is an adventurer, who, after two marriages, has many children and an uncertain future in the trade of gems and stones. That is mostly Ingrid's family, and we stay in touch.

My family is much smaller. My brother Gerhard is a professor in Vienna. My brave sister died recently after a long and difficult struggle with MS. Her son Martin is a doctor, and she would be so proud of him.

Here in Minnesota we have no family, but so many wonderful friends. First and foremost, Mark and Susie McKeon, who stand by in good times and in trouble. She is a fine teacher, and he is a good attorney. Ingrid's great support is Eileen Haeg, a P.A. of exquisite skill and married to a retired teacher who loves to farm and do projects that would take two hundred years to finish. He is so supportive and generous to us. He is also one of the best gardeners. There were always—somewhat reticent—Joe and Jill Farry, who would often share times and meals with us, do trips together and enjoy our children growing up. There are Judy and Mark Twomey, who sold us land and invite us to their condo in Florida. There is Fr. John Kulas, O.S.B., a wonderfully kind man and a true member of our family. There are Kathy Fischer and Neil; they bring so much good conversation, advice and support, including the Sunday *NYT* every week. And Bruce and Marcia Hanson! Life would be much less fun without them. There are our neighbors Al and Bertha Eich, who live on a Century Farm that dates back to 1864. They share their splendid land with us and let us use the Gator and run the dogs. They love our boys and help when they can. Nobody could be more generous. There are Greg and Tim Haeg, Megan McNair and Kelly, the young generation, who give us the illusion of eternal youth with their cheerful presence. It is a friendly world, and we love it.

In short, we could be content with the way the 20th century ended. My retirement account had been doing well on the stock market. In the summer of 2000, we celebrated the glorious wedding of Dimitri and Kara with many friends from here and relatives from Austria. We had a fine band to dance to, good weather and a background of the imposing Bauhaus architecture of Saint John's Abbey Church.

In December 2000, we all met again in Aspen, where Natascha and Glenn were married in Alpine style in a mountain chapel. The groom's dinner was in a Gasthaus way up in the mountains, and the wedding banquet was held at the splendid Hotel Jerome. Several days of skiing were a perk. During the ceremony, a Catholic-light clergyman asked the children what good wishes they would extend to the couple. Our Nikolaus raised his hand and solemnly said, "No divorce!" His father, our son Thomas, was shaken.

We flew to Alaska for the wedding of our neighbors Greg and Megan in the summer of 2001. It was the most spectacular week one could have up there at the Cook Inlet. We took the excursion boat to the glaciers and watched seals and dolphins, whales and birds. We saw the moose herds and the fish jumping. It was a paradise untouched. A bush pilot finally flew us around the top of Denali Mountain. It was awesome! Bigger, better and more majestic than Mont Blanc, which is not bad either! Then add twenty-four hours of daylight. The eyes cannot get enough of so much beauty and pristine nature! It was landscape á la Bruckner: mighty, majestic and intoxicating.

XXV

The 21st Century. Then came 9/11, the greatest attack on the U.S. mainland ever. The splendid World Trade Center Towers collapsed. We had stood on top of them in 1998, when Thomas worked in a New York clinic, and watched the beginning of the New York City Marathon crossing the Verrazano-Narrows Bridge. What was left now was dust and disbelief.

The real tragedy happened soon thereafter. Mr. Bush, a Texan of modest talent, had been anointed President by the Supreme Court, ignoring the outcome of the elections. He would have remained a nobody, a nothing, a joke, a buffoon. However, he managed to highjack the grief of the nation. He floated on the wave of global sympathy, and he transformed all that into a wicked commercial presenting himself as the protector on the white horse, a man who listens to a "higher father" and fights against the "evildoers" around us. You are "with us or with the terrorists." A crusade of apocalyptic dimensions was about to begin. His cronies, Wolfowitz, Rumsfeld, Condoleezza Rice and Dick Cheney started a new "Evil Empire." This time, it would be the U.S., which the world would learn to fear and distrust.

I thought the 20th century was sinister. It was only enlightened by the light from liberal America and the enduring civility of Europe after so much darkness. But the beginning of the 21st century bears no good omen for America.

With the elections stolen in Florida in 2000, Mr. Bush quickly moved to solidify his bastion of reactionary Bible readers, rich plutocrats (his base), and a greedy *Lumpenproletariat* (those trailer-home residents who rant against the death tax) expecting future riches from tax cuts, which in fact only benefited the very rich. In no time it was obvious, he wanted to strike Saddam, the man his father had failed to remove!

In March 2003 the time had come. He attacked Iraq. However, the war had been waged with so much incompetence that it soon turned into a disaster. The rest can be viewed in Michael Moore's great movie *Fahrenheit 9/11*. The seven deadly sins of the Texas Cowboy became painfully visible:

He recklessly and cynically disengaged from the Middle-East peace efforts with Israel and the Palestinians—just to be different from Mr. Clinton. Thus, the simmering conflict exploded into full-fledged bloodshed during his term. Palestinians killed one thousand Israelis and Israelis killed three thousand Palestinians. There is no end in sight, and without addressing this problem first, there will be no hope to stabilize the Middle East.

He waged an ill-fated, costly and incompetently led war against Saddam. A preemptive strike against a nation that was no threat to anybody as the U.N. sanctions worked. A war built on blatant lies and deceptions that led into an ever increasing mess.

He destroyed many alliances he had and all the good will and sympathy that existed after 9/11. He condescendingly mocked and offended the U.N. and his European allies, not to mention the Arab street, which seemed simply an extension of his "axis of evil" picture.

He humiliated his military forces by chasing them into a no-win situation. The U.S. fails to pacify Iraq, as the Soviet Union failed to stabilize Afghanistan in the '80s, thus starting the beginning of the disintegration of the Soviet Union. Will the U.S. face a similar decline?

He unified the Arab world in their crusade against the West. Osama bin Laden became a much more powerful force because of Bush's ill-fated "bring-it-on" strategy. He made Osama big, and Osama, in turn, made Bush seem important as the "defender of freedom."

By waging calamitous wars unilaterally and raising the fears of new attacks, he drove the budget into the biggest deficit ever amassed in U.S. history. That is a grave burden for future generations. Clinton had left him a large surplus. Now it is all gone and debts explode.

By misleading his nation into phony escapades, he made many more new enemies and, thus, made the U.S. and the world less secure than it was three years ago. Mr. Brzezinski said, "In times of crisis, you attempt to divide the enemy and unify your friends. He managed to unify his enemies and divided his friends. A President who misleads must not lead." Right on!

With Mr. Bush winning on November 2, 2004, America is at the beginning of a very dangerous century. It sends a nation sliding into shame and disgrace as shown in the brilliant *Fahrenheit 9/11*. It could become a very scary nation. The 21st century started with bad omens, similar to those of Sarajevo in 1914 or the sinking of the *Titanic* in 1912, and nobody knows how it might end. I am but an old man of seventy. For me, every good day is a day I much enjoy. Fall in Minnesota is one of the most glorious seasons.

I know old men often tend to get pessimistic and gloomy. Not me! There is so much to enjoy as a retired guy. There is so much to do with the chainsaw and the pickup, the mower and keeping the lake cabin open. For at least two years, I felt utterly free and relieved from any duties whatsoever.

Somehow, we also were victims of 9/11. We had planned a family reunion in the Caymans in October 2001 for our 40th wedding anniversary, but nobody wanted to fly after that event. We had to cancel and lost some money. But later, we transformed the bookings into a New York weekend. A day in the big city, even without the Twin Towers, is always a feast, such as stopping in the fine coffee shop of the elegant St. Moritz Hotel near Central Park. It is my favorite in New York. Then it is only a short walk to the Metropolitan Museum. Just around the comer on 86th Street is the "Neue Gallery" of Mr. Lauder with the genuine Viennese Café Sabarsky. Down on 52nd Street is the stunning new skyscraper by Mr. Abraham from Lienz, Austria, which houses the "Austrian Forum," the cultural embassy of Austria in the U.S. Hopping on the subway, it takes you to the Bronx Art Museum with a fine exhibit of "Victorian Nudes" from Great Britain. Bela Petheo enjoyed the catalogue.

New York is a city for walking, looking and inhaling the stunning architectural landscape inhabited by lively people easy to chat with in the breakfast cafes or delis. Everyone has an accent, so one fits in easily. At night I saw a great performance of the musical *Cabaret* at 55th Street. It was better than the movie and haunting as a document of Berlin in the scary '30s. Flying out of La Guardia one gets such a magnificent view of the skyline—minus the Towers!

In the summer of 2002, I did something wild. I accepted an invitation for a cruise on the new yacht of Ingrid's stepbrother Alfred. His wonderful wife Felicitas had died in the spring from a brain tumor. She had never set foot on the new boat anchored in Croatia.

I was no sailor, but I learned a few things, and Alfred was a great captain. We left Punat, the harbor. The wind was stiff, and the boat bobbed in white-capped waves, leaving the barren coast behind. We anchored in secluded bays and enjoyed the clean turquoise water. At night we would stop on some islands with a crummy restaurant and order some fish and wine. Down we sailed to the Kornati Islands: barren and splendid, powerful and poetic, those humps sticking out of the azure waters. We even climbed some stony, shrubby hills. A few donkeys and sheep try to make a living off the sun-scorched slopes. Sometimes one runs into an old chapel dating back to the Venetians, or monuments in remembrance of the Yugoslav resistance against German occupation in WW II. Occasionally we sailed into a harbor to take on water or fuel, not to mention a cup of good espresso or a shot of Slivovitz.

Time meant nothing. The sun and the sea were everything. It was glorious! And it was a good distraction for Alfred to overcome his grief. Life is better than death, and life on the ocean is about as close to being in heaven as one can feel. Gazing as far as the eye can see, feeling the breeze and listening to the waves caress the boat make you feel one with the world around you. Content. Without a wish. Happy with every hour one is awake and aware of the splendor and power of nature. I am so grateful to Alfred!

Back home we told our friends how it was. We would have them join us for picnics at the lake and serve my favorite junk food, Kentucky Fried Chicken. Read the *NYT* there.

Strangely, I became panicky in the water. I had difficulty with breathing. What could that be?

Finally, I confessed to Ingrid that I felt weak and out of breath easily. I did not think much of it. I was just getting closer to seventy. But our good friend Rebecca Hafner, our doctor, saw a red light flicker; she sent us to the neurologists at Mayo. In March 2003, we checked into this city of the sick. On that day, Bush started his ill-fated and illegal war against Iraq, and the doctors had news for us. Dimitri, Ingrid and I heard it: ALS!

For the first time I realized that I am no longer indestructible and will not live forever. Worse, we had tickets for *La Traviata*. Not good entertainment for someone learning of such a nasty disease. But I will not wilt as quickly as the soprano does in Act Three in this sad and sentimental opera.

And guess what my neighbors did? On my November birthday, they came with a "little" gift. In the driveway stood a brand-new John Deere Gator, a four-wheel all-terrain vehicle! A $7,000.00 gift from our neighbors and children who are not rich, but kind and caring! It makes you feel humble and grateful to have such friends! Ever since, the dogs and I jet through the Avon Hills, and we have so much fun in the splendid landscape in and around the 260-acre-farm of Al Eich. I am as mobile again as I was before. It feels like being on the boat with the splendor of nature around, and I enjoy the sky, the wind, the colors and the trails in the woods. Thanks many times to so many for so much!

Ingrid came up with an even wilder and bolder idea. How about building a light, bright and level home, a "studio," where I could move freely should a day come when I need a wheel chair. The permit was hard to obtain, but we did it. The construction is underway. It will be a glorious retreat with a giant deck, huge windows and easy access. Ingrid looks bravely into the future. We know we will face hardships, but we try everything we can to remain kicking. Thomas provides us with medication from Austria that would be hideously expensive here. We take part in a medical study with an experimental medication. I might be getting the placebo, but we might also benefit. God only knows. I am feeling fine, but I miss my chainsaw, playing an instrument and hiking in the Avon Hills.

I was a reader at the wedding of Meghan McKeon and Paul Hunt in the fall, and afterwards we enjoyed dancing to the Louis Armstrong tune "What a Wonderful World." A fine slow tune with lyrics that sound so true when one looks back on a wonderful life. I am just plain lucky!

We celebrated the 70th birthday of the writer and good friend Jon Hassler at the St. Paul Historical Society. He, too, is slowed down by system failures, but he keeps writing. As I do now, remembering his good advice: Keep it simple and never do more than one or two pages per day. It is a very helpful hint. Write every day—but not too much! That is what I am doing. Thank you, Mr. Hassler!

I am reading at leisure Garrison Keillor's *Homegrown Democrat*, Clinton's great memoirs, *My Life,* and Udo Jürgens' memoirs, *The Man with the Bassoon.* Great!

XXVI

My shaky condition notwithstanding, a few things have yet to be taken care of. In 1960 or so, while I was a student at Innsbruck University, I became interested in Guido Zernatto. Born in 1903 to a wealthy farmer, he went to school with my father in Treffen. I knew the Zernatto house from the days when I wrote a thesis on painted farm furniture. They had exquisite pieces that I had copied for my work.

In 1919, Guido joined the local militias who were fighting the invading Yugoslavs after WW I. He was sixteen. At eighteen, he became editor of a magazine that went into the red, and his father kicked him out. He worked for a lumber company, but finally ended up in an elite prep school near Vienna and then started to study law in the early '30s. He had very little if any money and contracted a kidney infection from which he never healed completely.

He met a wonderful and intelligent Jewish woman, Prague-born Riccarda Weidenhaus, whom he married in 1931. With her help he bought shares in a major bookstore and shifted to the world of literature. He was himself a fine poet and wrote novels, stories and political commentaries. Politics was in his blood.

The '30s were unruly times in Central Europe. The Weimar Republic was shaky. The First Republic of Austria was moribund. Mussolini was on the rise in Italy. In 1933, Austria became a clerical-fascist corporate state under Dollfuss. In February 1934, there was a military uprising of the now outlawed Social Democrats, which led to open civil war that was then crushed by Dollfuss's military. In July of the same year, the Austrian Nazis wanted to make a gift to the rising Adolf Hitler and tried a putsch, during which Dollfuss was assassinated. Again, the Austrian Army prevailed and the ringleader escaped to Germany. Schuschnigg took over. He needed a secretary of state not contaminated with the bloody uprisings.

In 1936, Zernatto became a minister in the cabinet of Kurt von Schuschnigg and soon after, Secretary General of the "Fatherland Front," the one and only unity party that controlled the political and cultural life. Zernatto was a fierce defender of Austrian independence vis-à-vis Nazi Germany. Schuschnigg was soft and looked for a compromise. Hitler had little taste for compromises. In 1938, he issued an ultimatum that demanded cancellation of a Zernatto-inspired referendum on Austria's future. Zernatto was willing to fight. Schuschnigg caved in and in March 1938, Hitler's Wehrmacht invaded Austria. Schuschnigg was arrested and put in a concentration camp. Zernatto managed to beat the Gestapo by just a few hours and escaped with Riccarda to Czechoslovakia. He was on Hitler's hit list.

The Czechs gave them fake French passports, with which they escaped to Paris. There, he tried to establish an Austrian exile government and wrote fine essays about Central Europe: *"Le Dossier de L'Europe Centrale"* and others. He also wrote accusatory articles against Hitler in the *Paris Match*.

Soon, the Germans invaded France, and the Zernattos had to run again, always staying a day or two ahead of the German tanks. They found shelter in Mentone on the Riviera. There he wrote the definitive book on the Anschluss and the last days of Austria for Longman's Green in Toronto/Stockholm. It appeared in America, and for the first time his name was noticed across the Atlantic.

With the emerging of the Vichy government collaborating with Hitler, staying in Mentone became dangerous. Again, with fake passports to escape the most-wanted list, they made it to Portugal, where they obtained papers as refugees and sailed to New York together with Franz Werfel, Alma Mahler and Erich Schuschnigg. In New York, he met with other exiles, among them Otto von Habsburg, and they tried again to establish an exile government. However, the contamination of having been a member of the corporate state made him unacceptable for the political Left with Otto Bauer in New York. He found shelter at Fordham University where he wrote his great analytical book, *The Problem of Nationalities and the Future of Nations*.

I was the first to find this manuscript in New York in 1962, when I visited Riccarda Zernatto as a Fulbright scholar. At that time she was working at the Austrian Institute on 52nd Street. In 1966, I published it with Wolf in der Maur in Vienna. But only a fragment of this manuscript was there. There were reams of letters, drafts, articles, documents and poems that have never been published so far. Above all and foremost, he was a fine poet ranking with Georg Trakl, Theodor Kramer or Christine Lavant. All those papers became the basis for my dissertation at Salzburg University. When it was done, I donated those papers to Saint John's University. That was thirty years ago. Riccarda agreed, and she said neither the papers nor Guido would have survived in Europe. It is good and proper, she said, that they stay in America.

Two years ago, Mrs. Zernatto died in Vienna. I went to her funeral. She was a great woman and a wise observer of human frailty and also of human courage, excellence and civility. She was cremated at the *Zentralfriedhof*, thus marking the end of an era.

It was then that the University of Klagenfurt became aware of the location of the papers here. Vice President Martin Hitz, a relative of Ingrid's, asked whether those papers could be brought "home." I mentioned this to our librarian. Would he return the gift, and let it go back to Europe? In the end, SJU agreed, and the University of Klagenfurt flew us back in business class with the boxes of materials. It was a very pleasant trip in June. My brother Gerhard and his wife Edith Darnhofer-Demar arranged a reception with the publisher Heyn, the University of Klagenfurt, the Bachmann Archives headed by the good professor Klaus Amann, the media, Austrian TV, friends and relatives. It was a fine event, and I must thank my brother and Edith for their good work. That night I was on Austrian TV for thirty seconds. How much more famous can you get without robbing a bank?

Zernatto is back home, so to speak, even though he is buried in the Bronx in the St. Raymond Cemetery. Some day, I am sure, Heyn will publish his work, including poems, novels, essays and political texts shedding light on a most tumultuous time in Austrian and European politics. I did my small share in bringing his work to the attention of the public and making it accessible.

He was a great man who had died just short of forty years in 1943 in New York. Many say it was from "homesickness." It was the old kidney condition that got worse from the constant stress of being on the run, being dislocated and being haunted by political activities that made him be rejected by the Left and the fascist Right. In the end, he is remembered for his sublime poems that have become a legacy of Austrian literary achievement beyond any doubt.

XXVII

We did not fly home right away. There was also the 50th anniversary of my graduation from the Klagenfurt Teachers' Training College in 1953. Those were spartan times after the war. We enjoyed excellent instruction in practical teaching, in music and in art. Other than that, the curriculum was a bit dreary. Literature was hardly covered. Theology stayed abstract, rather than asking about the Holocaust and war and peace issues. Physical education was important, but I was always slow to move and was glad to earn a "C." I was much happier in the conservatory, where the LBA paid for my instruction in theory and woodwind instruments. I became quite good in this area, but there was also that rising superstar Udo Jürgens, who taught us all humility. Many years later, the director of the conservatory, Professor Kehldorfer, would visit us in the U.S. and confide, "I had only two divinely gifted students over the years, Günther Mittergradnegger (the splendid conductor of the Klagenfurt Madrigal Choir, which I joined later for several years) and Udo Jürgens. And neither got anywhere!" So he bemoaned. Udo became a superstar and stayed so for fifty years, but none became a Gustav Mahler.

While I enjoyed the celebrity-filled halls of the conservatory, which gave me the illusion of being one of the rising stars, I barely tolerated the somewhat stuffy indoctrination of the LBA, the teachers' training college. During the Nazi years, the LBA was a cadre training institution for future little Nazis. Now, after the war, it was marked by a Catholic-conservative mentality that prevailed. It was repressive, a bit moralistic and shaped by an ethos of duty, obedience and respect for authority and shared belief. In fact, it was not at all that different from the Nazi years—just differently focused. In all fairness, we got a fine education for being future country school teachers, who could also play the organ during Mass on Sunday, teach vocational school for agriculture and direct the local men's chorus. I did all that, for a while. After three years, I left a tenured position and started doing other things—that eventually got me to America.

Now, fifty years later, I met with some forty comrades from those years in a lovely mountain Gasthaus on the Magdalensberg, a place with a lovely eight hundred-year-old church and Celtic and Roman ruins. It is a sacred place with a spectacular view and a deep sense of history. Many of my friends I had not seen again since 1953. I had stayed in touch with some, Franz V., Wolfram E. and Lorenz K., who is the father of a now famous theater producer. There were also women with whom I had enjoyed the first love affairs in a rather innocent, but no less passionate manner, Lore P. and especially Gerlinde G. I suffered a mad addiction to her in Florence during a choir competition in Arezzo, Tuscany, but in the end, I was too shy, too arrogant, too stupid or too chicken to court this elusive woman.

Others were friendly and distant: Hertha T., who came from Denmark and mocked her husband who pursues bliss and lust on ski slopes. Heidi W., who was on our fine *Doppel-Quartett* in the LBA years, as was Lore and Gerlinde, Gerhard J. and Lorenz. We were good back then! But nobody sings anymore—too much alcohol, too many cigarettes.

All of them seemed to be in good shape, especially the blond Herlinde P., who was the Austrian champion in javelin and discus back then. Lorenz was trim and elegant in a well-tailored white jacket. Gitti S. was elegant and urbane. All of them have been in retirement for quite a while. I was the one who had worked the longest, until 2001. No wonder I am the shakiest. But others are dead, at least seven of them. So I could not complain but instead enjoyed the good food up there. We all did. It was a nice get-together, even if a bit hot and muggy on a stormy summer day drenched in rain and nostalgia, mixed with a sense of solidarity and a tender notion of love.

The return home to Minnesota was a pleasant one. We flew business class and enjoyed the view from the front cabin over the glaciers of Greenland, the tundra of Labrador with all the green humps and blue lakes in summer. Slowly signs of human settlements come into view—fishing villages on the rough coast of Newfoundland, and eventually woods, farms, roads, the vast expanse of Lake Superior. We came in low over Duluth, one of the most idyllic harbor cities in the States. From there it is only a short snack until MSP, where we connect with the small turbo-prop to St. Cloud, and then we are home.

There our friends welcome us. Mark McKeon, who cares for me with brotherly love and concern, with Susie, his cheerful wife. Mark Twomey, our generous and soft-spoken neighbor, with Judy. There is Fr. John Kulas, O.S.B., one of the most civil gentlemen in our midst. There is the outspoken Kathy Fischer and her tough-looking Neil with a heart of chocolate. The Haegs are always happy to see us and the reticent Farrys, kind and good to our dogs and cat which they took care off while we were gone. Yes, the dogs are the most ecstatic about our return and not at all reticent. You get jumped on and licked. We have trouble keeping them out of our beds.

Eventually, we retire for the night. Jet-lag should not bother us too much since our fatigue is noticeable. With the sounds of Mozart's *Violin Concerto No. 3*, the slow movement of Mahler's *Fourth* or Miles Davis's horn, we shift from day to a calm summer night. The frogs are singing in the slough. The loons talk at the lake, and the stars are as bright as can be. Minnesota has us again, and we are happy and thankful.

Soon, the boys would be here from Salzburg, as always in summer. They are big and fly alone, with the help of an especially friendly ground stewardess in Minneapolis called Mary. A visit in Denver with Natascha and Glenn is part of the routine.

In November, we go back to the Grand Caymans with Glenn and Natascha. They have to leave early, but Maxi comes and stays with us on the island. This time, we rented a house on the dunes near Rum Point on the stormy East Coast. The waves break on the reef and produce a haunting base sound. Coconut trees, casuarina trees, blooming shrubs and the sounds of waves beating the beach surround us day and night. I am getting a bit weak, but I still can walk and inhale the splendid salty air. Only swimming is becoming a no-no, because my breathing is hard without a functioning chest. But the feast for the eyes is ample compensation for the lack of motion in and under water.

Life is wonderful! I am convinced the book *Treasure Island* was written here. Everything fits and reminds me of the reading pleasure when I was the age of our grandchildren.

The seasons do not change in the Caymans, but in Minnesota they do! Winter is always the most noticeable part of the year. I try to take good care of my condition. Dr. Lu does acupuncture every week, and Marianne Graeve does a massage every Tuesday. That keeps my stuttering body going. Ingrid does her part to make every day a feast of some sort: guests, meals, concerts, books, the *New York Times*, the *New Yorker*, the *Nation* . . . . Everything I can dream of is offered to me, and I am thankful for so much kindness.

For the last two years, I have been writing. The end of my narrative is in sight. I regularly write my comments in the local papers. Maybe it helps? I do hope so.

No, I am under no illusion; I cannot change the outcome of the U.S. election by writing a few missives for a local paper. All I have is ONE vote on November 2nd, so does my wife Ingrid, as we are both now U.S. citizens. I cannot change the fate of the country I adopted as my new home. I cannot force reality to follow my whims and wishes. But my wishes are for a more civil, a more honest, a more lawful and a more peaceful country. A friendlier world, in short, like the one we enjoy in our small world around Lake Wobegon. Here we have friendly neighbors and can reciprocate by being hospitable and friendly.

Here, Ingrid can beautify the environment with her flowers. Here, we can help friends and neighbors as they help us. Here, we can console people who recover from sickness like Father John, and they console us while struggling with my diminishing strength. Here, Bruce and Marcia Hanson bring vegetables and help with yard work. Axel Theimer comes to split wood. Dick and Eileen come to share the events of the day and supply us with the surplus of Dick's garden. The Farrys come and race to the airport when we forget my breathing device and race back to tend to our dogs. Here, Kathy Fischer comes with the *NYT* and advice when needed. Neil tells stories in his inimical manner. Mark McKeon comes and elopes with me to the coffee house. Susie is always there with cheerfulness when things are dim. And Mark and Judy Twomey sell us land when we need it and invite us to Florida when it gets cold. Father John comes with the latest news from my old workplace, from SJU. He even proofreads my manuscript! Al and Bertha Eich let us roam with the dogs and the Gator on their farm, which is about the most beautiful around here. So much kindness in so many forms and shapes! Who would not love to live in such a world made civil by people and beautiful by God's nature?! If only America could pay more attention to Minnesota, the land of Hubert Humphrey, Paul Wellstone and Garrison Keillor. Here are the "Homegrown Democrats"!

Even with all the wonders Minnesota provided to us and our children, we never neglected our Central European roots. All our children crossed the Atlantic many times to establish family ties there. I crossed the Atlantic many times in my declaration of love to this splendid part of Europe. After 1989, this area underwent so many astounding changes, mostly for the better, if one subtracts the pains of the changes in Yugoslavia and Romania. Maybe the next century will be kinder to this part of the world with Habsburgian traces and scars from too many wars.

In 1999, I made another trip to the by-then unified Berlin without the Wall and presented a few thoughts and questions for the future of Central Europe. It was on July 4th, the American Independence Day, that I presented my paper, "Europe: Visions and Realities Ten Years after the Fall of the Wall," at the Berlin Campus of Teiko University. It contained my farewell thoughts and best wishes to Europe before settling down in the tranquility of Minnesota. I am no Mr. Kohl, Mr. Reagan or Mr. Gorbachev. They made the changes; I can only comment and appreciate.

It was a wonderful occasion to see the changed Berlin after the hardships of fascism and Communism. It could mark the beginning of a peaceful era, but it would be easier without a man called George W. Bush. My grandchildren took a sticker from a junkyard in Holdingford that reads, "Kick the Son of a Bush Out of Office."

Here are my thoughts on Europe.

> This is the place where my roots are. I am an American, yes, but I am
> also a European with an unmistakable accent and cosmopolitan traits.
> My children share that openness and multilingual adaptability which I
> admire. They all deserve a good future. May they be more fortunate
> than my fathers' generation. I do hope so.

Being back in Berlin a decade after what was considered the least
likely event in European history—the fall of the Wall on October 9,
1989—offers a reminder for observers of current affairs that time can
move rather swiftly, and without much ado. Where we are now con-
gregated, only ten years ago, budding *Stasi* agents would have enjoyed
the care and attention this pristine place offers to us now; S-Bahn stations, rather bleak then, are now equipped with infrastructures filled
with flowers, fruit and foreign papers; where the Wall once was—and
nobody can trace that place accurately any more—is now a jungle of
cranes for the biggest construction site anywhere in Europe; the Palast
der Republik is not yet torn down, but boarded up—while the *Dom*
across the Spree is completed in its reconstruction; *Unter den Linden*
and *Friedrichstrasse* are quiet streets. What once was the hub of the
capital of the GDR is now a low-key part of town with mostly buildings closed until further notice; even *Friedrich der Grosse* is not on display. Nor is the HERDER Institute in operation any more, and the
baroque building next to the opera stands empty and idle.

Let me take the case of the Herder Institute and its meaning then
and now. During the GDR, this *Sprachinstitut* (language institute) sailed
under this name, because GOETHE was already used for the West
German equivalent (Goethe-Institut), even though the GDR would see
itself as the caretaker and guardian of the heritage of Goethe and *DAS
GROSSE ERBE*, and thus legitimize the existence of that other German
state as the more noble, its economic anemia and STASI omnipresence
notwithstanding. It was the Herder Institute that carried the sound of
German to Vietnam, Angola and Mozambique. The name "Herder"
conjured the Romantic spirit and its political ramification so useful for
the GDR and the Eastern allies. Why?

Johann Gottfried Herder (1744–1803) gave Central European nationalism a distinct twist, especially those Eastern nations of Central Europe long under imperial structures by the Romanoffs, the Habsburgs
or the Ottomans. He defined *Volksseele* as unique to each people. As a

proto-Romantic, Herder rejected many of the principles of the rationalistic version of enlightenment and also the cosmopolitan form of civilization it propagated. He had great reservations about the linear idea of progress because he saw it as a destructive agent that was leveling differences between peoples, each of which had its own authentic nature and soul. He saw the modern centralized state as robbing people of their natural freedoms. The manifestation of the national soul was not so much resting with the cultural elites but rather in the common people, their songs, fairytales and legends. It was manifested in their collective voice, and he proclaimed the mystical function of language, SPRACHE. And since languages are different, he propagated the creation of "nation-states." Herder's fascination with language as a creative medium made a deep impression on his Central European contemporaries. Herder's aesthetics of populism and Romanticism added a strong retrospective and introspective dimension to the idea of belonging to a particular nation. While he did not openly propagate "nation-states" in the later revolutionary spirit of 1848, he spoke of *Kulturnation*, thus advocating small communities, stressing the local rather than the universal. He is in fact the founder of modern "regionalism." . . .

The most interesting "nation" in this discussion is the Jewish nation. They were the ones who held out the longest against forming their own "national" identity. European Jews provided the cultural elites in their host nation, until Zionism emerged as a defining myth for a Jewish state yet to be born. But Jews were an exception in the rise of nationalism during the 19th century. Jews, instead of being more "Jewish," assimilated into dominant national cultures by becoming pronounced Germans, or Magyars, or Czechs and Poles. Moreover, Jews had no unifying linguistic roots. Their cultural elites chose German, disregarding their origins in Galicia, Romania, Slovenia or Bohemia.

By passport, Central European Jews were either Russians or Prussians or Austrians. They got their education and pursued their—often brilliant— careers in Berlin, Prague, Budapest and Vienna. The *fin de siècle* in Central Europe was essentially the product of assimilated Jews. They were, as Milan Kundera says, "the principal cosmopolitan, integrating element in Central Europe: They were its intellectual cement, a condensed version of its spirit." These Jews (Mahler, Kraus, Wittgenstein, Kafka, Freud, Schönberg, Adler, Zweig . . . made great contributions to enlightened and humanistic German culture. But German nationalists in a Wagnerian mythical mold, who soon adopted anti-Semitic and

RACIST doctrines, adamantly refused to recognize those contributions as "German." Rather, they condemned them, along with many of the precepts of cosmopolitan enlightenment and secular humanism that had fascinated Jewish assimilation, as Jewish. For a while, it looked as if Jews would be immune against the "parochial" dreams of Herder and its extreme forms of misinterpretations. But what started with Theodor Herzl soon led to "Bibi" Netanyahu. . . .

The second phase in the middle of the 19th century was shaped by national elites, who propagated a "national awakening" in Hungary, Italy, Poland, on the Balkans and in the Baltic. It also happened in Germany but was resisted in Habsburgian Austria and its ally Czarist Russia. "National traditions" were discovered and turned into powerful political dynamite. The revolutions of 1848 were fought over "national ideas." It was the springtime of nations that produced massive centrifugal forces. Around 1900, those forces became politically volatile when they found mass support for national movements. And that popular support was no longer inspired by the national elites of 1848, but rather by able demagogues dreaming of final solutions.

None of this can be blamed on Gottfried Herder and his seminal book *Ideas for the History of Mankind* (1784–1791) , translated by Hans Kohn, New York: 1965. But it is obvious what I try to demonstrate with the case of Herder: a diagnosis of a Central European pathology.

Johann Gottfried Herder helps us to diagnose the root of European resistance to European integration and cooperation because:

1) "Nations" do not make states and nationalism, but the other way around. Nations are imagined communities, but 19th-century nationalism was able to invent age-old national identities and conflicts where none had previously existed.

2) Western Europe is different from Central Europe. There, states provided the institutional framework for the articulation of nationalism and the process of nation-building. But in Central Europe nationalism triggered the process of forming national identities and the creation of states, a process brought to completion by Woodrow Wilson.

Ernest Renan diagnosed the ultimate flaw in the Herder argument in 1802: "Historical error is an essential factor in the formation of na tions." For Serbia, this means 1389, for Hungary 1848, for Germany this means Siegfried and Brunhilde and for Poland it means Sobieski. Ernest Geller adds, "a shared amnesia, a collective forgetfulness, is at least as essential for the emergence of what we now consider to be a nation." Getting history wrong, including forgetting what came before nationalism, frequently plays a greater role for a nation in forming its cultural and political identity than getting history right.

Thus, Central Europe has yet to learn from its history. Otherwise, we would not have to worry today about Bosnia-Herzegovina, Croatia, Slovenia or Kosovo. Religion, imperial superstructures, fascism and Communism have failed to provide an inclusive European model, its suave rhetoric notwithstanding. Nor has the bureaucracy of Brussels succeeded in convincing Europeans that harmonious cooperation is more important than the defense of agrarian policies, regional interests and ethnic purity.

Possible remedies

If Europe hopes to become more cohesive ten years after the unexpected fall of the Wall, then it would require some therapeutic remedies. None of which might be of the miraculous dimension of the fall of the Wall—but all are of a somewhat elusive nature that suggest proper caution. Let me propose ten remedies to contemplate:

1) Europe would need strategies and assimilatory techniques as demonstrated by Central European Jews in the pre-Zionist era. How Europe can find such cohesiveness in the absence of Jews as a cultural ferment and as a cultural elite which was understating its own national identity is far from clear.

2) Common interests have to be defined in monetary policy, defense and trade. All three are more important than regional or national identities. This hierarchy of needs is far from commonly understood;

3) The building of European cultural elites willing to be transnational and cosmopolitan would be a task for European universities. But those universities are mostly state institutions serving national interests, and whose ivory tower at times resembles paper-mâché.

4) There has to be a definition of values commonly shared by Europeans, e.g., human rights, solidarity, humanist traditions and the liberal dream of the autonomy of the individual and the civility of the state. Can those values become stronger than chauvinist pride, self-interest, religious and ideological purity?

5) Ideas will only be heard if there are compelling and convincing voices that proclaim them. Certain things will not sink in until articulated authoritatively, e.g., Brzezinski's statement at the recent Vienna

Conference on Security, "Europe is a U.S. protectorate . . . ," or Gorbachev's line, "He who comes too late will be punished by history. . . ."

6) Europe must be able to take initiative on its own. Can it act without America? Is there a likelihood of success without the U.S.? Bosnia or Kosovo did not make Europe shine.

7) Europe must come to terms with Russia—and Russia with Europe. Can Russia's economic abyss be bridged by European initiatives and funds? Can the Russian paranoia and insecurity be healed by arrogant and affluent Europeans? Do Europeans learn Russian? Do Russians learn Polish?

8) Germany will have to play a lead role—as it did in the imperial past, the Reformation, the age of Goethe, the Romantic era with the formulation of "German Idealism." Will Germany be able to overcome its reticence, timidity, guilt and occasional outbursts of arrogance and insensitivity? Can there be another "Weimar"?

9) Europe needs a pluralist rather than a conformist conscience. Can that be achieved in the absence of Jews and with Europe's history of vulnerability vis-à-vis ideologies, religious purity and simplistic totalitarian lures?

10) In spite of a pluralist conscience, Europe needs a commonly understood and shared linguistic model. It has to become a "community of language" in the Herderian sense. French, the old transcending language of aristocracy, is no longer operative. Latin, the ecclesiastic communality, is gone, especially since Vatican II. German is for many—including many Germans—a stigmatized language, though commonly understood in Central Europe and the East. Russian is even more stigmatized. English clearly is the language of Brussels, but it reeks of U.S. patronage. Italian is moot outside opera houses. Can Esperanto ever become a European language? A forbidding thought which would make Herder shiver because of its "rootlessness"! In the meantime, conflicts have to be settled in Albanian and Basque.

Central Europe has escaped the split of the Cold War. It has yet to find a way where a Jew from Galicia or Transylvania can again become a European voice in German, where a Jew from Bohemia can conduct in Vienna, where Russian Jews no longer use Europe as a mere transition on their way to the U.S. or Israel—and where participants of a symposium in Berlin can talk a common language with ease, its many accents and regional inflections notwithstanding. The anxiety of a possible *Stasi* agent behind the Wall is certainly no longer a concern, fortunately.

Summary:

I have tried to use the paradigm of Herder's Romanticism in order to diagnose a peculiarly Central European pathology as it moves from the permafrost of the Cold War to a more integrative role in Europe. Much of that diagnosed pathology has to do with the especially delicate relationship between nation and state, which can be explained by referring to Herder's assertion that the "soul" of a nation rests in its regional, linguistic and cultural communality. That this belief was used to legitimize emerging smaller states in Central Europe not only can be illustrated in the revolutionary efforts of 1848, but also proved to be useful in legitimizing the GDR via the Herder Institute as that other German state, which has since vanished.

I have also highlighted the fact that Central European Jews provided some immunity from a "nationalistic" translation of Romantic beliefs into political structures of exclusive nature as long as Central European nationalism was "liberal, linguistic and cultural." In rejecting self-contained orthodoxy and a "backward" form of seclusion, Jews opted for assimilation, liberalism, even Socialism and Communism, but definitely for a Western form of cosmopolitan European thought. By rejecting separate statehood for a long time, they became an integrative ferment in Europe, which has vanished after the rise of Zionism and especially the Holocaust.

In my generosity, I have offered ten possible remedies for the Central European condition—fully aware of the fact and under no illusion that nothing of what I say will help to expedite a more integrative Central Europe. But what I would like to initiate with my remarks is a deconstruction of the myths and dogmas resulting from a misinterpretation of Herder's thoughts. The deconstruction of the ideologically burdened Herder Institute has been accomplished swiftly after the disintegration of the GDR. The decontamination of places afflicted with "historical error" has barely begun in Sarajevo, Pristina—and here in Berlin, where the tangible sign of reorientation can be seen in the angular and edgy structure of the new Jewish Museum. It is as visible as is the abundance of fresh fruit, flowers and foreign papers in the formerly dismal S-Bahn stations below the no man's land of the Wall—which is by now ancient history.

XXVIII

The future is always an unknown entity. One cannot live in this climate of uncertainty. One has to live NOW. However, one cannot fall for the temptation of Faust either, "If I could say to the moment, 'stay, you are so beautiful . . . ,'" then this everlasting presence would be without a vision, without a notion of change, without hope for better things to come. It would be Faust's doom. Only the subjunctive mood saves him from damnation. Permanent presence without change is something for granite, limestone or slate. Human beings are less durable and more in need of hope and ongoing improvement. The future is simply a present tense that has not yet arrived. But its design has to be envisioned in dreams and hopes. That is why I am in America rather than in the Lesachtal. That is why I participate in politics rather than go fishing. That is why I left the security of a confined existence as a country school teacher and moved into uncharted terrain where life turned out to be wonderful and exciting.

What can be more rewarding than leaving class after a successful lecture, or leaving the opera pit after playing in the orchestra or after presenting a good paper in New York, Berlin, Chicago or Los Angeles! What can be more glorious than listening to Dave Brubeck, Gerry Mulligan, Miles Davis or a performance of *Porgy and Bess* live! What can be more fortunate than sitting across the table from Nobel Laureates like Isaac Bashevis Singer or Saul Bellow and have them sign and dedicate a book to you! What can be more delightful than introducing Peter Handke or Bernd Felderer to a U.S. audience!

When I bother my patient readers with my anti-Bush missives in local papers, it should indicate that I look into the future with some trepidation and concern. The 21ˢᵗ century simply did not start well for America. My angst about the future is made a bit more bearable with Michael Moore's thoughts on November 2ⁿᵈ.

The future of America will only improve with the removal of the Bushes from power. Otherwise, the 21ˢᵗ century will continue as it started, very poorly. It will no longer be the "American Century." Maybe the dawn of the European era? Or China? Or India? Remember how the "Evil Empire," the Soviet Union started to unravel? It was in Afghanistan, where the seemingly invincible Red Army failed to secure a stretch of desert in the mountains. First, James Bond glorified those romantic jihads, but then the disintegration of the Soviet Union became unstoppable. America is risking its good name—or whatever is left of its reputation, its strength and viability in a catastrophic military adventure in Iraq that cannot be won. The sole remaining superpower is being transformed into a victim of its arrogance. It deserves better than that! There must be another way!

Here is Michael Moore. He says it better than I could, and he gives a nation hope when it is needed the most:*

Dear Friends,

Enough of the handwringing! Enough of the doomsaying! Do I have to come there and personally calm you down? Stop with all the defeatism, OK? Bush is a goner—IF we all just quit our whining and bellyaching and stop shaking like a bunch of nervous ninnies. Geez, this is embarrassing! The Republicans are laughing at us. Do you ever see them cry, "Oh, it's all over! We are finished! Bush can't win! Waaaaaa!"

Hell no. It's never over for them until the last ballot is shredded. They are never finished—they just keep moving forward like sharks that never sleep, always pushing, pulling, kicking, blocking, lying.

They are relentless and that is why we secretly admire them—they just simply never, ever give up. Only 30% of the country calls itself "Republican," yet the Republicans own it all—the White House, both houses of Congress, the Supreme Court and the majority of the governorships. How do you think they've been able to pull that off considering they are a minority? It's because they eat you and me and every other liberal for breakfast and then spend the rest of the day wreaking havoc on the planet.

Look at us—what a bunch of crybabies. Bush gets a bounce after his convention and you would have thought the Germans had run through Poland again. The Bushies are coming, the Bushies are coming! Yes, they caught Kerry asleep on the Swift Boat thing. Yes, they found the frequency in Dan Rather and ran with it. Suddenly it's like, "THE END IS NEAR! THE SKY IS FALLING!"

No, it is not. If I hear one more person tell me how lousy a candidate Kerry is and how he can't win . . . Dammit, of COURSE he's a lousy candidate—he's a Democrat, for heaven's sake! That party is so pathetic, they even lose the elections they win! What were you expecting, Bruce Springsteen heading up the ticket? Bruce would make a helluva president, but guys like him don't run—and neither do you or I. People like Kerry run.

Yes, OF COURSE any of us would have run a better, smarter, kick-ass campaign. Of course we would have smacked each and every one of those phony swifty boaty bastards down. But WE are not running for president—Kerry is. So quit complaining and work with what we have. Oprah just gave 300 women a . . . Pontiac! Did you see any of them frowning and moaning and screaming, "O God, NOT a friggin' Pontiac!" Of course not, they were happy. The Pontiacs all had four wheels, an engine and a gas pedal. You want more than that, well, I can't help you. I had a Pontiac once and it lasted a good year. And it was a VERY good year.

My friends, it is time for a reality check.

1. The polls are wrong. They are all over the map like diarrhea. On Friday, one poll had Bush 13 points ahead—and another poll had them both tied. There are three reasons why the polls are b.s.: One, they are polling "likely voters." "Likely" means those who have consistently voted in the past few elections. So that cuts out young people who are voting for the first time and a ton of non-voters who are definitely going to vote in THIS election. Second, they are not polling people who use their cell phone as their primary phone. Again, that means *they are not talking to young people.* Finally, most of the polls are weighted with too many Republicans, as pollster *John Zogby revealed last week.* You are being snookered if you believe any of these polls.

2. Kerry has brought in the Clinton A-team. Instead of shunning Clinton (as Gore did), Kerry has decided to not make that mistake.

3. Traveling around the country, as I've been doing, I gotta tell ya, there is a hell of a lot of unrest out there. Much of it is not being captured by the mainstream press. But it is simmering and it is real. Do not let those well-produced Bush rallies of angry white people scare you. Turn off the TV! (Except Jon Stewart and Bill Moyers—everything else is just a sugar-coated lie).

4. Conventional wisdom says if the election is decided on "9/11" (the fear of terrorism), Bush wins. But if it is decided on the job we are doing in Iraq, then Bush loses. And folks, that "job," you might have noticed, has descended into the third level of a hell we used to call Vietnam. There is no way out. It is a full-blown mess of a quagmire and the body bags will sadly only mount higher. Regardless of what Kerry

meant by his original war vote, he ain't the one who sent those kids to their deaths and Mr. and Mrs. Middle America knows it. Had Bush bothered to show up when he was in the "service," he might have somewhat of a clue as to how to recognize an immoral war that cannot be "won." All he has delivered to Iraq was that plasticized turkey last Thanksgiving. It is this failure of monumental proportions that is going to cook his goose come this November.

So, do not despair. All is not over. Far from it. The Bush people need you to believe that it is over. They need you to slump back into your easy chair and feel that sick pain in your gut as you contemplate another four years of George W. Bush. They need you to wish we had a candidate who didn't windsurf and who was just as smart as we were when WE knew Bush was lying about WMD and Saddam planning 9/11. It's like Karl Rove is hypnotizing you—"Kerry voted for the war . . . Kerry voted for the war . . . Kerrrrrryyy vooootted fooooor theee warrrrrr . . ."

Yes . . .Yes . . . Yesssss . . . He did! HE DID! No sense in fighting now . . . what I need is sleep . . . sleep . . . sleeeeeeppppp . . .

WAKE UP! The majority are with us! More than half of all Americans are pro-choice, want stronger environmental laws, are appalled that assault weapons are back on the street—and 54% now believe the war is wrong. YOU DON'T EVEN HAVE TO CONVINCE THEM OF ANY OF THIS—YOU JUST HAVE TO GIVE THEM A RAY OF HOPE AND A RIDE TO THE POLLS. CAN YOU DO THAT? WILL YOU DO THAT?

Just for me, please? Buck up. The country is almost back in our hands. Not another negative word until Nov. 3rd! Then you can bitch all you want about how you wish Kerry was still that long-haired kid who once had the courage to stand up for something. Personally, I think that kid is still inside him. Instead of the wailing and gnashing of your teeth, why not hold out a hand to him and help the inner soldier/protester come out and defeat the forces of evil we now so desperately face. Do we have any other choice?

Yours,
Michael Moore

www.michaelmoore.com
mmflint@aol.com

*Reprinted here, with thanks, from MichaelMoore.com, Mike's Letter of September 20, 2004, entitled "Put Away Your Hankies . . . a message from Michael Moore."

Unfortunately, neither I nor Michael Moore was able to stop the Texas cowboy from moving back into the White House. When even Michael Moore fails, I should not feel that bad myself. Let me simply add a concession speech in which I humbly accept the outcome and warn against what might happen during "Four more years."

Four More Years? It Will Be Scary.

Mr. Bush has claimed victory and said, "I have political capital, and I am going to spend it!"

His early appointments give us a clue. He rewards, first and foremost, toadies and loyalists.

Mr. Gross, the man who tried to bury the 9/11 report, is now head of the CIA. A yes man.

Mr. Gonzales, the man who concocted legal briefs for Bush on how to torture without saying so, called the Geneva Conventions "quaint and obsolete." Speedy Gonzales is now going to be attorney general even though the Supreme Court slapped Bush's wrist three times so far for his transgressions: detaining people indefinitely without trial or legal procedures, detaining United States citizens indefinitely without stating charges and encouraging abuse.

Condi Rice, whose incompetence for providing reliable intelligence for the President can be topped only by the incompetence of warlord Rumsfeld or the Iraq-occupier Paul Bremer. Rice was patently unable to differentiate between fact and fiction, belief and reality. As National Security Advisor she has fabricated fairy tales for four years. Now she is going to replace Powell as Secretary of State. Not a pretty picture, nor a good omen for four more years to come.

If Bush were a reader of books, he might have learned a few things from history. For example, once upon a time there was an Austrian corporal who inhaled too much mustard gas in the trenches of WW I, which made him resentful and delusional. The guy did not amount to much after the war. He failed in most things he tried. He had run-ins with the law and spent time in jail where he wrote an unreadable book named *Mein Kampf*.

But he knew one thing: He could do terrific stump speeches. People looked at him as a buffoon, but an entertaining one. In January 1933, he won elections. Legitimately, fair and square. No problem there. He became Statesman A. But he had little authority. He needed a 9/11 kind of boost. He got it when the Reichstag was torched. By whom? Who cares?! Now, Statesman A. started to warn against Bolshevik terrorists, that lurking wolf pack, out to destroy Western civilization. Cunningly, he enacted the "War Powers Act," which neutralized the parliament and made him the all-powerful "protector."

In 1935, he passed a "Patriot Act," according to which only Aryans could be patriots. Not Jews! He also knew he had to pander to pious believers. In 1936 he implemented a concordat with the Vatican, according to which the churches were assured of fiscal stability in return for refraining from any and all political activities. (The treaty is still in effect.)

He also was "pro-life" and awarded Aryan mothers a cross of distinction for producing four or more children.

He was emphatically pro-gun and loved the military. This made him the darling of the industrial complex.

He was a Wagnerian opera freak, which made him the darling of high society.

But people became increasingly concerned about his militant rhetoric. He wanted to show he was really a "Man of Peace" with a mission from "God the Almighty." He signed a non-aggression treaty with his Bolshevist "brother" Josef Stalin. Everybody was stunned. But the two winked at each other and in 1939 attacked Poland simultaneously, Stalin from the East, Statesman A. from the West. Smilingly, they signaled "mission accomplished" and divided Poland up among themselves.

But peace did not come. There were blitzkriegs for Stalin in Finland and for Statesman A. in Norway, France and the Balkans. But Statesman A. was driven by strong beliefs and convictions about this future mission. He needed only "to stay the course." He had four more years left in 1941, and then attacked the Soviet Union, the non-aggression pact notwithstanding. He wanted to rid the world once and for all of the scourge of the Bolshevist terrorist threat. He formed a grand alliance with Bulgarians,

Italians, Romanians, Hungarians and Slovaks (all those nice statesmen who now help Statesman B. with our debacle in Iraq). Four more years and Statesman A. would be hailed as the savior of Western civilization. Well, in 1945 it was all over, and it was not pretty. Twenty million dead Russians, six million dead Jews, six million dead Germans. We now know what "four more years" meant for Statesman A, but nobody knows yet what "four more years" will amount to for Statesman B. One thing is certain; Statesman B. will face very little, if any, dissent. His toadies will nod and stay the course, wherever that might take our deeply divided nation. It is going to be scary. God bless America!

XXIX

The past is different; it is unchangeable. The Romans knew this and referred to it as *Perfectum*. When I return so often to Central Europe, is it not Habsburg nostalgia or sentimentality or an inability on my part to become an American without umbilical ties to my origins? However, since the past is unchangeable, it is also a permanent part of my soul, my personality and my mind. *The Past in the Present* is one of the several books by Lonnie Johnson. How fitting a title? As if you could sever yourself from it.

The "Nervous Splendor" of Central Europe is as impressive as it is addictive. Not just from the aesthetic point of view like the splendid cityscapes Kokoschka painted of Prague, Dresden, Vienna and Salzburg! All of them became victims of WW II, with the exception of Prague! Central Europe is the place where the assimilated Jews created a cultural manifestation of their host-nations around 1900. It is the place that gave birth to virtually everything of substance—classical music: Mozart, Beethoven, Haydn, Dvorak, Smetana, Verdi, Puccini, Brahms, Mahler, Strauss Richard and the Johanns, Bach, Berg . . . . . Hubert von Goisern and Udo Jürgens! What would MPR transmit without the repertoire of Central Europe?

For me, k.u.k. "Kakania," as Robert Musil calls it, is the essence of civility, but also the proximity of chaos. Auschwitz is close to wonderful Krakow with the splendid Wawel, and Buchenwald is just around the corner from Goethe's garden house in the Ilm Park.

It is the world of my father in the white uniform of a sailor for the k.k. Imperial Navy of WW I. It is the world of the opera houses in Prague, Budapest and Vienna. It is the world of the Venetian palazzos and Viennese boulevards. It is the world of the coffee houses and parks, the sumptuous museums and concert halls. It is the world of sailboats off the coast of Croatia and the glaciers in the Alps. It is Rome and Berlin, the spiritual and political centers of powers, past and present. It is the world linked with magnificent railroads leading to palatial rail stations in downtown cities that have healed all the terrible scars of 1914, 1939, 1945, 1953, 1956, 1991 and 1995.

Central Europe is a reminder that in the end, civility is stronger than barbaric interludes. It gives hope to those who would otherwise despair looking at the past. That is why it was so important for American students to make those pilgrimages with me in January over the years. The past is not only "perfectum," it is also permanent and indestructible, unforgettable and precious. This is why I love Central Europe as an American. We can learn so much from it, and it can give us hope.

How is the future of Europe going to be? Is it a hopeful one? A better one than the last century presented? It is yet to be seen, but my children and grandchildren will thank us, if we help to put America and Central Europe on a steady course. We owe it to them, to Alexander and Nikolaus, to little Maxi and to Thomas, Natascha and Dimitri with their partners. We owe it to all our friends and relatives, to my former students and all those who helped me so much finding my way through the obstacles of turbulent times. I owe so much to so many people! Thank you!

XXX

Indian summer in Minnesota is like taking a cruise on the *Titanic*. It is magnificent, opulent, hallucinating, spell-binding, awe-inspiring, overwhelming and wonderful. The Titian-red of the sumac, the bronze of the long-stemmed prairie grass, the orange glow of the maples, the golden light of the ashes, the blue of the lakes and the shining light of the bright sky. If Trakl had been here instead of the Russian front in WW I, he would not have overdosed in despair. He would have added many more fall poems. It is the best time in Minnesota—and on board the *Titanic*. But you know that ice is ahead six weeks from now.

Rilke would say that "he who has no house will not build one anymore. Will be awake, read and write long letters and restlessly stroll through the avenues strewn with drifting leaves. . . ." Retirement feels somewhat like this, too. But Ingrid is building my studio, a flat house without steps and ample light. It will be great for the two of us, and I am so grateful to my good wife who joins me on my cruise on the *Titanic*. We will avoid the ice and sit close to the fire when it gets grey and cold. My strength is not what it once was, but my spirits are good. I much enjoy every single good day, of which I have so many yet to come.

Today, Thomas got his divorce. His boys are so happy to have him back undivided and unburdened. It was a long and painful process, but good prevails in the end. He is such a wonderful, kind soul who deserves better than what he had.

Dimitri and Kara are in Paris and love it. Then, Dimitri will do his internship at an Austrian clinic for five weeks. They are a lovely couple and delivered a fine boy, Andreas, in February.

Natascha and Glenn in Denver delivered a baby too, also in February. A wonderful girl, Stephanie. All of a sudden, we have four instead of two grandchildren!

Ingrid protects the many flowers from early frost. And she protects me from the ravages of a nasty disease that we will not let interfere with our lives. Life is wonderful. Remember that good old Louis Armstrong tune, "Oh what a wonderful world . . . ."

My story has to end. There are so many memories from the past that stay with me. I cannot count my blessings enough: a wonderful wife who followed me on my unpredictable trails, three fine children of whom I am immensely proud, the two boys, Alex and Nick, who give me so much pleasure every summer here. What is left is just a collage of splendid moments that made my life a rich and happy one.

Sailing aboard the splendid *Titanic*. I look for what is on in the salon. I order tickets for October 14, "Eaglen sings Wagner." The Minnesota Orchestra will play all those sumptuous, seductive, decadent and magnificent Wagnerian hits: *Flying Dutchman Overture*, *"Du bist der Lenz"* from *Walküre*, *"Prelude and Liebestod"* from *Tristan*, *Der Ring*, an arrangement, and above all, *"Brunhildes Immolation and Die Götterdämmerung"*! I am an addict, when it comes to Wagner. This will be an orgy of luscious sound! Yes, and I have to order tickets for April at the Ordway, *Carmen*. I am lusting after those magnificent expressions of love, life and death. Some go to church; I go to the opera and feel redeemed!

My life is filled with past moments of great joy that make sitting now on the deck of the cruise ship sailing through the Indian summer so delicious:

I see myself with my children on top of mountains here and there: Grossglockner, Mangart, Rax, Long's Peak in the Rockies, Cloud Peak, the Tetons in Wyoming.

I see myself at the beaches with Ingrid and the children off the coast of Cape Hatteras, the Oregon Coast at the Pacific, along Boca Raton or Long Island.

I see myself in Paris, where Ingrid taught me the *ars amandi*.

I see myself in the splendid cities of America with my children and Ingrid, on a tour of the now vanished WTC Towers in New York, on the Staten Island Ferry approaching Manhattan, in San Francisco, San Diego or Boston, Duluth, Washington, D.C., Westport.

I see myself in the "nervous splendor" of Central Europe with my cosmopolitan children and Ingrid, my students and my friends as we experience Venice, Florence, Vienna, Andalusia, Carinthia.

I see myself playing the clarinet in the orchestra pit of the St. Cloud Opera Company.

I see Ingrid and Eileen painting ornaments while I play Mozart's clarinet concerto.

I see myself being welcomed by the University of Klagenfurt, where I returned the Zernatto papers after so many decades in the U.S. Add to that thirty seconds of ORF TV immortality!

I see myself in the Bela Petheo portrait with the Austrian award, *Das Österreichische Ehrenkreuz für Wissenschaft und Kunst Erster Klasse*. (Do I look good on that painting!)

I see myself on the title page of the SJU brochures as the model face for "good teaching."

I feel secure in the arms of my wife who whispers, "I need you, you belong to me, I love you," and she keeps me on my wobbly feet in our lovely home. I am so fortunate!

I see myself at the graduation of Thomas at the Vienna Medical School, of Natascha at the Hamline Law School and of Dimitri at the University of Minnesota Medical School. I am so proud of our children! And I love Alexander, Nikolaus, Stephanie and Andreas—the most precious grandchildren!

I see myself on the top of mountains in France, Switzerland, Italy and Slovenia. It was in the Alpine Club, where Fritz Turnowsky introduced me to the habit of walking uphill. There I learned the ethos that any peak is reachable if you keep at it one step at a time.

I see myself in the ensembles of Hilde Mayr, Günther Mittergradnegger, Günther Theuring, Kurt Schmidt and Norbert Artner performing Mozart operas, Schubert Masses and Haydn oratories and radio productions for Sunday shows at the ORF studios.

I see myself playing clarinet in the ORF ensemble and traveling with the Madrigal Choir to Arezzo, Llangollen and Ljubljana.

I see myself mesmerized, sitting in the Theater an der Wien at my first encounter with Gershwin's *Porgy and Bess*. It changed my musical orientation forever!

I see myself in the Linz Concert Hall, hearing Bruckner for the first time. That was majestic!

I see myself with my young family at the campground at the beach in Caorle, Italy.

I see myself in our wonderful condo in Innsbruck with a view of the Serles, the Castle of Ambras and the Inn River. Tyrol is a paradise!

I see myself with a pregnant Ingrid on board the *Statendam* bringing us to the U.S. for the first time as Fulbrighters. We sailed back home with Thomas on the *Constitution*.

I see myself with Ingrid in the hospitals after the birth of our wonderful children in Ravenna, Ohio, Solbad Hall, Tyrol and St. Cloud, Minnesota. All above average children!

I see myself at the graduation of Ingrid at St. Cloud State and the St. Cloud Hospital School of Nursing. I am so proud of my wife. Yes, she has a master's degree—in SCIENCE!

I see myself riding the Gator around the Avon Hills with the dogs.

I see myself with my clan on our lovely Lake Achmann, alias Lake Wobegon. Where else could we have found a more peaceful, more beautiful and more friendly place with neighbors, trees, horses, dogs, friends and colleagues!

I see myself in the arms of my future wife dancing at the Café Lerch, at the formals in the Konzerthaus, sipping champagne, enjoying the sounds of Udo Jürgens.

I see myself on the beaches of the Costa del Sol with my family on a spectacular sabbatical at Marbella, looking at the snow-capped mountains of Morocco and the Rock of Gibraltar in the distance while resting on the sundeck of our house on the beach.

I see myself on a flimsy Puch scooter with Ingrid, driving in the rain from England to Austria, from Krems to Zwettl—not comfortable, but wonderful!

Sitting on the sundeck in the glistening light of the Indian summer brings back all those past pictures in present clarity. It makes me happy and content. No, I am not really on the *Titanic*. Rather, I hop in my pick-up, turn left at the mailbox with Eich's "1864 Century Farm" sign, and follow Fruit Farm Road past the friendly Collegeville Community Credit Union. At Flynntown, I look right and see the imposing concrete structures of Breuer's Bauhaus design. I turn left and head toward I-94. The service road turns left and half a mile later, I turn into our lakeshore lot with the garden house "Kärnten" on Achmann Lake. There, I can lean back on the veranda, read the *New York Times*, get drowsy and feel at home. The sun sparkles in the waves. Indian summer colors glow on the other side.

As I fall asleep in the breezy shade, I am dreaming of a remote valley in Austria, the Lesachtal. The sound of the wild river Gail deep down in the valley in my ears, the smell of pine and tamarack trees in my nose, I see the splendid white of the limestone formations in the Carnian Alps at the Italian border. Next to them is the mighty hump of the Plenge and the glorious Wolayer Valley, leading to the tranquil lake of the same name way up high. The road, after many turns and bridges takes me to a village with two inns, one store, one post office and a few houses with four-hundred-year-old beams. That is BIRNBAUM.

I know the place. In the distance I could see the farm of Ambros Lamprecht. I lived there while attending high school far from home in Kornat. I would hike for days in the Carnian Mountains along the Italian border and count my blessings. I have been so close to paradise.

Further up the road on a steep path is the village of Kornat with a six-hundred-year-old Gothic church. Next to it is a yellow stone house, the old schoolhouse. It is no longer a school. Few people live there. Even fewer have children. I was born there seventy years ago. Five minutes from there is the graveyard surrounding the church and a war memorial for WW I on the left side and WW II on the right side. The view of the Carnian Range is awesome from there. The last line of the right side of the war memorial says, "Obl. Max Drekonja, MIA 1944."

Sixty years ago, he died somewhere, somehow in Yugoslavia. Thirty-four years ago, my sister Hildegard died. Nineteen years ago, my brave mother died. Two years ago, my sister Erika died. Forty-four years ago, I married Ingrid. Thirty-seven years ago, we came back to Saint John's University. It has been a good place for all of us. I feel at home here. I am happy and doze surrounded by an unspoiled nature filled with trees, lakes and loons, deer, beaver and . . . skunks. I wake up. Yes, that is that aroma! Well, if I were not so lazy, I would get the chainsaw and cut some dead elms, but I have learned to slow down. Less is more. Small is beautiful. I drive home and listen to Frank Sinatra. He is the greatest!

Max Birnbaum is done with his story. Oh, yes—I have to tell you who he is. I know him well. The profile on the next page will fill you in. Maybe some of you have met him before? I bet some have! Visit him and Ingrid at Lake Wobegon! They are hospitable and kind. The dogs will love visits especially. As do I. Thank you so much for so many things! I am just a very lucky man, a guy who made the long journey from that remote Lesachtal to Minnesota. A fella could do worse! Much worse indeed.

My pickup is rumbling back home from the lake. Pickups don't last forever. Mine is still very good. The car radio plays that special Louis Armstrong tune, "Oh what a wonderful world . . . ." I hum along and feel like playing along with the clarinet. I take a deep breath, and keep going, going, going . . . as long as I can. Isn't that what life is all about?

Psycho-profile
of Max Birnbaum

Astrological sign	Sagittarius
Preferred food	fried polenta, KFC
Preferred drink	buttermilk, Andechs beer
Preferred vehicle	Toyota pickup, John Deere Gator
Best skiing	Vail, Aspen, Arapahoe Basin, or anywhere in Tyrol
Preferred periodicals	*New York Times, The Nation, New Yorker*
Best vacations	Grand Cayman, Voyageurs National Park, Cape Hatteras, Montana
Best cities	New York, Prague, Venice, Duluth, Trieste, Berlin, San Diego, Krems
Best mountains	Mont Blanc area, France; Tetons, Wyoming; Red Lodge area, Montana
Best peaks climbed	Zebru, Italy; Cloud Peak in the Big Horns, Aiguille de Bionnassay, France
Best hiking	Avon Hills, Lake Wobegon; Lesachtal, Carinthia
Favorite authors	Stefan Zweig, John Grisham, Thomas Bernhard, Elfriede Jelinek
Favorite movies	*The Pianist, Fahrenheit 9/11, Fargo, An American in Paris*
Favorite composers	Mozart, Gershwin, Dvorak, Schubert, Strauss, Mahler, Udo Jürgens
Favorite calendar	*Sports Illustrated* Swim Suit
Favorite radio station	Minnesota Public Radio (MPR)
Least offensive TV shows	Charlie Rose, Jim Lehrer News Hour
Favorite season	Fall/ Indian summer in Minnesota
Best public figures	Bruno Kreisky, Paul Wellstone, Bill Clinton, Maximilian I (d. 1519)
Best artists	Bela Petheo, Oskar Kokoschka, Alfons Walde, Klimt (drawings)
Best students	Too many to mention everybody! Love them all!

Best colleagues	John Kulas, O.S.B.; Alexander Andrews, O.S.B.; Ray Larson, Joe Farry, Gerhard Weiss, Frank Hirschbach, Donald Daviau, Mark Thamert, O.S.B.
Best mentors	Volkmar and Harald Haselbach, K.H. Rossbacher, Walther Weiss, Erika Weinzierl, Chester E. Eisinger, F. Achberger, Frank Hirschbach
Best brother	Gerhard, *Ordinarius* of the "Katz Chair" at the University of Vienna
Highest recognition	*Das Österreichische Ehrenkreuz für Wissenschaft und Kunst Erster Klasse*
Best boss	Fr. Colman Barry O.S.B., president of Saint John's University
Best publication	on Guido Zernatto, Lion Feuchtwanger, Helene Scheu-Riesz
Greatest wish	to be a better clarinet player, pianist, watercolorist . . . . but . . . .
Most proud of	my wife Ingrid, my three children: Thomas, Natascha, Dimitri, and my brave, most caring mother (1907–1985), a "Mother Courage"!
Most fun	being with Alexander and Nikolaus, my grandsons
Missed the most	my father Max, (1901–1944) MIA 1944
Greatest disappointment	too shaky to use chainsaw any more
Saddest moment	visiting Auschwitz and Buchenwald, leaving Tyrol
Greatest hope	to beat the prognosis of my doctors— "I am invincible!" (James Bond)
Greatest accomplishment	my German and English memoirs
Most thankful to	my wife Ingrid Luger, without whom I would not be what I am
Most confident in	son Thomas, orthopedic surgeon, Salzburg; daughter Natascha, attorney in Denver; son Dimitri, internist at the University of Minnesota
Most happy	sitting at our lake house *Kärnten* and reading the *NYT*
Most curious	checking the mailbox at noon and e-mail at night
Most eager	to see post-Bush America come back to civility